# THE LIBERALISATION OF PUBLIC PROCUREMENT AND ITS EFFECTS ON THE COMMON MARKET

# The Liberalisation of Public Procurement and its Effects on the Common Market

CHRISTOPHER BOVIS
*Professor of European Business Law*
*University of Central Lancashire*
*Visiting Professor of Trade and Commerce*
*The Queen's University of Belfast*

LONDON AND NEW YORK

First published 1998 by Ashgate Publishing

Reissued 2018 by Routledge
2 Park Square, Milton Park, Abingdon, Oxon, OX14 4RN
711 Third Avenue, New York, NY I 0017, USA

*Routledge is an imprint of the Taylor & Francis Group, an informa business*

Copyright © Christopher Bovis 1998

All rights reserved. No part of this book may be reprinted or reproduced or utilised in any form or by any electronic, mechanical, or other means, now known or hereafter invented, including photocopying and recording, or in any information storage or retrieval system, without permission in writing from the publishers.

Notice:
Product or corporate names may be trademarks or registered trademarks, and are used only for identification and explanation without intent to infringe.

Publisher's Note
The publisher has gone to great lengths to ensure the quality of this reprint but points out that some imperfections in the original copies may be apparent.

Disclaimer
The publisher has made every effort to trace copyright holders and welcomes correspondence from those they have been unable to contact.

A Library of Congress record exists under LC control number: 98020665

ISBN 13: 978-1-138-33794-7 (hbk)
ISBN 13: 978-1-138-33797-8 (pbk)
ISBN 13: 978-0-429-44205-6 (ebk)

# Contents

**Table of Cases** ix

**Acknowledgements** xiii

**Chapter 1**
**Introduction** 1

The European Integration Process as the forum for the regulation
of Public Procurement 1
Some fundamental conceptual elements in the regulation of public
markets 5
The case of public procurement in the European Community 11

**Chapter 2**
**The Intellectual and the Policy Approaches to the Regulation
of Public Procurement** 23

The new approach towards the integration of public markets 26
The regulatory background of public procurement 32
Inherent dangers in the process of integration of the European
public markets 37
The structure of public procurement of Member States 41

## Chapter 3
## The Evolution of European Public Procurement Law 53

| | |
|---|---|
| The Public Supplies Regime | 53 |
| The Public Works Regime | 59 |
| The Public Utilities Regime | 65 |
| The Public Services Regime | 73 |
| The Compliance Directives | 79 |
| The GATT Agreement on Government Procurement | 81 |
| The new WTO Government Procurement Agreement | 86 |

## Chapter 4
## The Mechanism of Integration of the European Public Markets 90

| | |
|---|---|
| The principle mandatory advertisement and publication of public contracts | 93 |
| The monetary applicability of the Public Procurement Directives | 95 |
| Selection and Qualification Criteria | 98 |
|     Legal requirements for the qualification of contractors | 101 |
|     The list of recognised contractors | 102 |
| The Award of Public Contracts | 103 |
|     Tendering procedures | 103 |
|     The Award Criteria | 107 |
|     Framework Agreements | 109 |
|     In-house Contracts and Contracts to Affiliated Undertakings | 109 |
|     Design Contests | 110 |
|     Concession Contracts | 111 |
|     Additional award criteria | 112 |
|         Sub-contracting and public procurement | 112 |
|         Local labour employment and Public Procurement | 112 |
|         The award of Public Housing Schemes | 112 |

## Chapter 5
## Enforcement of and Compliance with Public Procurement Law: A Critique of the System — 114

| | |
|---|---|
| Judicial control at centralised level | 115 |
| Proceedings before the European Court of Justice | 119 |
|     The consequences of a judgment by the Court of Justice | 120 |
|     Interim measures | 122 |
| Judicial control at domestic level | 128 |
|     The award of damages under Community law | 130 |
| The judicial structure of Member States with reference to public procurement litigation | 135 |
| A critique of the national judicial structures in relation to public procurement cases | 144 |
| The Compliance Directives | 146 |
|     The Award of Damages under the Compliance Directives | 150 |
|     The Role of the European Commission under the Compliance Directives | 153 |
| Compliance with and enforcement of the rules under the WTO Government Procurement Agreement | 156 |

## Chapter 6
## An Impact Assessment of the European Public Procurement Law and Policy — 159

| | |
|---|---|
| Inherent shortcomings in the Public Procurement rules | 160 |
|     The dimesnsionality of public procurement | 161 |
|     The effects of the principle of transparency | 163 |
|     The abuse of award procedures which may restrict competition in the public markets | 168 |
| Public monopolies | 175 |
| Standardisation and specification | 177 |
| Reluctance in initiating litigation: a taxonomy of case law on public procurement | 180 |
| The effect of competitiveness in public procurement on the sustainability of certain industries | 183 |

**Chapter 7**
**Policy Choices and the Regulation Public Procurement in the Common Market**     196

Social policy objectives in the award of public contracts     200
    The notion of contract compliance     200
    The transfer of undertakings and employees' protection in the context of public procurement     206
The interrelation of Public Procurement with Regional Development Policy     209
    Preference purchasing schemes     212
The industrial policy dimension in public procurement     219

**Concluding remarks**     224

**Index**     226

# Table of Cases

Case 13/61 *Kledingverkoopbedrijf de Geus en Uitdenbogerd v. Robert Bosch GmbH*, [1962] ECR 45
Case 26/62 *NV Algemene Transport-en Expeditie Onderneming Van Gend en Loos v. Nederlandse Administrtie der Belastigen*, [1963] ECR 1
Case 6/64 *Costa v. ENEL*, [1964] ECR 585
Case 48/65 *Alfons Luttucke GmbH v. Commission*, [1966] ECR 19
Case 57/65 *Alfons Luttucke GmbH v. Haupzollampt Saarlouis*, [1966] ECR 205
Case 27/67 *Firma Fink-Frucht GmbH v. Haupzollamt Munchen Landsbergerstrasse*, [1968] ECR 223
Case 28/67 *Firma Molkerei Zentrale Westfalen/Lippe GmbH v. Haupzollampt Paderborn*, [1968] ECR 143
Case 13/68 *SpA Salgoil v. Italian Ministry for Foreign Trade*, [1968] ECR 453
Case 14/68 *Wilhem v.Bundeskartellampt* [1969] ECR 1 at 27
Case 78/70 *Deutche Grammophon GmbH v.Metro-SB Grossmarkte GmbH* [1971] ECR 1 at 31
Case 21-24/72, *International Fruit Co NV v. Produktschap voor Groenten en Fruit*, [1972] ECR 1236
Case 167/73 *Commission v. France*, [1974] ECR 359
Case 40-48, 50, 54-56, 111, 113-114/73 *Cooperative Vereniging "Suiker Unie" UA v. Commission*, [1975] ECR 1663
Case 2/74 *Reyners v.Belgian State*, [1974] ECR 631
Case 33/74 *Van Bisbergen v.Bestuur van de Bedrijfsvereninging voor de Metaalinijverheid*, [1974] ECR 1299
Case 41/74 *Van Duyn v. Home Office*, [1974] ECR 1337

Case 36/74 *Walrave and Koch v. Association Union Cycliste International et al,* (1974) ECR 1423
Case 43/75, *Drefenne v. SABENA,* (1976) ECR 473
Case 74/76, *Ianelli & Volpi Spa v. Ditta Paola Meroni,* [1977] 2 CMLR 688
Case 38/77 *ENKA BV v. Inspecteur der Invoerrecht en Accijnzen,* [1977] ECR 2203
Case *61/77R, Commission v Ireland* [1977] ECR 1411
Case 102/79 *Commission v. Belgium,* [1980] ECR 1489
Case 300/81 *Commission v. Italy,* [1983] ECR 449
Case 314-316/81&82 *Procureur de la Republique et al. v.Waterkeyn,* [1982] ECR 4337
Case 249/81, *Commission v. Ireland,* [1982]ECR 4005
Case 244/81, *Commission v. Ireland,* [1982], ECR 4005
Case 76/81, *SA Transporoute et Travaux v. Minister of Public Works,* [1982] ECR 457
Case 283/81, *Srl CILFIT v. Minisrty of Health,* [1982] ECR 3415.
Case 286/82 & 26/83 *Luisi & Carbone v. Ministero del Tesoro,* [1984] ECR 377
Case 247/83, *Commission v. Italy,* [1985] ECR 1077
Case 118/83R, *CMC Co-operativa Muratori e Cementisti v. Commission* [1983] ECR 2583
Case 44/84 *Hurd v. Jones* [1986] ECR 29
Case 152/84 *Marshall v. Southampton and South West Hampshire Area Health Authority,* [1986] ECR 723
Case 18/84, *Commission v. France,* [1985], ECR 1339
Case 103/84, *Commission v. Italy,* [1986], ECR 1759
Case 239/85 *Commission v. Belgium,* [1986] ECR 1473
Case 199/85, *Commission v Italy* [1987] ECR 1039
Case 24/85, *Spijkers v. Gebroders Benedik Abbatoir CV,* [1986] ECR 1, 1123
Case 147/86 *Commission v. Hellenic Republic,* [1988] ECR 765
Case 308/86 *Ministere Public v. Lambert,* [1988] ECR 478
Case 27/86, 28/86, 29/86. Case 27/86, *Constructions et Enterprises Industrielles S.A (CEI) v. Association Intercommunale pour les Autoroutes des Ardennes*; 27, 28, 29/86, *CEI and Bellini,* [1987] ECR 3347
Case 84/86, *Commission v. Hellenic Republic,* not reported

Case 28/86, *Ing.A. Bellini & Co. S.p.A. v. Regie de Betiments* [1987] ECR 3347

Case 29/86, *Ing.A. Bellini & Co. S.p.A. v. Belgian State*, [1987] ECR 3347

Case 45/87, *Commission v. Ireland*, [1988] ECR 4929

Case 31/87, *Gebroeders Beenjes B.V v. The Netherlands*, [1989] ECR 4365

Case 45/87R, *Commission v Ireland* [1987] ECR 1369

Case 3/88, *Commission v. Italy*, [1989] ECR 4035

Case C 21/88, *Du Pont de Nemours Italiana SpA v. Unita Sanitaria Locale N.2 di Carrara*, [1990] ECR 889

Case 103/88, *Fratelli Costanzo S.p.A. v. Comune di Milano*, [1989] ECR 1839

Case 351/88, *Lavatori Bruneau Slr. v. Unita Sanitaria Locale RM/24 di Monterotondo*, judgment of July 11, 1991

Case 194/88R, *Commission v Italy* [1988] ECR 5647

Case 213/89 *The Queen v.Minister of Agriculture Fisheries and Food* [1990] ECR I-2433

Case 247/89, *Commission v. Portugal*, [1991] ECR I 3659

Case 360/89, *Commission v. Italy*, [1992] ECR I 3401

Case 179/89, *Farmaindusrtia v. Consejeria de salud de la Junta de Andalucia*, [1989] O.J. C 160/10

Case 296/89, *Impresa Dona Alfonso di Dona Alfonso & Figli s.n.c. v. Consorzio per lo Sviluppo Industriale del Comune di Monfalcone*, judgment of June 18, 1991

Case *188/89, Foster v British Gas* [1990] ECR-1313

Case 6/90 and 9/90 *Francovich and Bonifaci v. Italian Republic*, [1993] ECR 61

Case 362/90, *Commission v. Italy*, judgment of March 31, 1992

Case 24/91, *Commission v. Kingdom of Spain*, [1994] CMLR 621

Case C 29/91, *Dr Sophie Redmond Stichting v. Bartol*, [1992] IRLR 369

Case C 209/91, *Rask v. ISS Kantinservice*, [1993] ECR 1

Case 272/91R, *Commission v. Italian Republic*, order of June 12, 1992

Case C 389/92, *Ballast Nedam Groep NV v. Belgische Staat*, [1994] 2 CMLR

Case 107/92, *Commission v. Italy*, judgment of August 2, 1993

Case 296/92, *Commission v. Italy*, judgment of January 12, 1994

Case C-71/92, *Commission v. Spain*, judgment of June 30, 1993

Case C 382/92, *Commission v. United Kingdom*, [1994] ECR 1

Case C 392/92, *Schmidt v. Spar und Leihkasse der fruherer Amter Bordersholm, Kiel und Cronshagen*, [1994] ECR 1, 1320

Case C 46 & 48/93 *Brasserie du Pecheur SA v. Germany, Regina v. Secretary of State for Transport, ex parte Factortame LTD*, 5 March 1996: [1996] 1 CMLR 889

Case C 359/93, *Commission v. The Netherlands*, judgment of January 24, 1995

Case C-280/93, *Germany v. Council*, judgment of 5 October 1994

Case C 324/93, *R. v. The Secretary of State for the Home Department, ex.p . Evans Medical Ltd and Macfarlan Smith Ltd*

Case C 392/93, *The Queen and H.M. Treasury, ex parte British Telecommunications PLC*, O.J. [1993], C 287/6

Case 79/94, *Commission v. Greece*, judgment of May 4, 1995

Case C 57/94, *Commission v. Italy*, judgment of May 18, 1995

Case C 48/94, *Rygaard v. Stro Molle Akustik*, judgment of September 19, 1995

Case C 87/94R, *Commission v. Belgium*, order of April 22, 1994

# Acknowledgements

Public procurement and its regulation within the European Community emerge as elements of *European Economic Law*, to the extent that the impact of the relevant law and policy making can be recorded upon a number of social stakeholders in the common market.

Assessing a law and policy framework such as public procurement in the European Community would certainly involve empirical research of various academic disciplines. It was the complexity and the technicalities of the law, as well as the serious underlying socio-economic parameters that intrigued me to study and research the regime of public purchasing and its effects on the common market. I decided to embark upon this assessment work with a view to exposing as many facets of the public procurement regime as I could. It has been a demanding but exciting exercise. During the stage of the empirical research, I had the unique opportunity to apply my preliminary findings and test their validity on a number of occasions, having performed several assignments relating to legal and policy aspects of public procurement for the European Commission, as well as public and private sector organisations. This exercise has been most useful to me, as it enabled the development of a critical - and sometimes perhaps a cynical approach - to the regulation of public sector purchasing in Europe, as well as to economic integration process in the Community. Times have changed dramatically and the economic interaction amongst the Member States has created a completely new regime which has taken many by surprise. The public sector ethos has been undergoing dramatic changes as a result of cost savings and efficiency related objectives in the delivery of public services.

It would have been very difficult to complete this project without the involvement of a number of people to whom here I record my great indebtedness. First of all, I would like to thank the Publishers for their professionalism and the assistance they provided. It is also with deep appreciation that I express my gratitude to Dr Christine Cnossen who stood by me and did so much to further the completion of this book through her invaluable support and encouragement. Finally, I am under the greatest debt of gratitude to Messrs T. Bramall, R. Watson and D. Blunt for their trust and esteem.


Professor Christopher Bovis
Summer 1998

# 1 Introduction

## The European Integration Process as the forum for the regulation of Public Procurement

The establishment of the *common market*, as the core objective envisaged by the Treaty of Rome (the treaty creating the European Economic Communities) and reinforced by the Treaty of Maastricht (the treaty creating the European Union) is to be achieved through the progressive approximation of the economic policies of Member States.[1] The concept of the *common market* embraces legal and economic dynamics of the European integration process, with clear political spillover effects from its accomplishment, and unfolds the characteristics of a genuine integral market, where unobstructed mobility of factors of production,[2] is guaranteed and a regime of effective and undistorted competition regulates its operation. These characteristics embrace the four basic freedoms of a customs union (free movement of goods, persons, capital and services)[3] and, to the extent that the customs union tends to become an economic and

---

[1] Articles 2 and 3 of the Treaty of Rome (EC).
[2] Articles 48 and 67 EC respectively.
[3] The Court of Justice has recognised a fifth freedom, the free movement of payments, which is closely related to the freedom of movement of capital, see cases 286/82 & 26/83 *Luisi & Carbone v. Ministero del Tesoro*, [1984] ECR 377, *308/86 Ministere Public v. Lambert*, [1988] ECR 478. The Treaty of Rome provides also for the accomplishment of this freedom in Articles 67(2) and 106. The free movement of payments, a complementary principle of the free mobility of capital as a production factor plays an extremely important role in the process of integration of public markets, and in particular in financing public projects either through indirect or direct investment.

a monetary one,[4] the adoption of a common economic policy and the introduction of a single currency. Adherence by Member States to the above-mentioned fundamental principles of economic integration would ensure the abolition of any restriction, protection or obstacle to inter-State trade. The level of success of economic integration in Europe would determine the level of success in political integration, as the ultimate objective stipulated in the Treaties.

The Law of the European Community has conceived the creation of a legal -supranational - system alongside existing domestic ones, where the supremacy of the former over national laws has been declared by the European Court of Justice.[5] The economic integration of the European Community requires the assistance of a legal order that can facilitate and observe its development with a view to achieving the ultimate aim which is the establishment of a political union. The *new legal order* is a conglomerate of mutual rights and duties between the Community and its subjects, both Member States and private persons, and also amongst these subjects themselves and provides for the procedures which are necessary for determining and adjudicating infringements of law. The *new legal order* does confer rights and obligations not only to Member States but also to individuals (physical or legal persons). Both Member States and individuals are the subjects of European Community law, with respect to compliance and observance, and in as much as Member States participate in market activities, they have the same rights and obligations as those of individuals.

Two strategic plans have facilitated the economic integration of the Member States. These plans were enacted by European Institutions and have been subsequently transposed into national laws and policies by Member States. The first plan has comprised of a series of actions, measures and mechanisms aiming at the abolition of all *tariff* and *non-tariff barriers* to intra-community trade (trade amongst Member States). The second plan has focused on the establishment of an effective, workable and undistorted regime of competition within the common market, in order to prevent possible abuse of market dominance and cartelisation, factors which could have serious economic implications in its functioning. The first plan, the abolition of all *tariff* and *non-tariff barriers*

---

[4] Article 102a EC
[5] See case 26/62 *NV Algemene Transport-en Expeditie Onderneming Van Gend en Loos v. Nederlandse Administrtie der Belastigen*, [1963] ECR 1.

to intra-community trade, appears to have a static effect aimed at eliminating all administrative and legal obstacles to free trade and had as its focal point Member States and their national administrations, whereas the second plan, the establishment of an effective, workable and undistorted regime of competition within the common market, has been addressed at industry level and has a more on-going and dynamic effect.

All tariff barriers appear to have been abolished by the end of the first transitional period,[6] so customs duties, quotas and other forms of quantitative restrictions could no longer hinder the free flow of trade amongst Member States. Non-tariff barriers, however, have proved more difficult to eliminate, as they involve long-established market practices and patterns that could not change overnight. Non-tariff protection represents a disguised form of discrimination and can take place through a wide spectrum of administrative or legislative frameworks relating to public monopolies, fiscal factors such as indirect taxation, state aids and subsidisation, technical standards and last but not least public procurement. Non-tariff barriers are by no means confined to the European Integration process only. The existence of non-tariff barriers is a common phenomenon in world markets and the main objective of regulatory instruments of international trade is their elimination. However, non-tariff barriers could seriously distort the operation of the common market and its fundamental freedoms and derail the process of European integration.

The European Commission's White Paper for the Completion of the Internal market[7] identified existing non-tariff protection and provided the framework for specific legislative measures[8] in order to address the issue at national level. A set of Directives have been deemed necessary for the completion of the internal market by the end of 1992, and the time table was set out in the Single European Act, which in fact amended the Treaty of Rome by introducing *inter alia* the concept of the *internal market*. The internal market, in quantifiable terms, could be considered as something less than the common market but, perhaps the first and most important part

---

[6] The period from the establishment of the European Communities until 31/12/1969. See Art. 8(7) EC.

[7] European Commission, *White Paper for the Completion of the Internal Market*, (COM) 85 310 fin., 1985.

[8] The completion of the internal market required the adoption at Community level and the implementation at national level of some 300 Directives on the subjects specified in the Commission's White Paper. See also the *Third Report of the Commission to the European Parliament on the Implementation of the White Paper*, (COM) 88, 134 fin.

of the latter, as it "...... *would provide the economic context for the regeneration of the European industry in both goods and services and it would give a permanent boost to the prosperity of the people of Europe and indeed the world as a whole*".[9]

The internal market, as an economic concept could be described as an area without internal frontiers, where the free circulation of goods and the unhindered provision of services in conjunction with the unobstructed mobility of factors of production are ensured. Literally speaking the concept of the internal market is a reinforcement of the customs union principle as the foundation stone of the common market. The internal market embraces, obviously, less than the common market to the extent that the economic and monetary integration elements are missing. The whole Single European Act, as an instrument amending the Treaties, revealed strong public law characteristics. The regulatory and interventionist feature of its provisions indicate the importance of certain fields that had been overlooked during the past. There has been both centralised and decentralised regulatory control by Community Institutions over environmental policy, industrial policy, regional policy and the regulation of public procurement. These areas represented the priority objectives in the process of completing the internal market. Public procurement was pointed out as a significant non-tariff barrier and action was scheduled to address the issue. The European Commission based its momentum on two notable studies,[10] where empirical proof of the distorted market situation in the public sector was highlighted and the benefits of the regulation of public procurement were emphasised.

---

[9] Lord Cockfield's quotation in the Cechinni Report *1992 The European Challenge, The Benefits of a Single Market*, Aldershot, Wildwood House, 1988.
[10] See Commission of the European Communities, *The Cost of Non-Europe, Basic Findings, Vol.5, Part.A; The Cost of Non-Europe in Public Sector Procurement*, Official Publications of the European Communities, Luxembourg, 1988. Also the Cechinni Report *1992 The European Challenge*, Aldershot, Wildwood House, 1988.

## Some fundamental conceptual elements in the regulation of public markets

State participation in free markets would normally take place on behalf or in pursuit of public interest.[11] The concept of the state embraces an entrepreneurial dimension to the extent that it exercises *dominium*.[12] Where state participation in the market place exists, the relevant markets can be described as public markets. Although the state as entrepreneur enters into transactions with a view to providing goods, services and works for the public, this kind of action does not resemble the commercial characteristics of entrepreneurship, in as much as the aim of the state's activities is not the maximisation of profits but the observance of public interest. In contrast, private markets comprise of firms whose only reason of staying in the market place is profit maximisation. *Public interest* substitutes *profit maximisation* and justifies state participation in public markets.

Apart from the above fundamental differentiating factor, a number of striking variances distinguish private from public markets. These variances focus on structural elements of the market place, competitiveness, demand conditions, supply conditions, the production process, and finally pricing and risk. They also provide for an indication as to the different methods and approaches employed in their regulation.

Private markets are generally structured as a result of competitive pressures originating in the buyer / supplier interaction and their configuration can vary from monopoly / oligopoly to perfect competition. Demand arises from heterogeneous buyers with a variety of specific needs. It is based on expectations and is multiple for each product. Supply, on the other hand, is offered through various product ranges, where products are standardised using known technology, but constantly improved through research and development processes. The production process is based on mass-production patterns and the product range represents a large choice including substitutes, whereas the critical production factor is cost level. The development cycle appears to be short to medium-term and finally, the

---

[11] The relevant market place is then defined as public markets. See M. L. Harrison, *Corporatism and the Welfare State*, Aldershot, Gower 1984, Chapter 1.
[12] T. Daintith in *The Changing Constitution*, Oxford University Press 1985, p.140-212, elaborates on the distiction between *dominium* and *imperium* as functions of a modern state.

technology of products destined for the private markets is evolutionary. Purchases are made when an acceptable balance between price and quality is achieved. Purchase orders are multitude and at limited intervals. Pricing policy in private markets is determined by competitive forces and the purchasing decision is focused on the price-quality relation. The risk factor is highly present.

On the other hand, public markets tend to be organised in a different way. The market structure often reveals a monopsony / oligopsony character. In terms of its origins, demand in public markets is institutionalised and operates mainly under budgetary considerations rather than price mechanisms. It is also based on fulfilment of tasks (pursuit of public interest) and it is single for many products. Supply also has limited origins, in terms of the establishment of close ties between the public sector and industries supplying it and there is often a limited product range. Products are rarely innovative and technologically advanced and pricing is determined through tendering and negotiations. The purchasing decision is primarily based upon the life-time cycle, reliability, price and political considerations. Purchasing patterns follow tendering and negotiations and often purchases are dictated by policy rather than price/quality considerations.

Whereas the regulatory weaponry for private markets is dominated by anti-trust law and policy, public markets are *fora* where the structural and behavioural remedial tools of competition law emerge as a rather inappropriate regulatory framework. The applicability of competition law is limited, mainly due to the fact that anti-trust often clashes with monopolistic structures which exist in public markets. State participation in market activities is regularly assisted through exclusive exploitation of a product or a service within a geographical market. The market activities of the state are protected from competition by virtue of laws on trading and production or by virtue of delegated monopolies. Another reason for the limited applicability of anti-trust law and policy in public markets is the fact that conceptual differences appear between the two categories of markets - private and public - in the eyes of anti-trust, which could be attributed to the very different nature between them. In private markets, anti-trust law and policy seek to punish cartels and abusive dominance of undertakings. The focus of the remedial instruments is the supply side, which is conceived as the commanding part in the supply / demand equation due to the fact that it instigates and controls demand for a product. In private markets, the demand side of the equation (the consumers in general) are susceptible to exploitation and the market equilibria are prone to distortion as a result of collusive behaviour of undertakings or abusive monopoly position. On the other hand, the structure of public markets reveals a different picture. In the supply / demand equation, the predominant part appears to be the demand side (the state and its organs as purchasers), which initialises demand through purchasing, whereas the supply side (the industry) fights for access to the relevant markets. Although this is normally the case, one should not exclude the possibility of market oligopolisation and the potential manipulation of the demand side.[13] These advanced market structures can occur more often in the future, as a result of the well established trends of industrial concentration.

Another argument in relation to the different regulatory approach in relation to public and private markets that deserves attention refers to the methods of market segmentation and abuse. In private markets segmentation occurs as a result of cartels and collusive behaviour, which would lead to abuse of dominance, with a view to driving competitors out of the relevant market, increasing market shares and increasing profits. It is maintained that the segmentation of private markets appears different than the partitioning of public ones. The difference lies in the fact that private markets can be segmented both geographically and by reference to product or service, whereas public ones can only be geographically segmented. This assumption can be substantiated by reference to the fact that the partition of the public markets would be probably the result of concerted practices attributed to the demand side. As such concerted practices focus on the origin of a product or a service or the nationality of a contractor, then the only way to effectively partition the relevant market would be by reference to its geographical remit. In contrast, in relation to private markets, the segmentation of the relevant market (either product or geographical) is attributed to the supply side. The argument goes further to reveal the fact that the balance of powers between the supply and the demand side are reversed when superimposed in private or public markets. In the latter, it is the demand side that has the dominant role in the equation by dictating terms and conditions in purchases, initiation of transactions, as well as by influencing production trends (supplies, works

---

[13] See P. Konstadacopoulos, *The linked oligopoly concept in the Single European Market*, Public Procurement Law Review, 1995, vol.4, p.p. 213.

and services destined for the public sector tend to shift from the traditional *inventory pattern* of production to *a custom made / build by order* one).[14]

In public markets, concerted practices of the demand side (e.g. excluding foreign competition, application of buy-national policies, application of national standards policies) represent geographical market segmentation, as they result in the division of the European public markets into different national public markets. It could also be maintained that public markets are subject to protection from rather than restriction of competition, to the extent that the latter are quasi-monopolistic and monopsonistic in structure. Indeed, the state and its organs, as contractors possess a monopoly position in the sense that no one competes against them in their market activities.[15] Even in cases of privatisation, the monopoly position is shifted from the public to private hands. The situation is slightly different in cases of an open privatised regime pursuing an operation of public interest. In that case, it would be more appropriate to refer to oligopolistic competition in the relevant market. Also in privatised regimes, interchangeability of supply is very limited, to an extent that monopoly position characteristics survive the transfer of ownership from public to private hands. The state and its organs also possess a monopsony position, as firms engaged in transactions with them have no alternatives to pursue business. Access barriers to geographical public markets are erected by states by means of exercising their discretion to conclude contracts with national undertakings. This sort of activity constitutes the partition of public markets in the Community, whereas, apparently, undertakings operating in private markets must enter into a restrictive agreement between themselves in order to split up the relevant markets. Due to their different integral nature, private and public markets require different control. The control in both cases has a strong public law character, but while anti-trust regulates private markets, it appears rather inappropriate for public ones. Anti-trust law and policy is a set of rules of a negative nature; undertakings must *restrain* their activities to an acceptable range pre-determined in due course by the competent authorities. On the other hand, public markets require a set of rules that have positive character. It should be recalled that the integration of public

---

[14] See C. Bovis, *The Regulation of Public Procurement as an element in the Evolution of European Economic Law*, European Law Journal, Spring 1998.
[15] See Denis Swann,*The Retreat of the State*, Harvester-Wheatsheaf 1988, Chapter 1-2.

markets is based on the abolition of barriers and obstacles to national markets; it then follows that the sort of competition envisaged for their regulation is mainly *market access competition*. This primarily indicates that price competition is expected to emerge in Community public markets, only after their integration.

It appears, however, that in both private and public markets, two elements have relevance when attempting their regulation. The first element is the *price differentiation* of similar products; the second element is *access* to the relevant markets. As the European integration is an economic process which aims at dismantling barriers to trade and approximating national economies, the need to create acceptable levels of competition in both public and private markets becomes more demanding. In fact, a regime of genuine competition in public markets would benefit the public interest as it will lower the price of goods and services for the public, as well as achieve substantial savings for the public purse.

If one accepts as point of departure the fact that the introduction of elements of competition in public markets would have desirable effects, a question which might arise is if, by dismantling public markets and entrusting private markets for the provision of goods and services destined for the public, the above desirable effects could be accomplished. As mentioned previously, private markets operate under the laws of demand and supply and the private sector is profit orientated. Privatisation, as a process of transfer of public assets and operations to private hands, on grounds of market efficiency and competition, as well as responsiveness to customer demand and quality considerations is often accompanied by simultaneous regulation by the state, in the form of a legal framework within which privatised industries will pursue public interest functions. It is not entirely clear that the process of privatisation would reclaim public markets and transform them to private ones. One should never underestimate the fact that the control of operations related to public interest remain within the competence of the state in the form of the regulatory regime, thus maintaining strong public market characteristics. To what extent the market freedom of a privatised entity could be curtailed by regulatory frameworks deserves a complex and thorough analysis which exceeds the thrust of this work. However, it could be maintained that through the privatisation process, the previously clear-cut distinction between public and private markets becomes blur, as a new market place emerges. This type of market embraces strong public law elements to the extent that it is regulated by the state with a view to observing public interest in the relevant operations. The economic freedom and the risks associated with such operations are also subject to regulation, a fact which implies that the above regulatory framework incorporates more than mere procedural rules. This market place reveals a transformation from traditional *corporatism* to a public management system where *governance is dispersed through contract* under terms and conditions determined by the state. It very much resembles the *principle of outsourcing* which is often utilised in restructuring exercises in the private sector. Outsourcing introduces elements of contractualisation in the production process, as sub-contracting takes over from the in-house operation in the production chain. Government by contract, along the same lines, introduces the principle of outsourcing in the dispersement of public service, but the *contractualised governance* appears far more stringent than outsourcing by virtue of regulation. Furthermore, apart from operational savings, outsourcing in the private sector would normally spread the risk factor amongst the operations in the production chain. If the sub-contractor could not deliver according to the expectations, the main operator could switch to an alternative with no major implications. Outsourcing, therefore, introduces an element of flexibility in the production process. It remains to be seen whether contractualised governance or government by contract conforms with the same parameters (savings, risk sharing, flexibility) as private sector outsourcing.

In addition to the above remarks, one should expect that the introduction of competitive forces in public markets through privatisation would result in a shift of the relevant regulatory instruments for these markets. However, within the European Union, the process of privatisation has not been approached in a uniform manner by the Member States. Although the element of competition in the relevant public markets, as well as the potential effects on public savings remains undisputed, the process and methods of privatisation has faced considerable criticism from the stakeholders of the European Community. Despite of the fact that European Institutions have in principle endorsed the process of privatisation as a means to reduce public debt and achieve a harmonious economic and budgetary policy throughout the common market,[16]

---

[16] See the response of the European Commission to a Parliamentary Question relating to the powers of a Member State to privatized publicly-controlled entities, O.J. 1997 No C72/82.

industrial relations in the Member States often have diluted both the principle and the effects of such transformation. Attempts to privatise state-controlled enterprises may have resulted in the regulation of their corporate performance through anti-trust, but apparently the purchasing relations are subject to the same regime as those of public sector bodies. The privatised utility, for example, although a private entity, has to comply with a rigorous purchasing system for its supply chain requirements.

## The case of public procurement in the European Community

Public procurement could be best described as the supply chain system for the acquisition of all necessary goods, works and services by the state and its organs when acting in pursuit of public interest. Public procurement stands as a procedural prerequisite for the delivery and dispersement of public service, to the extent that it constitutes a significant *modus operandi* of public markets. Public purchasing requirements cover supplies, works and services markets, categories which reveal the relevant *fora* where the state acts as a contractor in the market place. Apart from obvious reasons relating to accountability in public expenditure, avoidance of corruption and political manipulation, the regulation of public procurement within a legal system can acquire some quite high-powered dimensions. The regulation of public procurement, does not only represent a best practice in the delivery of public service by the state and its organs, it most importantly qualifies as an instrument of policy. The spill-over effects from the employment of a particular purchasing strategy in relation to the public sector can have significant implications for national administrations or alternatively can be detrimental in any integration process a state is committed to.

In the history of European economic integration, public procurement has been an important part of the Member States' industrial policy, to the extent that it was utilised as a tool with a view to supporting domestic policy considerations.[17] Protectionism from competition in public procurement and preferential award of public contracts to indigenous suppliers and contractors have reflected mainly a concern of Member

---

[17] See S. Arrowsmith, *The Legality of Secondary Procurement Policies under the Treaty of Rome and the Works Directive*, Public Procurement Law Review, 1992, Vol. 1. p. 410.

States for the preservation of national industries and the related workforce. The legislation on public procurement in the early days clearly allowed for "preference schemes" in less favoured regions which were experiencing industrial decline.[18] Such schemes required the application of award criteria based on considerations other than the lowest price or the most economically advantageous offer, subject to their compatibility with Community Law in as much as they did not run contrary to the principle of free movement of goods (Article 30 EC et seq) and to competition law considerations with respect to state aids. Preference schemes have been indissolubly linked with regional development policies, as they sought to guarantee a certain percentage of public procurement to local firms, a fact that has indicated the close interplay between public purchasing and state aids.[19] Along the above lines, protectionist public procurement practices, when strategically exercised, resulted in the evolution of vital industries for the state in question. The sustainability of *"national champions"* has brought about benefits for a sector or an industry, which, when protected from competition in the short-run, managed to achieve specialisation and internationalisation. Since the completion of the Internal market (1992) they have been abolished, as they have been deemed capable in contravening directly or indirectly the basic principle of non-discrimination on grounds of nationality stipulated in the Treaty of Rome.

It is interesting to see how preferential public procurement might acquire a double dimension. First, it appears in the form of an exercise which aims at preserving some domestic sectors or industries at the expense of the principles of the European integration process. In such a form, there is obviously no exit plan. Impact assessment studies undertaken by the European Commission showed that the operation of preference schemes had a minimal effect on the economies of the regions where they had been applied, both in terms of the volume of procurement contracts, as well as in terms of real economic growth attributed to the operation of such schemes.[20] Thus, in that form, preferential public procurement perpetuates the sub-optimal allocation of resources and

---

[18] See Articles 29(4) and 29(a) of the EC Public Works Directive 71/305; also Art.26 of EC Public Supplies Directive 77/62.

[19] For a thorough analysis see, J.M. Fernadez Martin and O. Stehmann, *Product Market Integration versus Regional Cohesion in the Community*, European Law Review, 1991, Vol. 16, p. 216.

[20] European Commission, *Public Procurement: Regional and Social Aspects (COM(89) 400)*

represents a welfare loss for the economy of the relevant state. On the other hand, preferential purchasing in the form of strategic sustainability of selected industries might represent a viable instrument of industrial policy, to the extent that the infant industry, when specialised and internationalised, would be in a position to counterbalance any welfare losses during its protected period. In the above form, preferential public procurement, as an integral part of industrial policy could possibly represent welfare gains.[21]

Whatever the dimension which preferential public procurement is looked at, its regulation requires a balancing exercise between related economic policies on the one hand and the objectives stipulated in the Treaty of Rome on the other. Public procurement, as a discipline involving legal, economic and public policy considerations has acquired a significant role within the context of the European integration, but more importantly at domestic level, where national administrations have been required to implement and comply with a legal regime which aims at integrating the public markets of the European Union and establishing a competitive regime similar to that envisaged for the private markets. The latter regime, the competition law and policy of the European Union has introduced a framework of effective and workable competition in the common market and has resulted in an industrial structure which reveals strong trends of industrial concentration through mergers and acquisitions, restructuring, outsourcing and optimisation of human and capital resources within the sectors of the European industries.

The volume of public procurement has been estimated at ECU 560 bn amongst the Europe of 12 Member States, an approximate 15% of the Community's Gross Domestic Product (GDP).[22] With the latest enlargement (the accession of Sweden, Finland and Austria) taken into account, the figures should approach ECU 750 bn at 1996 prices and an approximate 11% of the Community's GDP.[23] In real terms, public procurement represents a significant amount of the Member States' GDP, a fact that has been seen as very important by European Institutions for the

---

[21] Commission of the European Communities, *Statistical Performance for keeping watch over public procurement*, 1992.
[22] See *The Cost of Non-Europe, Basic Findings, Vol.5, Part.A; The Cost of Non-Europe in Public Sector Procurement*, Official Publications of the European Communities, Luxembourg, 1988.
[23] See the *Green Paper on Public Procurement in the European Union: Exploring the way forward*, European Commission 1996.

process of European integration. Given the level of infrastructure and the amount spent on it every financial year by contracting authorities of the Member States, the public sector has acquired a significant dimension within the European Integration process and the need to regulate it with the view to eliminate market distortions became imminent. Public procurement, as a dispersement of public service by the state and its organs not only does represent a substantial proportion of the European Union's GDP but, when viewed in the context of domestic budgetary frameworks, it may qualify as an instrument with a view to supporting national conjunctural (short-term economic policies) or even long-term economic policies relating to employment, regional development, industrial adjustment and performance. Such an application of public procurement by Member States in the direction of promoting domestic policies should always be weighted against the process of the completion of the common market through the progressive abolition of all existing non-tariff barriers which are deemed to inhibit the functioning of a genuinely integrated market in the Community. The regulation of public markets aims primarily at combating discrimination on grounds of nationality and also at the achievement of efficiency and optimal allocation of resources destined for the public sector Community wide, under a more competitive regime. The motive is again the pursuit of public interest, but through the regulation of public procurement public interest acquires a Community dimension with mainly economic characteristics.

The European Commission's White Paper for the Completion of the Internal Market has pointed out that public procurement in the Member States represented a serious threat to the process of economic integration of the European Community and could possibly derail the outcome of the common market. It should be mentioned that amongst the areas identified as actual or potential non-tariff barriers, public procurement was the most substantive and urgent discipline to be tackled by European Institutions and the Member States. The European Commission formulated a strategy for eliminating discriminatory public procurement amongst Member States which could pose significant obstacles to the fundamental principles of free movement of goods, the right of establishment and the freedom to provide services. That strategy was based on two principal assumptions: the first acknowledged the fact that in order to eliminate preferential and discriminatory purchasing practices in European public markets, a great deal of *transparency* and *openness* was needed; the second assumption rested on the premise that the only way to regulate public procurement in the Member States in an effective manner was through the process of *harmonisation* of existing laws and administrative practices which had been in operation, and not through a *uniform* regulatory pattern which would replace all existing laws and administrative practices throughout the Community. The latter assumption indirectly recognised the need for a decentralised system of regulation for public procurement in the Community, well ahead of the pronouncement of the principle of *subsidiarity*, which was introduced in the European law jargon some years later by virtue of the Maastricht Treaty on European Union.

Since harmonisation was adopted as the most appropriate method of regulation of public procurement in the common market, and the decentralised character of the regime was reinforced through legislation, the onus then was shifted to the national administrations of the Member States, which had to implement the Community principles into domestic law and give a certain degree of clarity and legitimate expectation to interested parties. Occasionally, the European Commission is criticised for not reserving for itself or other Community Institutions central powers, other than those already available and in its disposal as the guardian of the Treaty, in relation to the enforcement of and compliance with public procurement rules. The critics often refer to the applicability of competition law and policy of the European Community and the regime which legally implements it through specific Regulations. However, although in principle competition law of the European Community may apply to the award of public contracts,[24] the *effectiveness* and *efficiency* of a regulatory regime in the public markets through basic anti-trust remedies remains a challenge for the law and policy maker. A rigid regime in its application through a uniform way across the common market would not

---

[24] See case *Cooperative Vereniging "Suiker Unie" UA v. Commission*, [1975] ECR 1663, in which the European Court of Justice recognised the adverse effects of concerted practices in tendering procedures on competition in the common market. This case appears to have opened the way for the application of competition law on public procurement in the Community. The applicability of Competition Law provisions of the Treaty (Articles 85, 86) in controlling collusive tendering and anti-competitive behaviour of suppliers, was also the subject of Commission Decision 92/204, O.J. 1992 L92/1. It could be argued that competition law and policy applies equally to private as well as public markets, but the explicit provisions of the Directives on consortia participation in tendering procedures might limit the scope of Articles 85, 86 in public procurement.

take into account national particularities in public procurement and a highest common denominator would probably eliminate any elements of *flexibility* in the system. Public procurement, as a nexus of transactions in the supply chain of the public sector, differs no more than the purchasing management of the private sector, which remains unregulated.

The legal instruments opted for by Community Institutions to achieve the objective of flexibility are Directives. Public markets and their regulation are dominated by different legal regimes and legal approaches that diverge to a considerable extent from each other. Directives, as flexible Community legal instruments, leaving a great deal of discretion in the hands of Member States with respect to the forms and the methods of their implementation can harmonise public markets taking into account existing divergencies in domestic legal systems. The appropriateness of EC Directives to achieve the desired degree of competition in public markets and establish a regime where optimal resource allocation benefits the public interest is unquestionable. The nature and character of Directives, as *"framework"* legal instruments aims at harmonising existing legal systems, bringing them in conformity with Community envisaged objectives. Directives attempt to approximate different national laws and achieve a similar legal regime throughout the common market based on the lowest common denominator amongst the systems of the Member States. Divergencies will inevitably remain, as the Community lacks the powers to abolish existing domestic legal regimes and impose *ab initio* a different one.[25] On the other hand, it should be pointed out that Regulations aim at unification of the regimes governing the Member States' legal orders and have been exclusively used in the anti-trust field. It could be further argued that Regulations reveal all the characteristics of instruments of public law, in particular to the extent that they are directly applicable and produce vertical and horizontal direct effectiveness. Apart from the creation of a uniform system common to the internal legal orders of the Member States, other notable advantages by having recourse to Regulations instead of Directives would have been the fact that individuals could directly rely on

---

[25] For the constitutional aspects of the application of a Regulation in domestic legal orders see the reservations of the French Government after the adoption of the SEA and in particular Art.100A EC, which constitutes the legal basis of all Public Procurement Directives after 1986 in Kapteyn and Verloren van Themaat, *Introduction to the Law of the European Communities*, 2nd ed, 1989, Kluwer-Deventer p.470-479.

their provisions not only against the state but also against other individuals before domestic courts.

Directives, on the other hand, appear to have strong characteristics of instruments of public law, in as much as they constitute the legal framework within which the state must enact rules that regulate the relevant sector. Directives, unlike Regulations lay down duties and obligations addressed only to Member States. Regulations, in addition, introduce rights of individuals to be respected by Member States and also other individuals. Directives resemble circulars at domestic administrative level, to the extent that the latter provide the framework for action by central government to the competent decentralised authority. The difference is that Directives are binding legal instruments and may be relied upon before national courts by individuals under certain circumstances restrictively interpreted by the European Court of Justice (the case of direct effectiveness), whereas administrative circulars produce no binding effects. Directives, as Community legal instruments were thought to be the most appropriate method to regulate public markets in the European Community. As mentioned above, divergencies in existing national legal systems dictated the continuation of domestic public market regimes, but the main concern was their enforcement at national level. In fact, it was the range of procedural and substantive sensibilities and peculiarities found in the judicial infrastructure of the Member States, especially the system through which judicial review of public procurement is channelled, that prevented legal unification at Community level by means of Regulations.

If public markets are considered as a major component of the common market, the regulation of public procurement, as an essential feature for their implementation, obtains a crucial role for the whole European Integration process. Public markets comprise different geographical and product/services markets, but also embrace national ones. Thus, public market segmentation acquires a separate dimension, that of the national / domestic public market, as states often define their geographical public markets in accordance with their borders. The regulation of public procurement aims at dismantling national public markets and create a Community wide public market for products, works and services destined for the European public. It is useful here to explain the logic behind the tendency of Member States to partition public markets according to physical/geographical borders. The public sector in each

Member State represents transactions of almost 9% of the Gross Domestic Product. That reveals the fact that public expenditure in the relevant markets is a powerful tool of policy making. If public expenditure relating to procurement in a Member State is diverted back in the domestic economy, then the state in question enjoys a relatively strong and predictable industrial base, which in the short-run can attract foreign investment. In addition to that, in the long-run and if properly managed (promotion of research and development and product innovation), public markets segmentation through "buy-national" policies can lead to industrial specialisation and competitiveness of strategic industries, thus leaving the state in a position to plan not only conjunctural but also long term economic policies. The other effect for partitioning public markets and protecting them from outside competition is a control over domestic unemployment. If construction, supplies and services contracts are allocated between domestic contractors, the rate of production in the relevant sectors would be considerably high. There are also other, secondary-line effects for a state from protecting its public markets; economies of transport indicate better and more efficient delivery of products and after sales-services, or more efficient completion of a construction project or a service contract if the contractor is a domestic one. It appears that public markets segmentation often results in promoting firms engaged in transactions with the public sector and in supporting domestic economy as part of a carefully orchestrated industrial policy.

Public Procurement has been considered as the most important non-tariff barrier for the completion of the common market and its regulation received priority by the European Union Institutions and the Member States (*Commission's White Paper for the Internal market*). The liberalisation of public markets reflects the attempts of the European Institutions to enhance competitiveness in the public sector and industrial efficiency in order to achieve a uniform pattern of industrial policy at centralised level. Priority has been given by the European Community to the fact that Member States must embark upon a process of changing their public sector management ethos and adopting more market-oriented parameters in the delivery of public service. The objectives of such processes include: value for money (efficiency, risk management, savings, quality), transparency and competitiveness in public purchasing. Public procurement, as a fiscal discipline acquired a significant role within the context of the European integration, but more importantly at domestic level, where national administrations have been required to implement and comply with a newly established legal regime which aims at integrating the public markets of the European Union. Interestingly, at the same time of this evolutionary era in the direction of the regulation of public purchasing in the common market, the supply side has been facing considerable challenges. The industrial structure of the European Community reveals strong tendencies towards industrial concentration through mergers and acquisitions, rationalisation and restructuring of firms, downsizing, outsourcing and optimisation of human and capital resources within the sectors of the European industries.[26] The integration of public markets has threatened to bring about an end to long-standing dependency purchasing patterns which have undoubtedly sustained certain industries in the Member States of the European Community.[27]

The set of the Directives enacted by Community Institutions as the result of the Internal Market Programme and subsequently amended after its completion (the end of 1992) introduce a new regime that attempts to establish gradually[28] a public market in the Community without frontiers. This regime seeks to accomplish unobstructed access to public markets through transparency of public expenditure relating to procurement, improved market information, elimination of technical standards capable of discriminating against potential contractors and uniform application of objective criteria of participation in tendering and award procedures. The background and development of the legislative regime on Public Procurement in the Community will be examined in the following Chapters.

Public procurement has been considered one of the last obstacles - non tariff barriers for the establishment and proper functioning of the common market. Whether it still remains as the most substantial one should be rather the subject of exposure of the regime to empirical

---

[26] See the European Commission's *Concentration Memorandum*, Competition Series, Study no 3, Brussels 1966: *The problem of Industrial Concentration in the Common market*. For a detailed analysis of industrial concentration in the European Community see C. Bovis, *Business Law in the European Union*, Chapter 2, Sweet and Maxwell, 1997.

[27] See Commission of the European Communities, *Statistical Performance for keeping watch over public procurement*, 1992.

[28] The Utilities Directive 90/531 (O.J.1900 L297) and the Services 93/50 Directive (O.J.1992 L209/1) have been implemented by Spain, Portugal and Greece at a later stage in relation to the other Member States.

criticism.[29] A number of commentators have attempted to comprehend how the regime works in practice.[30] In this book, the author has attempted to provide a comprehensive background of the evolution and the actual operation of the public procurement rules in order:

- to expose and assess the impact of the regime on the demand and supply sides,
- to test the effect of the public procurement regime on purchasing patterns of the public sector,
- to criticise - in a constructive way - the interaction of public procurement rules with laws and policies of the European Union, and finally
- to answer the question *"How far has the public procurement legal regime accomplished the integration of the public markets of the European Community and how deep is this integration".*

This book aims to provide its readership with a comprehensive piece of literature which will pioneer interdisciplinary comparisons between the regulation of public procurement and the European Integration process. The main objective of the author is to introduce the concept of public purchasing as part of the emerging Economic Law of the European Union, as well as to introduce the regulation of public procurement from a *macro-perspective.* The legal and economic dynamics of the European Integration process have revealed a series of dramatic changes in the interaction amongst the Member States of the European Community which has taken many by surprise. The culture and ethos of public sector

---

[29] The Commission has accomplished a Mid-Term Assessment on the Functioning of Public Procurement in 1996, which has predominately resulted in the publication of the *Green Paper on Public Procurement in the European Union: Exploring the Way Forward.*

[30] See C. Bovis, *EC Public Procurement Law*, Longman, European Law Series, 1997. H.Fernandez Martin, *"EC Public Procurement Rules: A Critical Analysis*, OUP, 1996. S. Arrowsmith, *The Law of Public and Utilities Procurement*, Sweet & Maxwell, 1996. P. Armin-Trepte, *Public Procurement in the EC,* CCH Europe, 1993. A. Cox, *Public Procurement in the European Community: The internal market rules and the enforcement regime after 1992*, Earlsgate Press, 1993. Various authors, *Public Procurement: Legislation and Commentary*, Butterworths European Law Service, 1992. F. Weiss, *Public Procurement in European Community Law*, Athlone Publishers, 1992. P. Lee, Public Procurement, Current EC Legal Developments, Butterworths, 1992.

management have been the subject of fundamental transformation as a result of efficiency related objectives in the delivery of public service. Efficiency gains and cost savings in the public sector of the European Community could amount to a phenomenal sum equal, according to some calculations, to the budget attached to the Common Agricultural Policy.[31] These gains could be attributed to a liberalised public purchasing regime, where supply from a pan-European market will result in better prices for the public sector. The book also endeavours to familiarise its readership with the mechanisms and practices of achieving the desirable effects of integration of public markets in the European Community and to assess the impact of legislation on public procurement.

In Chapter 2, the author assesses the intellectual approach to the regulation of public procurement. He attempts to define the parameters of the European Integration process which are relevant to the public sector of the Member States and their subsequent regulation. Analysis of the public purchasing structures, the legal and socio-economic background of the reform of the public sector in the Member States, the method of legal integration of public markets, the motives and objectives of the process and the anticipated enhancement of competitiveness in the relevant markets through efficiency gains, the threats and dangers of the process are the main subjects of this chapter. In Chapter 3, the author presents and analyses the development, evolution and the principles of European Public Procurement Law, as well as the extra-territorial application and effects of the legal regime in its relation with other international agreements in which the European Community is signatory. The progress of the legal regime on public supplies, works and services contracts, the utilities procurement coverage, as well as the GATT regime on government procurement are covered in this chapter. In Chapter 4, an analysis of the process of the integration of public markets is provided by means of a thorough and detailed elaboration of the principles and applicability of the relevant law on the demand and supply sides. In Chapter 5, the author seeks to evaluate the enforcement of the public procurement law at European and domestic levels and the compliance of the demand and supply sides to the principles and objectives of the relevant rules. In Chapter 6, the author provides an impact assessment of the law and policy of public procurement. He

---

[31] Draft Communication from Commission to Council on the *Importance of Information for Monitoring in the Field of Public Procurement*, CCO 93/11, Brussels 1993.

addresses inherent constraints of the legislation, purchasing structures of public monopolies and the process of their privatisation in the Member States, the process and progress on harmonisation of standards and specifications, the reluctance of the supply side in initiating litigation and finally the effect of competitiveness on the possible sustainability of certain industries. In Chapter 7, the author places the regulation of public procurement in the European Community within the broader context of the whole integration process and examines the interplay of public purchasing with other related policies of the Community. Finally, in the Conclusions recent developments in the subject and in particular the European Commission's Green Paper on Public Procurement are summarised and the author provides his views on the way forward for this intriguing discipline.

# 2 The Intellectual and the Policy Approaches to the Regulation of Public Procurement

Reliance upon directly effective primary Community law and attempts to pronounce the incompatibility of domestic laws and administrative practices relevant to public procurement with Treaty rules and principles created a background for policy formulation and intervention in the sensitive field of domestic public purchasing.[1] Primary Treaty provisions on non-discrimination (Article 7), on the prohibition to barriers to intra-community trade (Article 30 et seq.), on the freedom to provide services (Articles 52, 53) and on the right of establishment (Articles 59, 60), on public undertakings and undertakings to which Member States grant special or exclusive rights and on state monopolies providing services of general economic interest (Article 90), although capable of embracing the legal relations arising form public procurement in the common market and regulating intra-community trade of public contracts according to the principles stipulated in the Treaties, seemed insufficient on their own in eliminating protection afforded to domestic undertakings through preferential public procurement. The diversity of legal systems within the

---

[1] Until the completion of the internal market, the European Commission had initiated 15 cases before the European Court of Justice against defaulting Member States under the compliance procedures based on Article 169 EC. Also, a number of landmark cases had reached the Court through reference procedures from national courts under Article 177 EC, seeking clarification or interpretation of provisions of Procurement Directives or requesting the Court to pronounce on their direct effectiveness.

Member States of the European Union and the differences in existing domestic public procurement rules, would have rendered the regulation of public markets ineffective, if recourse solely to primary Community legislation was sought. The negative character of the primary Community provisions which may apply to public procurement, to the extent that they provide for a legal framework which prohibits any obstructions, distortions and hindrances to intra-community trade and the relevant fundamental principles could be seen as the main reason for the need by Community Institutions to intervene and introduce a set of rules which, although based upon the above primary Community rules, have a positive character in the sense that they allow a margin of discretion in their implementation. Due to the decentralised nature of any regulatory form of public procurement in the common market, the normative character of the primary Community rules was diluted in favour of a process of harmonisation of existing laws and practices in the member states.

The existence of Community legislation in the form of Directives which aimed to co-ordinate the award of public contracts at national level[2], as well as the application of primary Treaty provisions to public procurement within the European Community appeared inadequate for the abolition of non-tariff barriers posed by preferential purchasing patterns of member states and their organs.[3] That particular inadequacy could be attributed to the fact that the secondary legislation (Directives) on public procurement mainly focused on procedural, and to some extent bureaucratic matters in the award of public contracts in the Member States,[4] while the substantive elements of the regulation of intra-community trade through public purchasing were left in the hands of national administrations, which, by exercising a great deal of discretion in selection and award procedures, discriminated against firms established in

---

[2] Reference is made here to the first generation of Public Procurement Directives: for Public Supplies, EC Directives 70/32 and 77/62 as amended by Directive 80/767 and 88/295; for Public Works, EC Directives 71/304 and 71/305 as amended by Directive 89/440. See Chapter 3 for more details.

[3] See the FIDE Congress on *The Application in the Member States of the Directives on Public Procurement*, Madrid 1990.

[4] See C. Bovis, *Public entities awarding procurement contracts under the framework of EC Public Procurement Directives*, Journal of Business Law, 1993, Vol.1, p.p. 56-78. Also, C. Bovis, *The eligibility of enterprises to participate in tenders for the award of Public Procurement contracts*, European Business Law Review, 1994, Vol.5, p.p. 1-36.

other member states and instead favoured domestic suppliers. The main factors responsible for the lack of success of the first generation of public procurement Directives according to the Commission's Communication to the Council[5] included *inter alia*: i) failure to advertise contracts above certain thresholds in the Official Journal, as a result of intentional splitting-up of contracts in order to avoid the mandatory advertisement requirement, although improvements had been made in the retrieval of information by the establishment of the Tenders Electronic Daily (TED) Data Bank; (however, the introduction of information technology to public procurement should be regarded as a means to facilitate the supply side (the industry) in determining the purchasing intentions of the demand side and not as a *panacea* in improving transparency ratios of contracting authorities); ii) ignorance of the relevant rules on the part of contracting authorities or deliberate omission of these rules; iii) excessive use of the exceptions permitting non-competitive tendering (negotiated procedures) instead of open or restricted procedures; iv) discriminatory requirements imposed by contracting authorities upon tenderers demanding compliance with national technical standards, to the exclusion of European standards or equivalent standards of other countries; and v) unlawful disqualification of suppliers or contractors or discriminatory use of the award criteria (either the lowest price or the most economically advantageous offer). Moreover, the Directives were inappropriately transposed into domestic legal systems, thus not conferring the envisaged access to justice and rights to individuals. Member States are obliged to implement Directives in a manner that satisfies the requirements of clarity, legal certainty and legitimate expectation, thus transposing their provisions into national ones by virtue of laws which have binding force.[6] Administrative circulars or administrative practices and official instructions which by their nature can always be changed as and when the authorities please and which do not confer rights to individuals are not considered sufficient to constitute proper fulfilment of the obligation to implement Directives. Even the direct effectiveness of the provisions of Directives does not exempt a Member State from the obligation to adopt the appropriate implementing measures within the period prescribed therein.[7] The inadequacy of primary

---

[5] COM(84) 717 fin.

[6] See case 239/85 *Commission v. Belgium*, [1986] ECR 1473; also case 300/81 *Commission v. Italy*, [1983] ECR 449.

[7] See case 102/79 *Commission v. Belgium*, [1980] ECR 1489; also case 147/86 *Commission v. Hellenic Republic*, [1988] ECR 765.

Community law to regulate public procurement within the common market was clearly augmented with the complexity of the legal regimes in operation in the member states, as well as their polarised nature and the character of national regulatory powers in relation to public purchasing. Thus, harmonisation and not uniformity was deemed to be the appropriate approach towards the integration of public markets in the European Community and the elimination of actual and potential non-tariff barriers arising therein.

**The new approach towards the integration of public markets**

The rationale behind the whole process of the integration of public markets of the Member States has been the establishment of an effectively competitive regime, similar to that envisaged for the operation of private markets.[8] European Institutions have intellectually supported such an attempt by reference to liberal economic theories,[9] where a regime of enhanced competition in public markets could bring about beneficial effects for the supply side of the equation (the industry), by means of optimal allocation of resources within the European industries, rationalisation of production and supply, promotion of mergers and acquisitions and elimination of sub-optimal firms and creation of globally competitive industries. These effects have been also deemed to yield substantial purchasing savings for the public sector.[10] The European Institutions envisaged the creation of such a competitive regime in public markets through the establishment of a legal framework which aims at abolishing discrimination on grounds of nationality and at eliminating preferential public procurement practices which favour "national champions". The above regime intends to introduce a strict regulatory framework of operations related to the supply chain of contracting authorities in the public sector. This indicates the fact that the demand side

---

[8] The adverse effects of concerted practices in tendering procedures on competition in the common market were recognised by the the European Court of Justice in case *Cooperative Vereniging "Suiker Unie" UA v. Commission,*, [1975] ECR 1663.

[9] See the Cechinni Report *1992 The European Challenge,* Aldershot, Wildwood House, 1988.

[10] See European Commission, *The Cost of Non-Europe, Basic Findings, Vol.5, Part.A; The Cost of Non-Europe in Public Sector Procurement*, Official Publications of the European Communities, Luxembourg, 1988.

in the supply / demand equation of public procurement is the dominant part and its regulation would materialise the objectives of the process.

However, the attempts to integrate the public markets of the European Community solely by reference to the regulation of the purchasing behaviour of the demand side (the contracting authorities) appear to have left the supply side of public procurement unaffected by the above regulatory framework. The behaviour of the supply side is not the subject of public procurement legislation, although its regulation appears equally important with reference to the integration of public markets in Europe. Theoretically speaking, the supply side in the public procurement equation is subject to the competition law and policy of the Treaties, but it is evident that there is lack of an integral mechanism in public procurement legislation capable of incorporating the results of the anti-trust rules when applied to the supply side. *Stricto sensu*, anti-competitive behaviour of undertakings or collusive tendering do not appear to be reasons for disqualification from the selection and award processes of public contracts. It seems that the assumptions of European Institutions concentrate on the fact that by forcing contracting authorities throughout the Community into a common purchasing behaviour which is based on the principles of openness, transparency and non-discrimination, industrial restructuring (in the supply side) will follow as a result of such stimulant and therefore all the above-mentioned desirable effects concerning efficiency gains and public sector savings will occur.

The European Commission has claimed that the regulation of public procurement throughout the Community and the resulting elimination of non-tariff barriers arising from discriminatory and preferential purchasing patterns of Member Sates could bring about substantial savings of ECU 20 bn or 0.5% of GDP to the (European) public sector. Combating discrimination on grounds of nationality in public procurement and eliminating domestic preferential purchasing schemes could result in efficiency gains at European and national levels through the emergence of three major effects which would primarily influence the supply side.[11] These include a *trade effect*, a *competition effect* and a *restructuring effect*.

The trade effect is associated with the actual and potential savings that the public sector will be able to achieve through lower cost purchasing. This effect appears to have a static dimension, since it emerges

---

[11] *ibid.*

as a consequence of enhanced market access in the relevant sector or industry. The trade effect emanates as a result of the principle of transparency in public markets (compulsory advertisement of public contracts above certain thresholds), a fact that constitutes an improvement from previously closed preferential regimes. However, the principle of transparency and the associated trade effect in public markets do not in themselves guarantee the establishment of competitive conditions in the relevant markets, as market access - a structural element in the process of integration of public markets in Europe - could be hindered by discriminatory behaviour of contracting authorities in the selection stages and the award stages of public procurement.

On the other hand, the competition effect relates to the changes of industrial performance as a result of changes in the price behaviour of national firms which had previously been protected from competition by means of preferential and discriminatory procurement practices. The competition effect derives also from the principle of transparency and appears to possess rather static characteristics. Transparency in public procurement breaks information and awareness barriers in public markets, and as mentioned above brings a trade effect in the relevant sectors or industries by means of price competitiveness. The competition effect comes as a natural sequence to price competitiveness and inserts an element of long-term competitiveness in the relevant industries in aspects other than price (e.g. research and development, innovation, customer care). The competition effect would materialise in the form of *price convergence* of goods, works and services destined for the public sector. Price convergence could take place both nationally and Community-wide, in as much as competition in the relevant market would equalise the prices of similar products.

Finally, the third effect (the restructuring effect) reflects the restructuring dimension in the supply side as a result of increased competition in the relevant markets. The restructuring effect is a dynamic one and refers to the long-term industrial and sectoral adjustment of industries that supply the public sector. The restructuring effect attempts to capture the reaction of the relevant sector or industry to the competitive regime imposed upon the demand and supply sides, as a result of openness and transparency and the sequential trade and competition effects. The response of the relevant sector or industry and the restructuring effect itself would depend on the efficiency of the industry to merge, diversify, convert or abort the relevant competitive markets and would also reflect contemporary national industrial policies.[12]

The above scenario represents the model envisaged by European Institutions on a macro-perspective and depicts the orientation of policy making towards the formation of a coherent industrial policy at European level. The regulation of the purchasing behaviour of the demand side in public markets seems to constitute an effective way of introducing competitive elements to the European industries, which apparently suffer from overcapacity and excessive compartmentalisation, when compared to rival industries in North America and Japan.[13] In addition, the cost of research and development in such a market structure builds up and it is reflected in pricing, particularly in high-tech products. Industrial restructuring and adjustment has been a priority for the European Commission for a long time, and attempts to control the structure of the European industrial base have been witnessed during the eighties with the introduction of the merger control regulation[14] and a number of regulations which provide for block exemptions from Article 85 EC of otherwise anti-competitive behaviour.[15] It is submitted that by the introduction of a regulatory regime for the public markets in Europe, a coherent policy towards industrial restructuring and adjustment has been put in place covering both private and public markets, with a view to establishing a more competitive interface amongst industries in the common market and vis-à-vis rivals in non-member states.[16]

---

[12] See European Commission, *The Opening-up of Public Procurement to Foreign Direct Investment* in the European Community, CC 93/79, 1995.

[13] See P. Nicolaides (ed), *"Industrial Policy in the European Community: A Necessary Response to Economic Integration"*, Martinus Nijhoff, 1993.

[14] EC Regulation 4064/89, [1989] O.J. L 391/1.

[15] See EC Regulation 1983/83 on exclusive distribution agreements ((O.J. 1984 L 173/1); EC Regulation 1984/83 on exclusive purchasing agreements (O.J. L 173/5); EC Regulation 2349/84 on patent licence agreements (O.J. 1984 L 219); EC Regulation 123/85 on motor vehicle distribution and servicing agreements (O.J. 1985 L 15/16); EC Regulation 417/85 on specialisation agreements (O.J. 1995 L 53/1); EC Regulation 418/85 on research and development agreements (O.J. 1985 L 53/5); EC Regulation 4087/88 on franchising agreements (O.J. 1988, L 369/46); EC Regulation 556/89 on know-how licensing agreements (O.J. 1989, L 61/1). See also C. Bovis, *Business Law in the European Union*, Chapters 2 and 3, Sweet and Maxwell, 1997.

[16] See C. Bovis, *The Regulation Public Procurement as an Instrument of Industrial Policy in the Common Market* in T. Lawton (ed) *European Industrial Policy and Competitiveness: concepts and instruments*, Macmillan Publishers, 1998.

As a result of the momentum gathered in the mid-eighties, the regulation of public procurement in the European Community became a priority overnight and the inefficiency of the relevant primary and secondary Community provisions to combat discriminatory practices and preferential public purchases of contracting authorities throughout the common market was disclosed as statistical results revealed considerably low cross border import penetration in public contracts. Furthermore, a disturbing picture emerged as to the extent of differentiation between a key element in the structures of private and public markets within the European Member States. Although it is correct to maintain that there are striking differences between demand and supply structures in private and public markets, one particular market structure element that had an interestingly low presence in public markets was the element of *market access*. Market access reflects the effectiveness of import penetration strategies (marketing, predatory pricing, venture alliances) of an undertaking and very much depends upon the regime of competition reigning in the relevant market place. Public markets differ considerably from private ones in terms of structure, demand and supply conditions as well as in terms of competitiveness.

If scale economies were important in defining the most desirable purchasing pattern for the public sector and competition increases amongst industries which supply the latter, an efficient European industrial structure would support less firms operating at full capacity.[17] Strategic mergers and cross-border investments would reshape the industries and reorganise the operation of firms. Within this reorganisation process, the structural adjustment would constantly change in order to adopt to the new market environment introduced by the legal regime on public procurement. In the process of developing new industrial strategies, two factors appear essential: the need for integration of industrial activities[18] and the need to meet local demands.

During the past many of the advantages offered to national champions and locally operating firms in public procurement markets had

---

[17] Dunning, J.H. (1979), *Explaining Changing Patterns of International Production: in Defence of the Eclectic Theory*, Oxford Bulletin of Economics and Statistics, Vol. 41, No. 4, pp. 269-295.
[18] Dunning, J.H. (1993), *The Globalisation of Business, The Challenge of the 1990s*, Routledge, London and New York.

discouraged the tradability of public contracts[19] amongst European industries.[20] Persistently low import penetration in protected public procurement sectors dictated a corporate strategy to the relevant industries. Before the opening-up of the public procurement in Europe, the typical strategic choice was low on integration and high on responsiveness, including the replication of all major corporate functions (production, R&D, marketing) in each Member State. The on-going realisation of the common market and the regulation of public procurement in the European Community has been forcing firms to revise those strategies and to build-up *network organisations*, which combine local responsiveness with a high degree of centralisation and co-ordination of major supporting activities. The new strategy has the characteristics of a multi-focal strategy.

The adoption of multi-focal strategies or global integration strategies involves a major shift in location patterns of key functions within firms.[21] The old decentralised multinational organisations which duplicated major functions in each country which they operated need to transform into an integrated system of which the key elements show a different degree of regional concentration.[22] As a consequence of the new organisational structure, different types of international transactions are expected to occur.[23] Specialisation and concentration of activities in certain regions will lead to more trade between certain Member States. In addition, as a result of the corporate network system, trade will increasingly develop into-intra-firm trade and intra-industry trade with greater exchange of intermediary products.[24] The organisational rationalisation following the development of network organisations poses the problem of ownership and location of the corporate headquarters. Some Member States may fear

---

[19] The term tradability of public contracts denotes the effectiveness of the supply side to engage in transactions with public authorities in Member States other than the State of its residence or nationality.

[20] McLachlan, D.L. (1985), *Discriminatory Public Procurement, Economic Integration and the Role of Bureaucracy*, Journal of Common Market Studies, Vol. 23, No. 4, pp. 357-372.

[21] Porter, M.E. (1990), *The Competitive Advantage of Nations*, MacMillan, London.

[22] Prahalad C.K. and Y. Doz (1987), *The Multinational Mission, Balancing Local Demands and Global Vision*, The Free Press.

[23] Dunning, J. (1982), *Multinational Enterprices in the 1970's*, in: K. Hopt, *European Merger Contract*, de Fruyter, Berlin.

[24] Vandermerwe, S., *A Framework for constructing Euro-networks*, European Management Journal, Vol. 11, No. 1, pp. 55-61.

losing strategic control in the restructuring process[25] and therefore may resist the rationalisation process that the industry has been undergoing, by imposing various restrictions in terms of ownership or control structures of locally operating firms.

## The regulatory background of public procurement

In recent years, the exercise of public procurement in the form of purchasing goods, works and services by the state and its organs has been through a phase of constructive criticism and has been the subject of an evolving transformation which has undoubtedly imposed considerable financial as well as performance burdens on both the demand and supply sides. The demand side in the public procurement equation is referred to as all the contracting authorities which are covered by law when they procure goods, services or works contracts. Contracting authorities thus cover the state and its organs (central and local government) and bodies governed by public law, as well as utilities (entities operating in the water, energy, transport and telecommunications sectors). On the other hand, the supply side in the public procurement equation is referred to as the industry that does business with the public sector. The Commission's White Paper for the Completion of the Internal Market[26] and two notable scientifically and empirically based studies during the mid-eighties[27] illustrated the fact that preferential public purchasing in the Member States of the European Community constituted a significant non-tariff barrier to trade, as well as a considerable obstacle for the uninhibited functioning of the common market. The underlying motivation behind the regulation of public procurement in uniform, non-discriminatory and transparent patterns throughout the common market has been the achievement of savings for the public sector, as preferential purchasing patterns for the public sector

---

[25] Tirole, J. (1988), *The theory of Industrial Organization*, The MIT Press, Cambridge.
[26] European Commission, *White Paper for the Completion of the Internal Market*, (COM) 85 310 fin., 1985.
[27] European Commission, *The Cost of Non-Europe, Basic Findings, Vol.5, Part.A; The Cost of Non-Europe in Public Sector Procurement*, Official Publications of the European Communities, Luxembourg, 1988; the Cechinni Report *1992 The European Challenge*, Aldershot, Wildwood House, 1988.

have been deemed to perpetuate price discrepancies attributed to factors other than quality.

Public procurement, as a dispersement of public service by the state and its organs represents a substantial proportion of the European Union's Gross Domestic Product (GDP)[28] and when examined in the context of domestic budgetary frameworks, it may qualify as an instrument which could support national conjunctural (short-term economic policies) or even long-term macro-economic policies relating to employment, regional development, industrial adjustment and industrial performance).[29]

The Commission's White Paper for the Completion of the Internal Market and the Single European Act formed the political and legal framework of the attempts of European Institutions to tackle the issue of public procurement more effectively. New legislation was introduced and priority was given to the inclusion of the so-far excluded public sectors (public utilities) into the regulatory regime of public procurement. The main improvements in relation to the previous regime are: i) with open and restricted tendering procedures as the norm, negotiated ones were allowed in exceptional circumstances; ii) the method of calculation of the thresholds was clarified; iii) purchasing authorities have to publish in advance information on their annual procurement programmes and their timetable, as well as a notice giving details of the outcome of each decision of award iv) the rules on technical standards have been brought in line with the new policy which is based on the mutual recognition of national requirements, through an objective process of legislative harmonisation of technical standards.

The new set of European Directives[30] have aimed at harmonisation of national provisions for the award of supplies, works and services

---

[28] Approximately 15% (at 1988 prices) and 11% (at 1996 prices) of the Community's Gross Domestic Product (GDP) respectively. See *The Cost of Non-Europe, Basic Findings, Vol.5, Part.A; The Cost of Non-Europe in Public Sector Procurement*, Official Publications of the European Communities, Luxembourg, 1988. Also the *Green Paper on Public Procurement in the European Union: Exploring the way forward*, European Commission 1996.

[29] See European Commission: *Public Procurement: Regional and Social Aspects* (COM(89) 400).

[30] Public Supplies Contracts: EC Directive 88/295 (O.J. 1988, L 127,1), consolidated by Directive 93/36, O.J. 1993, L 199. Public Works Contracts EC Directive 89/440 (O.J. 1989 L210,1), consolidated by Directive 93/37, O.J. 1993, L 199. Utilities Sectors: EC Directive 90/531 (O.J. 1990, L 297), as amended by Directive 93/38, O.J. 1993, L 199. Public Services Contracts EC Directive 92/50, O.J.1992 L 209.

contracts in the public sector (comprising of central and local government and bodies governed by public law) and the utilities (entities operating in the water, energy, transport and telecommunications sectors). Emphasis was also placed on compliance of the above Directives by Member States and their contracting authorities and the availability of remedies to interested parties and aggrieved tenderers, so Directives, which aim to ensure access to justice and sufficient compensation to tenderers that suffered damages because of illegal acts of contracting authorities have been enacted.[31] The public procurement regime can be classified into the public supplies sector,[32] the public works sector,[33] the public utilities sector[34] and the public services sector.[35] The principal objective of all Public Procurement Directives relies on the assumption that transparency and improved market information should enhance market efficiency by ensuring that conditions of competition are not distorted and that contracts are allocated to suppliers and contractors under the conditions which are most favourable for the contracting authorities. The Directives are based on three underlying fundamental principles: Community-wide advertising of public contracts above certain thresholds; prohibition of technical specifications capable of discriminating against potential bidders; and application of objective criteria of participation in tendering and award procedures. The underlying motivation behind the introduction of the European Directives as legal instruments to regulate public procurement in non-discriminatory and transparent patterns throughout the common market has been the achievements of savings for the public sector. The procurement Directives appear to possess a rather quasi-normative character and to balance the negative obligations deriving from primary Community law with the positive obligations deriving from the results to be achieved through the methods of their implementation. Justification of the above assumption could be sought by reference to the pronouncement of the direct effectivity of key provisions of the Directives by the European Court of Justice.[36]

---

[31] EC Directives 89/665, O.J.1989 L 395 and 92/13, O.J.1992 L 76/7.
[32] EC Directive 70/32, 77/62 as amended by Directive 80/767 and 88/295 and consolidated by Directive 93/36, O.J. 1993, L 199.
[33] EC Directive 71/304, 71/305 as amended by Directive 89/440, and consolidated by Directive 93/37, O.J. 1993, L 199.
[34] EC Directive 90/531, as amended by Directive 93/38, O.J. 1993, L 199.
[35] EC Directive 92/50 of 18/6/92, O.J.1992 L 209.
[36] See the analysis of *judicial control at domestic level in* Chapter 5.

Community Institutions have opted for Directives in order to regulate public markets since they are legal instruments which take into account existing sensibilities and particularities within the legal orders of the Member States. European Directives are flexible legal instruments not only because they leave the choice of the form and methods of their implementation in the hands of Member States, but also they provide for a period within which the latter should implement their provisions.[37] A Directive has binding force upon Member States to which it is addressed only with respect to the result to be achieved. The fact that the form and methods of its implementation are left at the discretion of the addressee Member State, reveals the unique character of such legal instruments, for which there is no parallel in national or international law.[38]

The definition of Directives poses some questions as to whether they imply a limitation, and to what extent, on the competence of Community Institutions.[39] A thorough reading of Article 189 EC leaves no doubt that such a limitation of competence is indeed implied. The real problems, however, arise in considering the extent of that limitation on the competence of the Institutions. A Directive's binding force is limited to the result to be achieved and in so far as it concerns the form and the methods it has no binding effect. The distinction between the "result" and the "forms and methods", or to put it in other words between the binding and non-binding character, is far from clear and has not yet received an answer from the Court of Justice.

A Directive serves to fetter the law-making power of Member States on certain points.[40] It is an instrument of Community intervention often with a view to harmonisation of national laws. This sort of intervention includes the insertion of a common denominator envisaged at Community level in national legal orders. Harmonisation of laws is a gradual approximation of Member States legal orders in a given complex of interrelated legislative provisions, which directly affects the establishment or functioning of the Common Market.[41] Therefore, the "result" to be achieved, the legally binding character of a Directive, may be defined as a legal or factual situation which does justice to the

---

[37] Article 189 EC.
[38] see Kapteyn and Verloren van Themaat, *Introduction to the Law of the European Communities*, 2nd ed. 1989, Kluwer, Deventer, pp.331 et seq.
[39] see R. Lauwaars, *Lawfulness and legal force of Community Decisions*, A.W.Sijthoff, Leiden 1973, pp.28-37.
[40] see Kapteyn and Verloren van Themaat, op.cit.
[41] Article 100 EC.

Community interest that the Directive is to ensure. The harmonisation process may sometimes necessitate amendments of national laws; a Directive then will contain instructions as to the content of such amendments. In that case, if not the actual "form", at least the "methods" by which the result should be achieved are envisaged at Community level.

The above-mentioned analysis reveals that the relationship between the "result" and the "form" and "methods" is a fluctuating one, although there is an inherent limit to that fluctuation; a Directive can never impose on Member States an obligation to introduce an exhaustive list of rules entirely unconnected with the national legislation in the context of which the field concerned is to be regulated.[42] Member States always are left with a margin of discretion as to the form and methods of implementation of a Directive. This implementation must be achieved in a manner that ensures the effective function of the Directive, with an account being taken of its aims. Member States are obliged to implement Directives in a manner that satisfies the requirements of clarity, legal certainty and legitimate expectation,[43] thus transposing their provisions into national ones which have binding force. Mere circulars or administrative practices, official instructions which by their nature can always be changed as and when the authorities please and which do not confer rights to individuals are not considered sufficient to constitute proper fulfilment of the obligation to implement Directives.[44] Even direct effectiveness of a Directive's provisions does not exempt a Member State from the obligation to adopt the appropriate implementing measures within the period prescribed therein.[45]

Although Directives generally aim at the harmonisation of national laws of Member States, the Directives on Public Procurement mention as their objective the co-ordination of national procedures for the award of public contracts. Using the term harmonisation of laws, the EC Treaty has envisaged the gradual approximation of existing national legal provisions.[46] These provisions are legally enforceable in Member States' legal orders conferring rights and duties upon individuals. On the other

---

[42] See case 38/77 *ENKA BV v. Inspecteur der Invoerrecht en Accijnzen*, [1977] ECR 2203.
[43] See case 239/85 *Commission v. Belgium*, [1986] ECR 1473; also case 300/81 *Commission v. Italy*, [1983] ECR 449.
[44] See case 102/79 *Commission v. Belgium*, [1980] ECR 1489; also case 147/86 *Commission v. Hellenic Republic*, [1988] ECR 765.
[45] Case 102/79, op.cit., at 1487.
[46] Article 100 EC.

hand, co-ordination as a term used by Community law appears relevant with respect to national policies. National policies are not always incorporated in legal instruments, but they may constitute governmental lines towards the achievement of an aim. The fact that a State prefers to regulate a sector through administrative practices and not statutorily reflects the complexity of the sector in question. Administrative practices are not legally enforceable instruments and do not confer rights and obligations upon individuals of Member States. They serve as legal guidelines, rather than as regulatory tools. Thus, co-ordination of national policies is a more relaxed procedure than harmonisation of laws. The latter is closer to uniformity amongst the Member States' legal orders, whereas the former rather attempts to remove striking differences between Member States' policies in order to achieve a smoother function of the sector in issue. Implementing measures related to public procurement Directives have taken the form of ministerial circulars, ministerial orders and administrative practices in many Member States. There is little doubt that the public procurement sector is dominated by national sensibilities that change continuously, thus requiring frequent governmental intervention. National decision-making with respect to regional and social development, anti-cyclical demand management and employment are less autonomous policy objectives[47] and has often dictated the need to implement EC Public Procurement Directives through administrative practices. On the other hand, statutory implementation of Public Procurement Directives provides for a clearer and more precise regime, as individuals in Member States may rely upon legally enforceable acts before national courts in a dispute that falls under the framework of those Directives.

**Inherent dangers in the process of integration of the European public markets**

The process of the integration of public markets in Europe and the integral mechanism of dismantling national borders in intra-community public trade have revealed a number of considerable threats amongst the potential benefits of the exercise. Firstly, the integration of public markets and the

---

[47] The effectiveness of government contracts as an instrument of public policy is questioned. For more details see the Commission's Communication (1989) fin. of 22 Sept.1990 *on Public Procurement, Regional and Social Aspects*, O.J.1989, C 311/7, Ch.IV.

opening-up of public procurement in the Member States do not seem to take fully into account the inherent danger of market concentration. As a result of such a stimulant to the demand side, sub-optimal firms would be forced to leave the market and the volume of industrial concentration through mergers and acquisitions of less competitive firms would inevitably grow, the danger of market oligopolisation becomes eminent.[48] The adverse effects of market concentration as a result of the oligopolistic structure of the relevant markets could seriously hinder the objectives of the exercise. It was mentioned previously that the restructuring effect would facilitate the clearing of the relevant markets of any sub-optimal firm or industry. However, there is no indication as to the market structure after the impact of the restructuring effect, and given the fact that the above effect has a dynamic character, the relevant market would present trends of continuous adjustment. Industrial adjustment and restructuring would inevitably lead to a more concentrated structure of the market place as a result of predation, take-overs and amalgamation of rival firms. The potential threats of market oligopolisation should be counterbalanced with the long-awaited desirable effects on the structure of the European industrial base. If the results of the market oligopolisation were translated to a more innovative and specialised production output along the supply chain system and if the expected industrial competitiveness across a European-wide basis could put firms in a position to compete directly with rival industries in other parts of the world, then the dangers arising from market concentration would be minimal. However, one should never underestimate the threats of collusive behaviour and the pricing policies that could emerge from oligopolistic structure.[49] Conspiratorial practices of oligopolists which supply the public sector could possibly lead to high prices, perhaps higher than those prior to the restructuring and adjustment exercise. Furthermore, even if prices of goods, works and services destined for the public sector would converge and settled at a higher level, this could result in supra-competitive profits for the oligopolists at the expense of the demand side. Another dimension of the concentration and oligopolisation of public markets reflects considerable socio-economic

---

[48] The applicability of Competition Law and Policy of the Treaty (Articles 85, 86) in controlling collusive tendering and anti-competitive behavior of suppliers, was the subject of Commission Decision 92/204, O.J. 1992 L92/1.

[49] See C. Bovis, *Business Law in the European Union*, Chapter 3, Sweet and Maxwell, 1997.

considerations. If one is to accept that industrial restructuring and adjustment emanate from the need to eliminate sub-optimal overcapacity, the factor of production which would be affected most is labour. Redundancies and reduction of workforce often follow market concentration in an attempt to minimise duplication, or to achieve rationalisation.

It is important here to distinguish high technology industries supplying public procurement markets from more "traditional" ones. The high-tech group of industries is characterised by strong technological developments and reinvestment of a considerable amount on research and development. Such industries include telecommunications, data-processing equipment, medical equipment, bio-tech and pharmaceutical products and aerospace. These industries have been demarcated by high cross-country investment patterns, with an important presence of Japanese and American interests.[50] The group of traditional industries supplying public procurement markets include industries dealing with railway equipment, heavy steel structures, shipbuilding, vehicles and textiles. Most of these industries have been "national champions"[51] and heavily protected from competition and sustained through public sector purchasing.[52] The high-tech public procurement industry has a tendency to operate in several national public procurement markets, thus having a large share of European production. This could be explained by the high levels of concentration observed for such industries over the last decade.[53] On the other hand, traditional public procurement industries have a strong tendency to operate at national level and enjoy the advantages of being national champions.

The second inherent threat of the process of integrating the public markets of the European Community reveals the vulnerable position of small and medium size firms as a consequence of their exposure to the

---

[50] Thomsen, S. and Nicolaides P. (1991), *The evolution of Japanese Direct Investment in Europe: Death of a Salesman*, Royal Institute of International Affairs, London.
[51] The term implies a firm with more than a third of its turnover made in its own country and has enjoyed formal or informal government protection. The term has been defined by Abravanel, R. and D. Ernst (1992), *Alliance and acquisition strategies for European national champions*, The McKinsey Quarterly, no. 2, pp. 45-62.
[52] Abravanel, R. and D. Ernst (1992), *Alliance and acquisition strategies for European national champions*, The McKinsey Quarterly, no. 2, pp. 45-62.
[53] Davies, S. and B. Lyons (1993), *The EC Industrial Organization Data Matrix*, Mimeo.

new regime. Small and medium firms would find it difficult to sustain existing market shares or penetrate product or geographical markets as a result of either collusive tendering of oligopolists suppliers, or inefficient own resources which could not be·compared with those of large firms (volume production and economies of scale, financial and economic standing). Arguably, if the enhanced competitive regime in public markets results in industrial concentration which could bring about efficiency gains for public sector purchasing, then there is little complaint about market inequalities concerning access and opportunities for small and medium firms. This, however, runs contrary to the declarations and undertakings[54] by European Institutions on the role of SMEs for the completion of the common market and its importance for regional and economic development, social cohesion and industrial adjustment. The fears of oligopolisation of public markets and its subsequent effect of marginalisation of SMEs have been confirmed.[55] Market access for SMEs in public procurement is limited and disproportionately low in relation to their numbers throughout the European Union.

In addition to the internal effects of the new regime, the integration of public markets has acquired an external dimension through the GATT Agreement on Government Procurement.[56] Exposure of the supply side to competitive forces form both within and outside the common market have intensified the impact and the effect of the new regime. Market access is guaranteed to firms established in signatories to the Agreement in an attempt to liberalise globally public procurement, although it was until recently that contracting entities, other than central authorities, as well as construction procurement and procurement of services and telecommunications equipment were included in the Agreement during the

---

[54] See European Commission, *SMEs participation in public procurement in the European Community* (SEC(92) 722). European *Commission Action Programme for SMEs* (COM(86) 445); (b) *Public Procurement: Regional and Social Aspects* (COM(89) 400); (c) *Promoting SME Participation in the Community* (COM(90) 166).

[55] See European Commission, *SME TASK FORCE: SMEs and Public Procurement*, Brussels 1988. European Commission, *Pan European Forum on Sub-Contracting in the Community*, Brussels 1993.

[56] See Council Decision 80/271, O.J. 1979 L 71/1 and Council Decision 87/565, O.J. 1987, L 345/24. Also the Agreement on Government Procurement as a result of the negotiations during the GATT Uruguay Round which was signed on April 15, 1996. The new Government Procurement Agreement (GPA), after ratification by its signatories, is in force since January 1, 1996

GATT / WTO Uruguay Round. Despite the fact that the GATT Agreement on Government Procurement has been in existence since the Tokyo Round (1980), the tradability of public contracts vis-à-vis member-signatories to the Agreement has been rather limited. Import penetration for the public sector has been marginal and, again, large conglomerates appear to be the beneficiaries.[57] European SMEs, particularly those in highly specialised industries, have been the target of US or Japanese take-overs, as the flow of direct investment within the European Union has been increased over the last years. Interestingly enough, the vulnerability of SMEs, as a result of the global integration of public markets follows similar patterns with those on internal public sector integration.[58]

## The structure of public procurement of Member States

The volume of public procurement in the Europe of 12 has been estimated at ECU 560 bn, an approximate 15% of the Community's Gross Domestic Product (GDP).[59] These figures were based on 1988 prices. With the latest enlargement[60] taken into account, the figures should approach ECU 750 bn at 1996 prices and an approximate 11% of the Community's GDP.[61] In real terms, public procurement represents a significant amount of the Member States' GDP, a fact that has been seen as very important by European Institutions for the process of European integration.[62] In the light of the level of infrastructure within the common market and the amount spent on it every financial year by contracting authorities of the Member

---

[57] European Commission, *Statistical Performance for keeping watch over public procurement*, 1992.
[58] For more details on the GATT AGP and the new WTO Government Procurement Agreement see Chapter 3.
[59] See *The Cost of Non-Europe, Basic Findings, Vol.5, Part.A; The Cost of Non-Europe in Public Sector Procurement*, Official Publications of the European Communities, Luxembourg, 1988.
[60] The accession of Sweden, Finland and Austria.
[61] See the Green Paper on *Public Procurement in the European Union: Exploring the way forward*, European Commission 1996.
[62] Public procurement at domestic level represents transactions which amount to almost 9% of the Gross Domestic Product of each Member State. See European Commission, *The Cost of Non-Europe, Basic Findings, Vol.5, Part.A; The Cost of Non-Europe in Public Sector Procurement*, Official Publications of the European Communities, Luxembourg, 1988.

States, the public sector has acquired a significant dimension within the European Integration process and the need to regulate it with the view to eliminate market distortions became imminent. Preferential public purchasing in the Member States of the European Community- in pursuit of national policies- constituted a significant non-tariff barrier to intra-Community trade[63] as well as a considerable obstacle for the establishment and the uninhibited functioning of the common market.[64]

In relation to the public purchasing structure of the Member States of the Community, two main categories of systems can be distinguished: the first depends on a centralised control of the procurement requirements of the contracting authorities, whereas the second allows for more autonomy at regional level. Of course, there are cases where a combination of centralised and decentralised procurement practices exist, as a result of long standing administrative structures which predate the European legislation. One could not easily criticise the operation of a domestic public purchasing system by reference to the centralised or decentralised nature of the national administration. Member States have their own administrative/public systems, which to a certain degree give priority to centrifugal or centripetal purchasing structures accordingly.[65] Public procurement and its regulaton could not escape such long and well established patterns and there is no substantial evidence that change in the structural nature of national administrations would benefit the state and its contracting authorities when purchasing supplies, works or services.[66] Bearing in mind that the principle of subsidiarity is well in place by virtue of the Maastricht Treaty on European Union, it would be a *contradictio in*

---

[63] European Commission, *White Paper for the Completion of the Internal Market*, (COM) 85 310 fin., 1985.
[64] see the Cechinni Report *1992 The European Challenge*, Aldershot, Wildwood House, 1988.
[65] see C. Bovis, *EC Public Procurement Law*, Longman, European Law Series, 1997, p.p. 10-12.
[66] The impact of public procurement liberalisation on *dominium* exceeds the scope of this work. However, for a comprehensive guide, the reader is referred to P.J. Birkinshaw, *"Corporatism and Accountability"* in *"Corporatism and the Corporate State"*, eds. N. O'Sullivan and A. Cox, Edward Elgar, 1988. Also see T. Daintith *"The Executive Power Today: Bargaining and Economic Control"* in *"The Changing Constitution"*, J. Jowell and D. Oliver eds., OUP, 1985, where reference is made to the distinction between *imperium* (the use of force by way of regulatory or criminal law) and *dominium* (the use of policy instruments involving the deployment of wealth by government) as two ways of policy implementation by the state.

*terminis* to deny peripheral responsibility throughout the common market, as far as procurement is concerned.

The only structural change in the domestic public systems that has been suggested by European Institutions and is not related to the division of powers between central and local goverenment, is the privatisation of state controlled enterprises. The reader will recall that public monopolies, often operating in the utilities sectors, have been considered as actual and potential non-tariff barriers. Privatisation will bring about changes in the ownership of such enterprises and raise capital for the government, but it is not expected to result in significant changes in structural purchasing patterns. Utilities, either in the form of a state controlled enterprise or a privatised one are subject to the public procurement Directives anyway.

The figures provided in Table 1 below show national public procurement above certain thresholds which trigger the application of the relevant Directives (dimensional public procurement). The volume of public procurement contracts which are not covered by the Directives (sub-dimensional public procurement) is higher and much more difficult to monitor with accuracy. The limited availability of data for the public sector purchasing of the new Member States (Sweden, Finland and Austria), at the time of writing, did not permit any comparisons with the public procurement volumes of other Member States. The figures in Table 1 shed light on the cumulative magnitude of public sector procurement in the European Union and reveal the relative importance of procurement of supplies and services for Member States in terms of volume.[67]

---

[67] see C. Bovis, *"The European Public Procurement Rules and their interplay with International Trade"*, Journal of World Trade, vol.31, no.3, p.p. 161 - 201 June 1997.

### Table 1. Public Procurement Markets in European Member States

| Member State | Total Public Procurement (ECU m) 1994-1995 | Total Public Procurement (ECU m) 1995 - 1997[68] | Supplies & Services Procurement (ECU m) 1994 - 1995 | Construction Procurement (ECU m) 1994 - 1995 |
|---|---|---|---|---|
| Belgium | 26,938 | (29,412) | 11,557 | 9,326 |
| Denmark | 21,482 | (27,785) | 9,216 | 6,493 |
| France | 69,897 | (72,653) | 45,433 | 24,464 |
| Germany | 176,927 | (182,174) | 51,310 | 24,891 |
| Greece | 6,531 | (8,211) | 3,830 | 1,027 |
| Ireland | 5,936 | (9,232) | 3,150 | 958 |
| Italy | 142,456 | (149,098) | 31,079 | 19,359 |
| Luxembourg | 1,253 | (1,987) | 538 | 124 |
| Portugal | 7,042 | (10,542) | 1,536 | 896 |
| Spain | 52,866 | (59,432) | 11,534 | 9,423 |
| Netherlands | 25,412 | (28,112) | 8,200 | 7,171 |
| United Kingdom | 65,206 | (71,583) | 51,904 | 13,302 |

Sources: The Cost of Non-Europe in Public Sector Procurement, Commission of the European Communities, 1990; Economic and Financial Outlook, National Westminster Bank 1994; Economic Outlook, OECD, December 1994; Tenders Electronic Daily Data Bank

---

[68] Data extrapolated from the Tenders Electronic Daily Data base of the European Communities and cover the period between January 1996 and March 1997.

An analysis of the public sector purchasing structure in the Member States is provided below.

The Belgian purchasing system is highly decentralised,[69] although there is a high degree of publicly owned and controlled procurement in Belgium through central ministries. Over half of public procurement is undertaken by local government. There is a high degree of purchasing autonomy, even down to the level of the 589 local *communes*. Electricity supply is mainly privately generated, but the distribution network is shared between the public and private sectors. Oil and gas are primarily publicly owned by *Detrofina* and *Distrigaz*. *The Societe Nationale de Distribution d'Eau* (SNDE) purchases goods and services for the water industry. Sewage and waste water treatment is provided by eight inter-communal companies. Rail transport is provided by the *Societe National de Chemin de Fer* (SNCB), which procures all of its own services and products. The federal government owns air transport services through the *Regie des Voies Aeriennes* (RVA); postal and telecommunication services are state controlled through the *Regie des Poste* and the *Regie des Telegraphes et des Telephones* respectively. Central government public purchasing accounts for 19.7 % of the total public procurement in Belgium. Local authorities are responsible for 57.5 % and public utilities for 22.8 % of the public procurement volume.[70] In Belgium 7.9 % of the total public contracts are advertised in the Official Journal. The total public procurement import penetration in Belgium is 17.7%.

The structure of the Danish public purchasing can be classified as a decentralised one.[71] Central and local government are responsible for their own procurement with 28.7 % and 36.9 % as a proportion of the total public procurement respectively. Local authorities own most of the energy companies in the electricity and gas sectors and there are several water authorities which are responsible for their procurement requirements. Public transport and telecommunications are in state control, through the *Danske Statsbauer* and the *Post os Telegrafvaesenet* respectively, although lately some telecommunication services including mobile telephony have been privatised. The public utilities procurement accounts

---

[69] Sources from *Institut National de Statistiques, Comptes Nationaux*.
[70] Extrapolated from the Tenders Electronic Daily data base.
[71] Sources from *Danske Statsbaner*.

for 34.4 % of the total public purchasing in Denmark.[72] In Denmark 18.1% of the total public contracts are advertised in the Official Journal. The total public procurement import penetration in Denmark is 9.2 %.

The structure of French public purchasing can be classified into three major types of contracting entities.[73] These include i) central government with its various departments and agencies including the Ministry of Defence in its purchasing capacity for civilian purposes; ii) local authorities; and iii) public corporations (utilities) operating in water, telecommunications, energy and transport sectors. French public procurement is a rather complex regime. The existing domestic procurement practices survived most of the changes brought about by the European Directives and provide for a very fragmented picture of the French public sector. The latter could be characterised as highly decentralised in principle, with complicated administrative structures. The only centralised feature of French public procurement is the *Union des Groupement d'Achats Publics*, which acts as a central procurement agency for public purchasing. Although in the past it was vested with significant powers and tasks, it is now used by few ministries for the purchases of specific products. Most of the government departments have their own procurement systems. Local and regional authorities as well as communes are also vested with procurement powers. Utilities are in the form of public corporations and have a monopoly status in both production and distribution, as well as in the form of concessions. The highly fragmented and decentralised French public sector presents considerable difficulties in its monitoring. Central government, local authorities have more or less equal shares in public procurement, accounting for 28 % and 25 % respectively. Public utilities are responsible for 47% of the total public procurement.[74] In France 14.7% of the total public contracts are advertised in the Official Journal. The total public procurement import penetration in France is 9.3%.

The structure of German public procurement has been highly decentralised.[75] The federal government has 16 ministries responsible for their own procurement. Federal states (Länder) possess autonomy in their procurement, whereas the same occurs for the police and educational

---

[72] Extrapolated from the Tenders Electronic Daily data base.
[73] Sources from *Commission Centrale des Marches*.
[74] Extrapolated from the Tenders Electronic Daily data base.
[75] Sources from *Bundesministerium der Finanzen*.

institutions. Electricity supply is provided by the *Deutsche Verbundgesellschaft* and distributed via distribution companies often owned by the Länder. Local authorities also own gas production and distribution companies. Water supply is undertaken at Länder level. Rail transport is controlled through the *Deutsche Bundesbanh*. Air transport is state controlled and the operation of civil airports is the responsibility of companies owned by the Länder. Telecommunications and postal services are the responsibility of the *Deutsche Bundesposte*. The central administration has 13.8 % share of the annual public procurement in Germany, whereas local authorities account for 39.5 %. Public utilities are responsible for 46.7 % of the total public procurement in Germany.[76] In Germany 16.8% of the total public contracts are advertised in the Official Journal. The total public procurement import penetration in Germany is 7.1%.

The structure of the Greek public procurement sector could be classified as a centralised one.[77] Central government purchasing is pursued through various ministries. They pursue public procurement by requests which are sent to one of four public purchasing directorates at the Ministry of Commerce. Greek public procurement is relatively transparent and competitive since it is mainly based on open tenders. In the Utilities sectors, most of the industries are publicly owned. For coal mining and for electricity generation and distribution the relevant authority is the Public Power Corporation. For oil and gas supply, the purchasing authority is the Public Petroleum Corporation (DEP); and, for distribution the *Athens Municipal Gas Enterprise (DEFA)* is responsible. The *Athens Water and Sewage Corporation (EYDAP), the Thessaloniki Water Authority* and the *Municipality of Patras* are the major purchasers in the sewerage sector. Railways are state owned through the *Organismos Sidirodomon Ellados (OSE)*. Air services are state owned and controlled by the Ministry of Transport and Communications. Postal and telecommunications services are provided by the state owned *Hellenic Post (ELTA)* and the *Hellenic Telecommunications Organisation (OTE)* respectively. Central government has a 25 % proportion in public purchasing whereas local authorities and public utilities are accountable for 38 % and 37 % of the total public procurement respectively. In Greece 8.2% of the total public

---

[76] Extrapolated from the Tenders Electronic Daily data base.
[77] Sources from the National Bank of Greece.

contracts are advertised in the Official Journal. The total public procurement import penetration in Greece is 19.1%.

The structure of Irish public purchasing can be classified as a centralised one.[78] The Government Supplies Agency is the official body responsible for Irish public procurement. In addition, however, most government departments maintain their own purchasing sections. Local authorities are divided into County Councils, County Borough Corporations, Borough Corporations and Urban District Councils. The Irish Republic's utilities sector includes six major purchasing authorities. *Gais Eireann* is responsible for the distribution of natural gas, whilst the Electricity Supply Board (ESB) generates and distributes electricity. Purchasing for the water sector is conducted at the local level. In the travel and transportation sectors, *Coras Iompair Eireann* is responsible for bus (Irish Bus, Dublin Bus) and train *(Iarnrod Eireann)* operations. *Aer Lingus* is the wholly state-owned national airline whilst the three major airports are managed by *Aer Rianta*. Postal services are provided by *An Post and Telecom Eireann* is responsible for telecommunications services. Central government, and public utilities have more or less equal shares in public purchasing with 25 % and 27.5 % respectively, while local authorities (including health boards) account for 47.5 % of the total public procurement.[79] In Ireland 11.5% of the total public contracts are advertised in the Official Journal. The total public procurement import penetration in Ireland is 20.4%.

The structure of Italian public purchasing is *sui generis*.[80] It can be described as a mixture of centralised and decentralised procurement control. At central level, the *Proveditorato Generale dello Stato* is responsible for procurement of government departments, although all major ministries have their own procurement responsibilities, which can be delegated at regional and local levels. At regional level, the *Agenzia per la Promozione dello Sviluppo del Mezzogiorno* is the body responsible for procurement of regional and local authorities, particularly in the southern part. Energy is generated by the state controlled company *Ente Nationale Energia Elettrica* (ENEL) and supplied by regional companies owned by municipalities. Water supplies are the responsibilities of local authorities,

---

[78] Sources from the Irish Trade Board.

[79] Extrapolated from the Tenders Electronic Daily data base and the *Guide to Public Procurement*, Irish Expost Board, 1991.

[80] Sources from *Proveditorato Generale dello Stato, Ministerio del Tesoro.*

which undertake the relevant procurement. Air and rail transport are state controlled by *Alitalia* and *Aero Trasporti* and *Ferrovie dello Stato* respectively. Telecommunications and postal services are also in public hands through the *Amministrazione delle Poste e Telecomunicazioni* and the *Societa Italiana per l' Esercizio delle Telecommunicazioni*. Central government is responsible for 16.8 % of the total public procurement, whereas local authorities for 24.8 %. Additionally, 27.9 % is spent on social security and health mainly through *enti pubblici*, a category of contracting authorities which usually are independent of central or local administration control. Utilities account for 30.4 % of Italian public purchasing volume.[81] In Italy 50.6% of the total public contracts are advertised in the Official Journal. The total public procurement import penetration in Italy is 8.6%.

Luxembourg has a mixture of centralised and decentralised procurement systems.[82] Each central Ministry undertakes its own purchasing. Central co-ordination occurs through the *Service Central des Imprimes et des Foumitures de Bureau de L'Etat* which purchases all office supplies; *the Administration des Batiments Publics* which procures all furniture and fuel; the *Centre Informatique de L'Etat* which purchases all data processing equipment; and, the *Ministere des Travaux Publics* is responsible for all roads, engineering and buildings. Only ten administrative districts of the 130 in the Grand Duchy have powers to place public contracts, although the smaller districts sometimes establish purchasing consortia for particular procurement projects. *The Societe Electrique de l'Our SA* imports electricity supplies mainly from Belgium and Germany. For oil and gas the principal supplier is *the Societe de Transport de Gaz (SOTEC)* which imports, transports and delivers gas. The water industry is controlled by ten inter-municipal syndicates which have extensive procurement powers. The railways are controlled by the *Societe Nationale des Chemins de Fer Luxembourgeois (SNCL)* which is publicly owned. The *Administration des Postes et Telecommunications* controls all postal and telecommunication services. Central government has a 38.8 % share of the total public procurement in Luxembourg, whereas local authorities are responsible for 24.5 %. Public utilities

---

[81] Extrapolated from the Tenders Electronic Daily data base and data from the *Ministerio delle Finanze*.
[82] Sources from *Service Central des Imprimes et des Foumitures de Bureau de L'Etat*.

account for 36.7 % of the total public procurement volume.[83] In Luxembourg 7.5% of the total public contracts are advertised in the Official Journal. The total public procurement import penetration in Luxembourg is 24.2 %.

In the Netherlands, the structure public purchasing can be classified as a de-centralised one.[84] The body which acts as the intermediary between suppliers and public entities is the *Rijkinskoopbureau*. The *Rijkinskoopbureau* was subject to privatisation and as a consequence, it currently charges public entities for the procurement services it provides. This resulted in a major restructuring of Dutch public procurement and many of the central government departments undertake their own public procurement. Decentralisation occurs in the utilities as well. For electricity there are provincial and municipal authorities. For oil and gas the main entities are *Nederlandse Gasuine*, and *Petroland BV* and a large number of distribution companies. For water, there are numerous local authorities *(Wanderleidings Wet)*. Transport is in the hands of *Nederlandse Spoorwegen NV* for railways and KLM for air services, and for post and telecommunications in *Staatsbedrijfer der Ponteijen, Telegraphie en Telefonie*. Central government has a modest proportion in public procurement (15 %), whereas local authorities and public utilities are accountable for 57.5 % and 27.5 % of the total public procurement respectively.[85] In The Netherlands 6.5% of the total public contracts are advertised in the Official Journal. The total public procurement import penetration in the Netherlands is 11.6%.

The Portuguese public procurement system appears rather centralised.[86] Public purchasing lies in the hands of five major ministries, which are responsible for central government procurement. In the electricity sector, the public monopoly *Electricidade de Portugal* controls the market, whereas there are no oil and gas industry at all. The *Correois e Telecommunicacoes de Portugal EP* provides most of the postal and telecommunication services, and *Telefones de Lisboa e Porto EP* handles the telephone services in Lisbon and Porto. Air services are state controlled by *Aeroportos E Navegacao (ANA)*, while the rail services are

---

[83] Extrapolated from the Tenders Electronic Daily data base.
[84] Sources from *Rijkinskoopbureau, Central Bureau of Statistics.*
[85] Extrapolated from the Tenders Electronic Daily data base.
[86] Sources from *Ministerio das Financas, Analyse do Sector Publico Administrativo em Empresarial.*

operated by *Caminhos de Ferro Portugueses EP*. Water supplies and services are purchased by the regional municipal authorities. Central government accounts for 29.4 % of the total public procurement, whilst local authorities have a modest 11.4 % share. Public utilities are responsible for 57.1 % of the public procurement volume in Portugal.[87] In Portugal 15.4% of the total public contracts are advertised in the Official Journal. The total public procurement import penetration in Portugal is 17.6%.

The structure of Spanish public purchasing has centralised characteristics.[88] Four major ministries are responsible for the bulk of procurement at central and regional level. Public utilities are state controlled. *ENHER* and *ENDESA* are the electricity companies, *ENGAS* the gas distributor. Water supplies are managed through 10 management authorities. Rail and air transport are controlled *by National de los Ferrocarriles Espanoles* and *Iberia* respectively. Postal and telecommunications services are controlled by *PTT* and *Companie Telephonica Nacional de Espana* respectively. Central government and local authorities public procurement account for 13.9 % and 18.1 % of the total public procurement respectively. An additional 10.9 % is spent on social security, mainly through the central government. Public utilities are responsible for 56.9 % of the public procurement volume in Spain.[89] In Spain 8.4% of the total public contracts are advertised in the Official Journal. The total public procurement import penetration in Spain is 15.7%.

The structure of the British public procurement can be classified into five major types of contracting entities.[90] These include central government with its various departments and agencies; local authorities which are subdivided into county, district and borough councils; the national health service (NHS); the Ministry of Defence (MoD) in its capacity as a procurer of supplies for non-military purposes; public utilities operating in water, telecommunications, energy and transport sectors, the majority of which have been privatised or are in the process of privatisation; and finally other types of public entities covered by public procurement

---

[87] Extrapolated from the Tenders Electronic Daily data base.
[88] Sources from *Ministerio de Economia y Hacienda, Intervencion General de la Administracion del Estado, Guendas de las Empresas Publicas*.
[89] Extrapolated from the Tenders Electronic Daily data base.
[90] Sources from the *Central Statistical Office*, United Kingdom National Accounts, (HMSO, London).

legislation, such as Quangos (Quasi-autonomous non-governmental organisations), universities and higher education institutions. With reference to the purchasing power of public authorities, central government is responsible for 27% of the total public procurement, local authorities (including the NHS) for 25% and the ministry of defence for 26%. Public utilities account for 15% and finally Quangos and other non-governmental bodies for 7% of total public procurement in the United Kingdom.[91] In the United Kingdom 16.4% of the total public contracts are advertised in the Official Journal. The total public procurement import penetration in the United Kingdom is 14.4%.

---

[91] Extrapolated from the Tenders Electronic Daily data base and National Statistics.

# 3 The Evolution of European Public Procurement Law

**The Public Supplies Regime**

Attempts to regulate public procurement in the European Community were recorded even before the end of the first transitional period.[1] For the purposes of giving guidance to Community Institutions and Member States in the implementation of Articles 52, 53 EC (right of establishment) and 59, 60 EC (freedom to provide services), in 1962 the Council of Ministers adopted two *General Programmes*[2] for the elimination of existing restrictions on inter-state trade. Among the restrictions to be abolished were rules and practices of Member States which '...*exclude, limit or impose conditions upon the capacity to submit offers or to participate as main contractors or subcontractors in contract awards by the State or legal persons governed by public law*'. Those rules and practices resulted in blunt discrimination based on nationality grounds and practically fragmented the entire common market in relation to public procurement. Both Programmes envisaged a gradual and balanced removal of restrictions in the form of quotas and the co-ordination of national procedures for the award of public contracts to nationals of other Member States through agencies or branches or directly to persons or undertakings established in other Member States.

---

[1] The period from the establishment of the European Communities until 31/12/1969. See Article 8(7) EC.
[2] See J.O. 1962,36/32.

With respect to the abolition of all quotas and measures having an effect equivalent to quantitative restrictions upon trade amongst Member States, the Commission in 1966 introduced Directive 66/683[3] which required the elimination of measures prohibiting the use of imported products or prescribing that of domestic products, thus favouring them. However, public supplies contracts were exempted pending the adoption of a specific Directive. Four years later, in 1970 the Commission enacted Directive 70/32[4] on the basis of Article 33(7) EC, hence introducing the prohibition of measures having an effect equivalent to quantitative restrictions in the public procurement arena. That Directive applied to all products of whatever description which were admitted to free circulation within the Community by virtue of Articles 9 and 10 EC. These were products originating in a Member State and third country products admitted to free circulation within the Community through a Member State. It indicated two types of barriers that States, territorial authorities and other public corporate bodies could impose upon procurement of public supplies[5]; i) those preventing or inhibiting the supply of imported products and ii) those favouring the supply of domestic products or granting preferential treatment (other than state aids which must be assessed under the framework of Article 92 EC and taxation) to domestic suppliers. In addition, the Directive [article 3(3)] listed a number of forms of discrimination against foreign goods. Among those were technical specifications, which though applicable to both domestic and imported products, had restrictive effects on trade. The aims behind the introduction of Directive 70/32 were similar to the aims and objectives of Directive 66/683. However, the very first Community instrument to regulate public supplies contracts (Directive 70/32) came into force when the transitional period had virtually expired (at end of 1969), thus rendering Article 30 EC directly effective. One might question the logic behind the decision of European Institution to introduce secondary legislation (Directive) which had as its main thrust the free movement of goods within the Community, when the primary Treaty provision which guarantees the principle of free movement of goods (Article 30) had become directly effective.

---

[3] J.O.1966, P.3748.
[4] J.O.1970, L 13/1.
[5] See Articles 3(1) and 3(2), of EC Directive 70/32, as well as the preamble of the Directive.

A possible answer could be that the direct effectivity of Article 30 EC would have facilitated the incorporation of the Directive into national legal orders. On the other hand, this delay on the part of the Community in adopting an instrument which aimed at regulating public supplies, revealed a highly complicated and sensitive regime that was related not only to the free movement of goods, but expanded further covering aspects in the fields of competition and common commercial policy. Directive 70/32 attempted to integrate markets relating to the supply of goods destined for the public sector from within and from outside the Community. It indirectly made clear to national administration and law and policy makers that public supplies markets could not be confined within the geographical territory of the Community, let alone the national border of Member States, but encompass a broader field of sourcing of goods, a fact that cultivated the ground for the introduction of common commercial policy consideration in public procurement.[6] Indeed, ten years later the European Commission was concluding on behalf of the Member States the Agreement on Government Procurement during the GATT Tokyo Round, thus expanding the territorial application of the EC internal regime to members / signatories to the Agreement.[7]

In 1977, the Council adopted Directive 77/62[8] pursuant to Articles 30 and 100 EC, concerning the co-ordination of procedures for the award of public supply contracts. This instrument, which came into force in 1978, was designed to ensure a more effective supervision of compliance with the negative obligations of Article 30 EC and Directive 70/32 by means of the imposition of a number of positive obligations on purchasing bodies [article 1(b): contracting authorities specified in Annex I].

The imposition of a positive obligation on a Member State by a Directive reveals that a margin of appreciation as to the forms and methods of the result to be achieved is allotted to it. Of course, there is no doubt that Directives are binding only with respect to the result to be achieved[9],

---

[6] See C. Bovis, *The extra-territorial effect of EC Public Procurement Directives- The situation under the GATT Uruguay Round*, Legal Issues of European Integration, 1993, Vol.II, p.p.83-93. Also, C. Bovis, *Public Procurement under the framework of the EC Common Commercial Policy*, Public Procurement Law Review, 1993, Vol.4, p.p. 211-220.
[7] For a detail analysis of the GATT AGP and its successor WTO GPA, see below in this Chapter.
[8] O.J.1977, L 13/1.
[9] Article 189 EC.

thus requiring Member States to opt for the appropriate methods and forms to implement their provisions into domestic law, but the fact that a Directive imposes a positive obligation may affect the direct effectiveness of its provisions, in case of wrongful or non implementation. Positive obligations, in contrast to negative ones, allot to Member States a greater margin of discretion. Member States should not only abstain from action that hinders a Community aim, but, in addition, they must take all the appropriate measures to enhance the function and operation of that aim. A positive obligation seems to contain two requirements: that of abstention and that of introduction of further measures to secure the results of the former. With respect to direct effectiveness of provisions of Directives imposing positive obligations on Member States, the Court, initially was reluctant[10] to accept that the margin of discretion deriving from a positive obligation was capable of rendering the provision in question directly effective. Interestingly, in two cases[11] it ruled that even positive obligations contained in a Directive may produce direct effect.

The fact that Directive 77/62 imposed a number of positive obligations on Member States raised a number of questions as to the direct effectiveness of its provisions. The principal aim of the Directive was to enhance public market efficiency by ensuring that conditions of competition were not distorted and that contracts were allocated to suppliers and contractors under the most favourable conditions for the contracting authorities. That aim could be achieved through transparency and improved market information. The Directive introduced three fundamental principles: 1) Community-wide advertising of contracts; 2) prohibition of technical specifications capable of discriminating against potential bidders; and 3) application of objective criteria of participation in tendering and award procedures. However, the scope of the Directive was rather limited. It explicitly excluded from its coverage public supplies contracts by public utilities (authorities in the transport, energy water and telecommunications sectors). Apparently the main legal reason for that exclusion was that these entities had different legal status and operated under different regimes in Member States. Some of them were completely covered by public law, others governed by private law, while some were in the process of privatisation, although the essential control remained in the

---

[10] See case 57/65 *Alfons Luttucke v. Hauptzollampt Saarlouis, [1966] ECR 205.*
[11] *Case 28/67 Firma Molkerei-Zentrale Westfalen/Lippe GmbH v. Haupzollampt Pederborn,* [1968] ECR 143; case 13/68 *SpA Salgoil v. Italian Ministry of Foreign Trade,* [1968] ECR 453.

hands of the State. On the other hand, it could be argued that this is not a valid argument, since the instruments employed for the regulation of this sort of entities were Directives, which implement Community envisaged standards into national law, taking into account existing national sensibilities. It appears that the regulation of the public utilities in respect to their purchasing requirements had been rather premature for the time.

Directive 77/62 contained a sort of *de minimis* rule; it was applicable only to public supply contracts with a value of more than 200.000 EUA[12]. Its legal basis (Articles 30 and 100 EC) rendered it inapplicable to products originating in and supplied by third countries. The Directive was also inapplicable to public supplies contracts awarded i) pursuant to an international agreement between a Member Sate and one or more non-Member countries; ii) pursuant to an international agreement relating to the stationing of troops between undertakings in a Member State or a non-Member country and iii) pursuant to a particular procedure of an international agreement[13].

In 1980 Directive 77/62 was amended by Directive 80/767[14] in order to take account of the 1979 GATT Agreement on Government Procurement.[15] The Agreement committed the Community and its Member States in providing suppliers from third countries better access, through the application of lower thresholds, to central government purchasing and to some defence procurement, than suppliers from the Community enjoyed under Directive 77/62. Clearly, Directive 80/767 instituted an element of multilaterality in access to international public markets based on the principle of *reciprocity*.[16] That Agreement became part of Community law as it was approved by Council Decision 80/271.[17]

In 1984 the Commission's Communication to the Council on Public Supply contracts[18] revealed an unsatisfactory situation with respect to the implementation of the Supplies Directives in the legal orders of Member

---

[12] Article 5(1)(a) EC Directive 77/62. EUA refers to the European Unit of Account, the predecessor of the ECU. The threshold of the Directive was exclusive of VAT.
[13] This may be the case of supplies under ECSC and Euratom Treaties.
[14] O.J.1980, L 215/1.
[15] O.J.1980, L 71/1.
[16] See P.J. Birkinshaw and C. Bovis, *The EC Public Supplies Directive*; *Public Procurement: Legislation and Commentary*, Butterworths European Law Service, 1992.
[17] O.J.1980, L 215/1.
[18] COM(84) 717 fin.

States. The list of factors responsible for the lack of success includes *inter alia*:
- failure to advertise contracts in the Official Journal, as a result of intentional or unintentional splitting up of contracts;[19]
- ignorance of the relevant rules on the part of contracting authorities or deliberate omission of these rules;
- excessive use of the exceptions permitting non-competitive tendering (negotiated procedures) instead of open or restricted procedures;
- discriminatory requirements posed by contracting authorities by means of compliance with national technical standards, to the exclusion of European standards or equivalent standards of other countries.
- unlawful disqualification of suppliers or contractors or discriminatory use of the award criteria.

The Commission's White Paper on the Completion of the Internal market[20] reiterated that there was a serious and urgent need for improvement and clarification of the relevant Public Procurement Directives. In accordance with the Commission's action programme, the Council in 1988 adopted Directive 88/295[21] amending all previous Supplies Directives. The main improvements were:
- with open tendering procedures as the norm, negotiated ones were allowed in exceptional circumstances[22];
- the definition of the types of supplies contracts was widened[23] and the method of calculation of the thresholds was clarified;[24]
- the exempted sectors were more strictly defined;[25]
- purchasing authorities had to publish in advance information on their annual procurement programmes and their timetable, as well as a notice giving details of the outcome of each decision of award.[26]
- the rules on technical standards were brought in line with the new policy on standards which is based on the mutual recognition of national requirements, where the objectives of national legislation are essentially

---

[19] It was anticipated that EC Directive 83/189, O.J.1983, L 165/1, enacted in order to assist suppliers to fulfil the requirements of norms and standards referred to EC Directive 77/62 and to eliminate discrimination arising through their use.
[20] COM(85) 310 fin.
[21] O.J.1988, L 127/1.
[22] Article 7(2) of Directive 88/295.
[23] Article 1(a) of Directive 88/295.
[24] Article 6(1)(c) of Directive 88/295.
[25] Article 3(2) (a)(b)(c) of Directive 88/295.
[26] Article 9 of Directive 88/295.

equivalent, and on the process of legislative harmonisation of technical standards through non-governmental standardisation organisations (CEPT, CEN, CENELEC).[27]

In an attempt to consolidate all previous legislation relating to public supplies and align it in conformity with the relevant Directives on Public Works[28] and Public Services[29] and the Utilities Sector[30], Directive 93/36[31] has been adopted since June 1993. The consolidated Directives aim at introducing a similar procedural regime in their relevant sectors and at enhancing clarity of some of the previously existing provisions.[32]

**The Public Works Regime**

The two General Programmes adopted by the Council for the purpose of guiding the Community Institutions in the implementation of the provisions of Articles 52, 53, 59 and 62 EC Treaty, took account of the special features of public works contracts. A gradual and balanced removal of restrictions based on quotas and the co-ordination of national procedures for awarding public works contracts to nationals of other Member States were the main aims envisaged therein.

The issue of public sector activities related to construction contracts after the transitional period was addressed by Directive 71/304,[33] which required Member States to abolish restrictions on participation of non-nationals in public procurement contracts. However, it came into force after the completion of the transitional period, when Articles 59 and 60 EC concerning the freedom to provide services became directly effective, thus leaving few aspects to be implemented by Member States. It now serves mainly to list professional trade activities which constitute public works.

The aims envisaged in Articles 52 et seq. on the right of establishment and 59 et seq. on the freedom to provide services were

---

[27] Article 7 of Directive 88/295. See the White Paper on Completing the Internal Market, paras.61-79; also Council Resolution of 7 May 1985, O.J.1985, C 136, on a new approach in the field of technical harmonisation and standards.
[28] Directive 93/37, O.J. 1993, L 199.
[29] Directive 92/50 of 18/6/92, O.J.1992 L 209.
[30] Directive 93/38, O.J. 1993, L 199.
[31] Directive 93/36, O.J. 1993, L 199.
[32] See P.J. Birkinshaw and C. Bovis, *Public Procurement: Legislation and Commentary*, Butterworths European Law Service, 1992.
[33] O.J.1971 L 185/1.

further enhanced by the adoption of Directive 71/305[34], which was the primary vehicle for the opening up of the public works contracts. Based on the prohibition of discriminatory technical specifications, the adequate and prompt advertising of contracts, the establishment of objective selection and award criteria and a procedure of joint supervision both by Member States' authorities and the EC Commission to ensure the observation of these principles,[35] the Directive sought the co-ordination of national procedures in the award of public works contracts. The Directive's major objective was the establishment and enhancement of a transparency regime in the public works sector, where conditions of undistorted competition would ensure that contracts are allocated to contractors under the most favourable terms for the contracting authorities. However, like the Supplies Directive 77/62, Directive 71/305 had a limited aim. It did not introduce new tendering procedures nor were existing national procedures and practices replaced by a set of Community rules. Member States remained free to maintain or adopt substantive and procedural rules on condition that they comply with all the relevant provisions of Community law and in particular, the prohibitions following from the principles laid down in the Treaty regarding the right of establishment and the freedom to provide services.[36]

The concept of public works contracts under the first Works Directive was very extensive[37] and covers those contracts concluded in writing between a contractor and a contracting authority for pecuniary interest concerning either the execution or both the execution and design of works related to building or civil engineering activities listed in class 50 of the NACE Classification[38], or the execution by whatever means of a work corresponding to the requirements specified by the contracting authority. The above formula was wide enough to embrace modern forms of works contracts such as project developing contracts, management contracts and concession contracts.[39] With reference to the latter type of contracts, a

---

[34] O.J.1971 L 185/5.
[35] See the Preamble of Directive 71/305.
[36] See cases 27, 28, 29/86, *CEI and Bellini*, [1987] ECR 3347.
[37] Article 1(a) of Directive 71/305 as amended by Directive 89/440.
[38] General Industrial Classification of Economic Activities within the European Communities, see Annex II Directive 71/305.
[39] Concession contracts are public works projects under which the consideration for the works consist in a franchise (concession) to operate the completed works or in a franchise plus payment. For more details see the Guide to the Community rules on opening government procurement, O.J.1987, L 358/1 at 28.

public works concession is defined by the Works Directive[40] as a written contract between a contractor and a contracting authority concerning either the execution or both the execution and design of a work and for which remunerative considerations consist, at least partly, in the right of the *concessionaire* to exploit exclusively the finished construction works for a period of time. The initial Works Directive 71/305 did not apply to concession contracts, except in the case that the concessionaire was a public authority covered by the Directive. In such situations, only the works subcontracted to third parties would be fully subject to its provisions. In any other case, the only provisions of the Directive applicable to works concessions were that the *concessionaire* should not discriminate on grounds of nationality when it itself awarded contracts to third parties[41]. The regulation of concession contracts was introduced to the *aquis communautaire* almost two decades later by virtue of Directive 89/440 which amended Directive 71/305. In fact, it incorporated the Voluntary Code of Practice, which was adopted by the Representatives of Member States meeting within the Council in 1971[42]. The Code was a non- binding instrument and contained rules on the advertising of contracts and the principle that contracting authorities awarding the principal contract to a concessionaire were to require him to subcontract to third parties at least 30% of the total work provided for by the principal contract. Obviously, these requirements could not easily be incorporated in a binding instrument such as Directive 89/440, thus a more relaxed regime occurred. As a result, the co-ordination rules of the Directive applied to concession contracts only in respect of their advertising. The Directive's rules on tendering procedures, suitability criteria, selection and qualification, technical specifications and award procedures and criteria were inapplicable. Interestingly, Article 3(3) of Directive 71/305 on the prohibition of discrimination on grounds of nationality by a *concessionaire* awarding subcontracts has disappeared from the text of the amending Directive 89/440. The reason could be that by the end of the transitional period Articles 7, 48, 52, 59 and 119 EC were directly effective and in addition, their horizontal direct effect had been pronounced by the European Court of Justice[43].

---

[40] Article 1(d) of Directive 93/37.
[41] Article 3(3) Directive 71/305.
[42] O.J.1971, C 82/13.
[43] See case 36/74 *Walrave and Koch v. Association Union Cycliste International et al*, (1974) ECR 1423; case 43/75, *Drefenne v. SABENA*, (1976) ECR 473.

The amended Works Directive has adopted a special, mitigated regime for the award of concession contracts.[44] The provisions of the Directive only apply to concession contracts when the value is at least 5 million ECU. No rules are given as to the way in which the contract value must be calculated. For the award of concession contracts, contracting authorities must apply similar rules on advertising as the advertising rules concerning open and restricted procedures for the award of every works contract. Also, the provisions on technical standards and on criteria for qualitative selection of candidates and tenderers do apply to the award of concession contracts. The Directive does not prescribe the use of specific award procedures for concession contracts. The Directive presupposes that concession contracts should be awarded in two rounds, such as in the case of restricted procedures or negotiated procedures for ordinary works contracts. Nothing, however, prevents contracting authorities from applying a one-round open procedure. The Directive contains no rules on the minimum number of candidates which have to be invited to negotiate or to submit a tender. It would seem that a contracting authority may limit itself to selecting only one single candidate, provided the intention to award a concession contract has been adequately published. A contracting authority may under no circumstances refrain from publicising a notice to the Official Journal indicating its intention to proceed with the award of a concession works contract.[45]

The definition of contractors comprised any legal or natural person involved in construction activities and for the purposes of the Directive, the contracting authority might impose a requirement as to the form and legal status of the contractor that won the award.[46] The above requirement covers the case of *consortia participation* in public procurement contracts. To facilitate market access and provide as many opportunities as possible for interested tenderers, the Directive specifically prohibits contracting authorities to disqualify groups or consortia of tenderers without corporate structure. This means that contracting authorities must equally apply all the relevant selection and qualification procedures in evaluating an offer made by a consortium and award the contract to the consortium, if the offer meets the award criteria. However, after the award of the contract and for

---

[44] Article 3 of Directive 93/37.

[45] See C. Bovis, *EC Public Procurement Law*, Longman, European Law Series, 1997, pp. 67-68.

[46] Article 21 of Directive 71/305 as amended. The same requirement is found also in the Supplies Directive (Article 18 of Directive 77/62).

reasons dictated by legal certainty and legitimate expectation, as well as for reasons associated with the supervision of the contract and its management, contracting authorities may require the incorporation of the consortium into a more concrete entity. As far as contracting authorities are concerned, their definition was very wide and covers bodies governed by public law which is defined as being any body *established for the specific purpose of meeting needs in the general interest and not having an industrial or commercial character, which has legal personality and is financed for the most part by the State or is subject to management supervision by the latter.*[47] There is a list of such bodies in Annex I of Directive 71/305, which is not an exhaustive one like that in the Supplies Directive, and Member States were under an obligation to notify the Commission of any changes in that list.

Works contracts in the utilities and defence sectors and those contracts awarded in pursuance of certain international agreements were explicitly excluded by virtue of Articles 4 and 5 of the Directive. These provisions are identical in effect to the corresponding ones of the Supplies Directive.[48] This revealed the fact that public contracts under the framework of the Works Directive covered mainly construction projects in the education, health, sports and leisure facilities sectors, in as much as the State or regional or local authorities undertake such projects. In cases that entities involved in this sort of activity (e.g. a hospital or a University) enjoyed considerable independence from the State or local government, as to the undertaking of works contracts, Directive 71/305 was inapplicable to them, since they were not included in its Annex I as bodies governed by public law for the purposes of the Directive in question. This seems to have limited the scope of the Directive only to cases where the State or local government had direct control over the above mentioned entities. Given the fact that works contracts in the utilities sectors were also excluded from the framework of the Directive, its applicability covered a rather modest portion of the construction sector. In order to moderate this apparently undesirable result, the amending Directive 89/440[49] provides for an obligation upon Member States to ensure compliance with its provisions when they subsidise directly by more than 50%, a works contract

---

[47] This definition resembles the Court's ruling on state controlled enterprises in case 152/84 *Marshall v. Southampton and South West Hampshire Area Health Authority*, [1986] ECR 723.
[48] Article 3 of Directive 77/62 as amended by Directive 88/295.
[49] Article 2 Directive 71/305 as amended by Directive 89/440.

awarded by an entity involved in activities relating to certain civil engineering works and to the building of hospitals, sports recreation and leisure facilities, school and university buildings and buildings used for administrative purposes. These conditions seem not to impose a heavy duty on Member States, as only direct subsidies trigger the applicability of the Directive. Indirect ways of subsidising the entities in question, such as tax exemptions, guaranteed loans, or provision of land free of charge, render it inapplicable. It should be noted that under both the original Supplies and Works Directives, preference schemes in the award of contracts were allowed. Such schemes required the application of award criteria based on considerations other than the lowest price or the most economically advantageous tender, which are common in both regimes.[50] However, preferences could only be compatible with Community Law in as much they did not run contrary to the principle of free movement of goods (Article 30 EC et seq.) and to competition law considerations in respect of state aids.[51] Preference schemes have been abolished since the completion of the internal market at the end of 1992.

Works contracts which are subsidised directly by more than 50 per cent by the States, can still fall within the scope of the Directive.[52] Works which are not subsidised directly, or for less than 50 per cent, fall outside this anti-circumvention provision. Not all subsidised works fall within the scope of the Directive: only civil engineering works, such as the construction of roads, bridges and railways, as well as building work for hospitals, facilities intended for sports, recreation and leisure and university buildings and buildings used for administrative purposes are referred to as subsidised works contracts.[53] This list is exhaustive. The Works Directive does not apply to works contracts which are declared secret or the execution of which must be accompanied by special security measures[54] in accordance with the laws, regulations or administrative provisions in force in the Member State concerned; nor does the Directive apply to works contracts when the protection of the basic interests of the Member States' security so requires. Finally, the Works Directive does not

---

[50] See Articles 29(4) and 29(a) of Directive 71/305; also Article 26 of Directive 77/62.
[51] See the Commission's Communication on the *Regional and Social Aspects of Public Procurement*, where it gives an overview of the preference schemes still existing in Member States, COM(89) 400 fin.
[52] Article 2(1) of Directive 93/37.
[53] Article 2(2) of Directive 93/37.
[54] Article 4(b) of Directive 93/37.

apply to public works contracts awarded in pursuance of certain international agreements;[55] nor does the Directive apply to public works contracts awarded pursuant to the particular procedure of an international organisation.[56] Several international organisations, such as NATO, have their own rules on the award of public works contracts.

In 1993, the Council enacted a Directive with a view to consolidating all existing legislation in the field of public works. The consolidated Directive 93/37[57] has embraced all relevant Community legislation relating to public works with some minor amendments and clarifications of existing provisions of Directive 89/440.

## The Public Utilities Regime

As previously mentioned, both supplies and works contracts in the transport, water, energy and telecommunications sectors were excluded from the relevant Supplies and Works Directives.[58] The exclusion of the above-mentioned sectors from the framework of Supplies Directives (77/62 and 88/295) had been attributed to the fact that the authorities entrusted with the operation of public utilities had been subject to different legal regimes in the Member States, varying from completely state controlled enterprises to private controlled ones. With respect to Works Directives, the above justification appears valid, although the apparent connection between construction projects and the excluded sectors leads to the conclusion that Directives 71/305 and 89/440 have very limited application.

As far as supplies contracts were concerned, a convincing reason behind the exclusion of these sectors is that the projects covered therein could not fall within the thresholds of Directives 77/62 and 88/295. Energy, telecommunications, transport and, to a lesser extent, the water industry, are technical sectors requiring state-of-the-art technology (especially telecommunications and energy). The prices in the contracts are very high, in comparison with (simple) supplies ones, so the only way these sectors could be brought within Directive 77/62 would have been

---

[55] Article 5(a) of Directive 93/37.
[56] Article 5(c) of Directive 93/37. Also see the relation between public procurement and Defence Policy in Chapter 7 below.
[57] Directive 93/37, O.J. 1993, L 199.
[58] Article 2 of Directive 77/62 as amended; Article 3 of Directive 89/440.

either to increase the thresholds (200.000 ECU) of the supplies contracts to such a level as to catch a substantial amount of contracts of the excluded sectors, or on the other hand, to lower the envisaged thresholds of contracts in telecommunications, energy, transport and water industry sectors[59] to the level of the (simple) supplies ones (200.000 ECU). Either option would have resulted in a very undesirable situation; if the first option was chosen, the bulk of supplies contracts would have escaped from the framework of Directive 77/62. On the other hand, reducing the thresholds of the excluded sectors to 200.000 ECU would have eliminated the *de minimis* rule for those sectors. A *de minimis* rule is a *conditio sine qua non* where quantitative criteria for regulation of a sector are chosen, thus the administrative burdens on contracting authorities would have made the award of public contracts a rather slow and costly exercise.

With respect to works contracts, the exclusion of the telecommunications, transport, energy and water industry sectors from Directives 71/305 and 89/440 could be justified, rather, due to the different legal positions of the entities in question in the Member States. If a private controlled entity operating in the above sectors were to be involved in a construction project, Works Directives would be inapplicable, as the former was not included among the contracting authorities specified in Annex I (bodies governed by public law). To cover both private and public controlled entities operating in the relevant utilities sectors, the Works Directives should have expanded the definition of contracting authorities; but this would have resulted in an internal disturbance in the operation of the Directives, which are envisaged as regulating construction project awards exclusively by the State or local government or bodies governed by public law. Thus, the only viable and reasonable solution was to introduce a separate instrument, applying the same principles as those found in Directive 77/62, in order to regulate the transport, telecommunications, energy and water sectors.

A more cynical explanation for the late regulation of utilities procurement could be attributed to the fact that due to their purchasing volume and relative magnitude, public utilities procurement constituted an important domestic industrial policy instrument. Member States appeared reluctant in subjecting the procurement of their utilities to the rigorous transparent and competitive regime of public works and supplies

---

[59] Article 12 of Directive 90/531; 400.000 ECU for water, energy and transport supplies and 600.000 ECU for telecommunications supplies.

purchasing, as they have relied upon preferential and closed utilities procurement in order to sustain certain strategic industries.[60]

The Commission was requested by the Council to follow the progress of the CEPT proceedings[61] on harmonisation in the field of telecommunications and to submit to the latter a timetable for measures ensuring effective competition in the field of supply contracts awarded for telecommunications services. The Commission, in its Recommendations on Telecommunications[62] also expressed its desire to ensure that the objective of an open market, in particular for suppliers within the Community, was being achieved without undesirable consequences for the pattern of Community trade with non-Member countries. In its Communication to the Council of 1984 on Public Supply contracts[63] and its White Paper on the Completion of the Internal Market,[64] the Commission reiterated the need to liberalise the so far excluded sectors, particularly telecommunications.

The European Parliament's Committee on Economic and Monetary Affairs and Industrial Policy presented a report in the European Parliament[65] stressing the need for extension of the scope of the Supplies Directives to cover excluded sectors. In its Resolution[66] the Parliament approved all the Commission's and Council's actions so far, and called them to submit a proposal for a directive to govern the excluded sectors. The Council, in its Recommendation 84/550[67] shared the Commission's considerations as to the opening of access to public telecommunications contracts, providing that Governments of Member States should offer opportunities for Community undertakings to tender on a non-discriminatory basis for the supply of specified telecommunications equipment and should also report to the Commission on implementing measures and practical effects. The Commission in 1988 issued Directive

---

[60] European Commission, *Statistical Performance Indicators for Keeping Watch over Public Procurement*, 1992. Also, see Chapter 6 below.
[61] CEPT is the European Conference of Postal and Telecommunications Administrations, established in Montreux in 1959 and aiming at closer relations between member administration to improve their administrative and technical services, O.J.1977 C 11/3.
[62] COM.(80) 422 fin.
[63] COM.(84) 717 fin.
[64] COM.(85) 310 fin.
[65] See the von Wogau report, DOC.A2-38/85.
[66] O.J.1985 C 175/241.
[67] O.J.1984 L 289/51.

88/301[68] on competition in the markets in telecommunications terminal equipment.

Finally, in 1990 the Council adopted Directive 90/531[69] on the procurement procedures of entities operating in the water, energy, transport and telecommunications sectors. The regime imposed is rather similar to the Supplies Directives with some important differences as to the flexibility given to the contracting authorities over the choice of methods to be used to make the award process competitive.[70] The Utilities Directive has been amended by Directive 93/38,[71] which mainly incorporates the newly enacted Public Services Directive 92/50[72] into the Utilities regime.

The legislative background of the utilities Directive and the ordeal of the regulation of public utilities procurement justify the high complexity of the regime. The fact that public utilities often have an unclear legal status or their legal nature varies within the Member States' legal systems has obviously rendered difficult to introduce a single legal instrument to regulate their purchasing, although such a prolonged delay should be attributed to other factors. It may be recalled that public utilities absorb the vast majority of high technology equipment designated to the public sector. Protectionism in strategic industrial sectors has been pursued through preferential purchasing with a view to either sustaining the relevant industries or to assisting the development of infant industries in Member States. The regulation of utilities purchasing not only had to overcome the significant legislative barriers accountable to their nature but also the abandoning of individual industrial policies of Member States through strategic procurement. In addition to these constraints, the fear of an uncontrolled flow of direct investment which would target vulnerable European-based high technology industries and the subsequent possible increase in take-overs and acquisitions, mainly from Japanese and American predators poured cold water on the attempts of European

---

[68] O.J.1988 L 131/73.
[69] O.J.1990 L 297.
[70] The Directive provides different implementing periods for Spain, Greece and Portugal. Spain has to implement its provisions by January 1, 1996 whereas Greece and Portugal by January 1, 1998 respectively. The delay in the uniform implementation of the Utilities Directive could be attributed to the preparations needed for the integration of the public utilities sectors in the respective countries.
[71] O.J. 1993, L 199.
[72] O.J. 92/50, O.J. 1992, L 209.

Institutions to integrate the utilities procurement within the common market.

The Utilities Directive has been the most radical approach to the public sector integration in Europe and its enactment coincided with the envisaged international liberalisation of public procurement during the Uruguay GATT negotiations. One could question such a strategy by European Institutions, particularly bearing in mind the vulnerability of Europe's high-tech industry in comparison with that in the USA and Japan. However, the GATT regime has introduced a new era in the accessibility of international public markets, to the extent that highly protectionist countries like the USA and Japan must, under the new regime, abolish their buy-national laws and policies and open, on a reciprocal basis, their public markets to international competition.

The ambit of the Utilities Directive and its field of application appear more complicated than those in the Supplies and Works Directives, although the internal legal structure among the three Directives is very similar. Articles 1 and 2 form the broad framework of the Directive's application, by providing various definitions and the scope of some preliminary exemptions. The Utilities Directive devotes a substantial amount of provisions in an attempt to exempt from its application certain contracts or activities that have been deemed ineligible for community-wide regulation.

Apart from the normal exemptions under the grounds of defence and security and confidentiality, the major exemptions are provided for under Articles 1 and 2. Radio and television broadcasting have not been classified as telecommunication activities and have been specifically excluded from the ambit of the Directive by virtue of Article 2. Also, bus transport services to the public are excluded on condition that their providers operate under a regime of competitive conditions, which means that other potential contractors or suppliers of similar services are allowed to enter the relevant geographical and product markets and compete against the existing utilities provider (Article 2 (4). A similar rule applies to telecommunication services which operate within a competitive market.[73]

Under the same Article (2) special exemptions are also provided to private entities supplying gas, heat, drinking water and electricity. Although the wording and spirit of the Directive covers private entities

---

[73] Article 2(4) and Article 8 of the Utilities Directive amended by Directive 93/38.

operating under exclusive and special rights in the utilities sectors, nevertheless under certain conditions, these entities can be exempted from the application of the rules of the Directive. In the case of the production of drinking water and electricity, if a private entity is able to show that it does so for its own purposes, which are not related to the provision of drinking water or electricity to the public, it is exempt. Similarly, if a private entity is able to show that it supplies to the public network drinking water or electricity which is destined for its own consumption, and that the total so supplied to the network is not more than 30% of the total produced by that network in any one year over a three year period, it is also exempt.[74]

In the case of gas and heat supplies, if the production by a private entity is related to an activity other than the supply to a network for public consumption, then these entities are also exempt. In the same line, if the supply of gas and heat by a private entity to a public network relates to economic exploitation only and does not exceed 20% of the firms turnover in any one year, taking an average of the preceding three years and the current year, then such an entity is also exempt.[75] These exemptions predominantly cover entities which have research and development as their main objective in the relevant utilities sector, or do not play a major role in supplying public networks with water or energy.[76]

There are also exemptions for entities exploring for gas, oil, coal and other solid fuels under Article 3. Entities operating in these sectors will not be regarded as having an exclusive right provided that certain conditions are fulfilled. These conditions are cumulative and stipulate that, when an exploitation right is granted to the entity in question, the latter is exempt from the Utilities Directives provided that other bodies are able to compete for the same exclusive rights under free competition; that the financial and technical criteria to be used in awarding rights are clearly spelt out before the award is made; that the objective criteria are specified as to the way in which exploitation is to be carried out; that these criteria are published before requests for tenders are made and applied in a non-discriminatory way; that all operating obligations, royalty and capital and

---

[74] Article 2(5) (a) of the Utilities Directive amended by Directive 93/38.
[75] Article 2(5) (b) of the Utilities Directive amended by Directive 93/38.
[76] See N. O'Loan, *Implementation of Directive 90/531 and Directive 92/50 in the United Kingdom*, Public Procurement Law Review, 1993, p. 29. Also, A. Cox, *Public Procurement in the European Community: The single market rules and the enforcement regime after 1992*, 1993, Erlsgate Press.

revenue participation agreements are being published in advance; and finally, that contracting authorities are not required to provide information on their intentions about procurement except at the request of national authorities.[77] Furthermore, Member States have to ensure that these exempted bodies apply, at least, the principles of non-discrimination and competition. They are obliged to provide a report to the EC on request about such contracts. However, this requirement is less stringent than the mandatory reporting rules in the Supply and Works Directives. It should be mentioned that the Utilities Directive does not apply to concession contracts granted to entities operating in utilities sectors, awarded prior to the coming into force of the Directive. All exemption provisions within the Utilities Directive are subject to assessment in the light of the four year overall review of the process.[78]

Other exemptions cover entities in the relevant sectors which can demonstrate that their service and network associated contracts are not related to the specific supply and works functions specified in the Directive, or if they are related, but they take place in a non-member State and they are not using an European public network or physical area.[79] The Member States are under an obligation to inform the European Commission, on request, of the cases when these exemptions have been allowed. There are also provisions which allows for resale and hire contracts to third parties to be exempt when the awarding body does not possess an exclusive or special right to hire or sell the subject of the contract, and there is competition already in the market from other suppliers or producers to provide the commodity or service to third parties.[80] Similar relaxed reporting and monitoring requirements are found in Article 8 which applies to telecommunication exemptions.[81]

In 1993 the Divisional Court of the Queen's Bench Division of the Supreme Court of England and Wales made a reference to the European Court of Justice on the interpretation of Directive 90/531 concerning procurement in public utilities. The national case[82] concerned with the definition of the relevant provision of the Directive relating to the

---

[77] Article 3(1) of the Utilities Directive amended by Directive 93/38.
[78] Article 3(2) to (4) of the Utilities Directive amended by Directive 93/38.
[79] Article 6(1) of the Utilities Directive amended by Directive 93/38.
[80] Article 7(2) of the Utilities Directive amended by Directive 93/38.
[81] Article 8(2) of the Utilities Directive amended by Directive 93/38.
[82] Case C-392/93, *The Queen and H.M. Treasury, ex parte British Telecommunications PLC*, O.J. 1993, C 287/6.

application of procurement rules to entities operating in the telecommunication sector. Article 8(1) of the Utilities Directive provide for an exemption from the regime and for the inapplicability of the Directive, when contracting authorities in the telecommunications sector operate under substantially the same competitive conditions within the same geographical market. The national court asked for an interpretation of Article 8(1) of the Utilities Directive and in particular the competence of Member States to determine the sufficiently genuine competitive regime and the criteria for such evaluation, in a geographical area between telecommunications operators in order to exclude them from the application of the Directive. In the preliminary ruling, the European Court of Justice elucidated the so far controversial interpretation of Article 8(1) and the exemption schemes within the Utilities Directive, as well as determine the Member States' obligation to award damages to individuals who suffered from wrongful implementation of Directives. The Court followed the Conclusions of the Advocate-General and held that a Member State could not decide, when implementing the Directive, which telecommunication services were excluded from the scope of the Directive, as that power was reserved to the telecommunications entities themselves. Answering the second question, the Court maintained that in order for the criterion in Article 8(1) to be satisfied, other contracting entities had, in all the circumstances of the case, to be able to compete as a matter of fact as well as of law.

Another set of significant exemptions is provided for water authorities under Article 9. Under this provision water authorities specified in Annex 1 are specifically exempt from the rules when they purchase water. They are however covered by the Directive when they purchase other supply and construction products.[83] Similarly, there are specific exemptions for the electricity, gas and heat, oil and gas and coal and other solid fuels entities outlined in Annex II, III, IV and V, but only when they award contracts for the supply of energy or for fuels for the production of energy. For all other relevant contracts these bodies are included in the rules. These exemptions were provided because of the need to allow contracting authorities to buy from local sources of supply, which may not always be the cheapest, but which are important on the basis of regional development policies or environmental grounds, and because these

---

[83] Article 9(1) (a) of the Utilities Directive amended by Directive 93/38.

purchases are central to the entities' operations and not part of normal supply and works procurement process.[206]

Finally, specific exemptions under the Utilities Directive are provided for those carriers of passengers and providers of transport services by air and by sea. In the preamble of the Directive it is stated that, under a series of measures adopted in 1987 with a view to introducing more competition between firms providing public air services, it was decided to exempt such carriers from the scope of the legislation. Similarly, because shipping has been subject to severe competitive pressures, it was decided to exempt certain types of contracts from the Directive.[207]

The Utilities Directive intends to open up procurement practices in the four previously excluded sectors mainly to EC-wide competition. With respect to goods (and services) originating in third countries, things are more complicated. A product outside the Community, in order to be subject to a public contract regulated by one of the EC Public Procurement Directives, must lawfully be put in free circulation in at least one Member State.[208] Except where there has been an international agreement which grants comparable and effective access for Community undertakings to public markets of a third country (reciprocity principle), Article 29 renders possible for European contracting authorities in the utilities sector to reject offers from outside the Community and requires Community preference where Community offers are equivalent to offers from third countries (where the price difference does not exceed 3%). With reference to an international agreement granting access to public markets, the Utilities Directive opens the door for the application of the GATT Agreement on Government Procurement in the utilities sector.

**The Public Services Regime**

Whilst the liberalisation of trade, as envisaged in international agreements

---

[206] It has been considered that these exemptions might be the appropriate framework to introduce a common energy policy.
[207] In the future sea-ferry operators would be excluded, but their position has been kept under review. Inland water ferry services and river ferry services operated by public authorities were to be brought within the rules.
[208] For the concept of origin of goods and their lawful free circulation in the Common Market, see Regulation 802/68, O.J. English Special Edition 1968 (1), p.165.

such as the GATT or in supranational organisations such as the European Communities, embraces primarily the free movement of goods, provisions regulating the provision of services are often described as inadequate. Modern economies have witnessed a shift in trade patterns from product manufacturing industries to markets where the provision of services is the predominant sector of the industry. The lack of regulation of services at a global level has given rise to economic controversies. Trade wars have been taking place and the international legal community currently attempts to adopt measures towards regulation of trade in services within the context of the GATT Uruguay Round of multilateral trade negotiations.

In line with the above considerations, European Institutions enacted Directive 92/50[209] on the award procedures relating to public services contracts attempts to pave the way for liberalisation of services in public markets. The Directive follows the same principles with the rest of the Community's legislation on Public Procurement, that is compulsory Community-wide advertising of public contracts, prohibition of technical specification capable of discriminating against potential bidders and uniform application of objective criteria of participation in tendering and award procedures. The Services Directive has introduced special type of award procedure, namely *design contests*, with reference to planning projects. According to Article 1 *(g), design contests* are those national procedures which enable the contracting authority to acquire in the fields of area planning, town planning, architecture and civil engineering, a plan or a design selected by a jury, after being put out to competition with or without the award of prizes. The award of *design contests*, according to the Services Directive must follow specific rules. The admission of participants to the contest shall not be limited either by reference to the territory or part of a Member State, or on the grounds that under the law of the Member State in which the contest is organised, participants would have been required to be either natural or legal persons. Furthermore, where design contests are restricted to a limited number of participants, the contracting authorities must lay down clear and non-discriminatory selection criteria which ensure sufficient and genuine competition among the participants. The jury shall be composed exclusively of natural persons who are independent.

---

[209] O.J. 92/50, O.J. 1992, L 209.

Under the Services Directive, public services contracts are contracts which have as their object the provision of services classified in the Common Product Classification (CPC) Nomenclature of the United Nations, as a Nomenclature for Classification of Services at Community level is lacking. The United Nations Common Product Classification covers almost every conceivable service an undertaking may provide, although the services description is rather plain.

The Services Directive is the first legal instrument which attempts to open the increasingly important public services sector to intra-community competition. It should be mentioned that the Directives on Public Supplies, Public Works and Utilities contain provisions where the provision of services is regarded as ancillary to the main contract under their regime, provided the value of the services are less than the value of the supplies or works. Such services are covered by the relevant Directive.

Specific services contracts are excluded from the scope of the Services Directive. It should be mentioned that not all of these specific exclusions are listed in the amended Utilities Directive 93/38, because they would not, in any event, fall within the ambit of a defined activity. Apart from those contracts which are covered by the relevant provisions of the Works, Supplies and Utilities Directives, and therefore not considered as services, the other contracts excluded from the Services Directive and amended Utilities Directive 93/38 are:

(i) contracts for the acquisition or rental, by whatever financial means, of land, existing buildings, or other immovable property or concerning rights thereon. (however, financial service contracts concluded at the same time as, before or after the contract of acquisition or rental, in whatever form, will be subject to the Directive);

(ii) contracts for the acquisition, development, production or joint production of programme material by broadcasters and contracts for broadcasting time;[88]

(iii) contracts for voice telephony, telex, radiotelephony, paging and satellite services;[89]

---

[88] This includes the purchase of, on the one hand, services producing audio-visual works such as films, videos and sound recording, including advertising and, on the other hand broadcasting time (transmission by air, satellite or cable). In principle, these services would be covered but are given derogations in so far as they are connected with broadcasting activities. see P. Armin-Trepte, *Public procurement in the EC*, CCH Europe, 1993, p. 101.

(iv) contracts for arbitration and conciliation services;

(v) contracts for financial services in connection with the issue, sale, purchase or transfer of securities or other financial instruments, and central bank services;[90]

(vi) employment contracts;

(vii) research and development service contracts other than those where the benefits accrue exclusively to the contracting authority for its use in the conduct of its own affairs, on condition that the service provided is mostly remunerated by the contracting authority.

Research and development services contracts are covered in identical terms in both. The exclusion of such contracts under both the Services and the Utilities Directives lies in the assumption that research and development projects should not be financed by public funds.[91] However, where research and development contracts are covered by the procurement rules, a provision in the Utilities Directive allows a contracting entity to award a contract without a prior call for competition where it is purely for the purpose of research, experiment, study or development and not for the purpose of ensuring profit or of recovering research and development costs and in so far as the award of such contract does not prejudice the competitive award of subsequent contracts which have in particular these purposes.[92]

---

[89] These have been excluded because they are not part of the Community liberalisation package for the telecommunications services market.

[90] This refers to contracts which constitute transactions concerning shares, for example. In the public sector, it will also include within the derogation contracts awarded to financial intermediaries to arrange such transactions because these are specifically excluded from the scope of investment services (Category 6 of annex IA). However, this exclusion does not appear in the Utilities Directive so that contracts for the services of intermediaries who will make the arrangements for such transactions would be subject to the provisions of the Utilities Directive; see de Graaf *The political agreement on a common position concerning the utilities services Directive*, Public Procurement Law Review, 1992, p. 473. Choice of such intermediaries is often difficult in practice since it is quite often made on the basis of the perceived quality of the intermediary or on references from existing clients and past experience. This choice will be made no easier by the application of the procurement rules which do not necessarily best fit such services; see P. Armin-Trepte, *Public procurement in the EC*, CCH Europe, 1993, p. 101.

[91] See de Graaf *The political agreement on a common position concerning the utilities services Directive*, and P. Armin-Trepte, *Public procurement in the EC*, op. cit.

[92] Article 20(2)(b) of amending Utilities Directive 93/38.

Interestingly, service concessions, although included in the draft Directive,[93] have been excluded from the provisions of Directive 92/50. The exclusion of service concessions falls short of the aspirations to regulate concession contracts for the public sector under the Works Directive and breaks the consistency in the two legal instruments. The reasons for the exclusion of service concessions from the regulatory regime of public procurement could be attributed to the different legal requirements in Member States to delegate powers to concessionaires. The delegation of services by public authorities to private undertakings in some Member States runs contrary to constitutional provisions.

The Directive adopts a two-tier approach in classifying services procured by contracting authorities. This classification is based on a "priority" and a "non-priority" list of services, according to the relative value of such services in intra-community trade. *Priority services* include: Maintenance and repair services, Land transport services (except for rail transport services), including armoured car services and courier services, except transport of mail, Air transport services of passengers and freight, except transport of mail, Transport of mail by land and by air, Telecommunications services (except voice telephony, telex, radiotelephony, paging and satellite services), Financial services including *(a)* Insurance services, *(b)* Banking and investment services (except contracts for financial services in connection with the issue, sale, purchase or transfer of securities or other financial instruments, and central bank services)[1], Computer and related services, Research and development services, Accounting, auditing and book-keeping services, Market research and public opinion polling services, Management consultant services (except arbitration and conciliation services) and related services, Architectural services; engineering services and integrated engineering services; urban planning and landscape architectural services; related scientific and technical consulting services; technical testing and analysis services, Advertising services, Building-cleaning services on a fee or contract basis, Publishing and printing services on a fee or contract basis, Sewage and refuse disposal services, Sanitation and similar services. *Non-Priority services* include: Hotel and restaurant services, Rail transport services, Water transport services, Supporting and auxiliary transport services, Legal services, Personnel placement and supply services, Investigation and security services, Education and vocational education

---

[93] See COM (90) 372 fin, SYN 293 and COM (91) 322 fin, SYN 293.

services, Health and social services, Recreational, cultural and sporting services.

The division is not permanent and the European Commission has under constant review the situation, by assessing the performance of "non-priority" services sectors. The two-tier approach, in practical terms, means that the award of priority services contracts are subject to the rigorous regime of the public procurement Directives (advertisement, selection of tenderers, award procedures, award criteria), whereas the award of non-priority services contracts must follow the basic rules of non-discrimination and publicity of the results of the award.

Article 6 of the Services Directive provides for the inapplicability of the Directive to service contracts which are awarded to an entity which is itself a contracting authority within the meaning of the Directive on the basis of an exclusive right which is granted to the contracting authority by a law, regulation or administrative provision of the Member State in question.[94] Article 13 of the Utilities Directive provides for the exclusion of certain contracts between contracting authorities and affiliated undertakings.[95] These are service contracts which are awarded to a service-provider which is affiliated to the contracting entity and service contracts which are awarded to a service-provider which is affiliated to a contracting entity participating in a joint venture formed for the purpose of carrying out an activity covered by the Directive.[96] The exclusion from the provisions of the Directive is subject, however, to two conditions: the service-provider must be an undertaking affiliated to the contracting authority and, at least 80 per cent of its average turnover arising within the European Community for the preceding three years, derives from the

---

[94] This practice resembles the market testing process often employed in the United Kingdom between a contracting authority and an in-house team; see I. Harden, *Defining the range of application of the public sector procurement Directives in the United Kingdom*, Public procurement Law Review 1992, Vol.1 p.362.

[95] An affiliated undertaking, for the purposes of Article 1(3) of the Utilities Directive, is an undertaking the annual accounts of which are consolidated with those of the contracting entity in accordance with the requirements of the seventh company law Directive (Council Directive 83/349 (OJ 1983 L193/1)).

[96] See the explanatory memorandum accompanying the text amending the Utilities Directive (COM (91) 347-SYN 36 1) which states that this provision relates, in particular, to three types of service provision within groups. These categories, which may or may not be distinct, are: the provision of common services such as accounting, recruitment and management; the provision of specialised services embodying the know how of the group; the provision of a specialised service to a joint venture.

provision of the same or similar services to undertakings with which it is affiliated. The Commission is empowered to monitor the application of this Article and to request the notification of the names of the undertakings concerned and the nature and value of the service contracts involved.

**The Compliance Directives**

European Community law remains silent as to the availability of remedies available to individuals at national level in cases of infringement of primary or secondary legislation. To address the issue of the protection of individuals under Community law when their rights have been violated, one should first seek clarification of a crucial factor: the direct effectiveness of Community Law and in particular whether an infringement of a directly effective primary or secondary Community provision may be used by individuals before national courts as sufficient ground for an action for damages against the State. As many provisions of Community legislation concerning public procurement (Directives) are deemed to produce direct effect, the question of whether an infringement of them can be considered as a sufficient ground for an action for damages at national level, is combined with the duty of national courts to afford an effective protection mechanism (remedies) of the rights conferred on individuals by directly effective Community law. In an attempt to complement the substantive Procurement rules enacted by virtue of the Supplies, Works and Services Directives and to provide a system of effective protection of individuals in cases of infringements of their provisions, European Institutions enacted the Compliance Directive on the harmonisation of laws, regulations and administrative provisions relating to the application of review procedures in the award of public works and public supply contracts (Directive 89/665 EC).[97] To encompass the Utilities procurement rules, Directive 92/13[98] extends the remedies and review procedures covered by Directive 89/665 to the water, energy, transport and telecommunication sectors.

The scope and thrust of the Compliance Directives focuses on the obligation of Member States to ensure effective and rapid review of decisions taken by contracting authorities which infringe public

---

[97] O.J. 1989 L 395.
[98] O.J. 1992 L 76/7.

procurement provisions. Undertakings seeking relief from damages in the context of a procedure for the award of a contract, should not be treated differently under national rules implementing European public procurement laws and under other national rules. This means that the measures to be taken concerning the review procedures should be similar to national review proceedings, without any discriminatory character. Any person having or having had an interest in obtaining a particular public supply or public works contract and who has been or risks being harmed by an alleged infringement of public procurement provision shall be entitled to seek review before national courts. This particular obligation is followed by a stand-still provision concerning the prior notification by the person seeking review to the contracting authority of the alleged infringement and of his intention to seek review. However, with respect to admissibility aspects, there is no qualitative or quantitative definition of the interest of a person in obtaining a public contract. As to the element of potential harm by an infringement of public procurement provisions, it should be cumulative with the first element, that of interest. The prior notification should intend to exhaust any possibility of amicable settlement before the parties have recourse to national courts. A novelty in the Compliance Directive of the Utilities sectors[99] is the introduction of the *attestation procedure*. Member States are required to give the contracting entities the possibility of having their purchasing procedures and practices *attested* by persons authorised by law to exercise this function. Indeed, this attestation mechanism, may investigate in advance possible irregularities identified in the award of a public contract and allow the contracting authorities to correct them. The latter may include the attestation statement in the notice inviting tenders published in the Official Journal. The system appears flexible and cost-efficient and may prevent wasteful litigation. Quite promisingly, the attestation procedure under Directive 92/13 will be the essential requirement for the development of European standards of attestation.[100] A more detailed analysis of the Compliance Directives follows in Chapter 5.

---

[99] Directive 92/13, O.J. 1992, L 76/7.
[100] See Article 7 of EC Directive 92/13.

## The GATT Agreement on Government Procurement

The Procurement legal regime of the European Union has been extended in order to cover signatories to the GATT Agreement on Government Procurement.[101] Foreign firms (from third countries) can participate in tendering procedures for the award of public contracts from public entities in the common market and vice-versa, European firms can participate in tendering procedures in foreign public markets. The GATT Agreement on Government Procurement embraces the following countries: the USA, Canada, Japan, EFTA countries, Singapore, Hong Kong and Israel and promises considerable improvement in reciprocal market access.

The first Public Procurement Directives were inapplicable to products originating in and supplied by third countries. In practical terms the meaning of this limitation was that a product outside the Community, in order to be subject to a public contract regulated by one of the Directives, had to be lawfully put in free circulation in at least one Member State.[102] The Council, being conscious of the above limitation adopted a Resolution[103] concerning access to Community public supply contracts for products originating in non-member states. At the same time, negotiations in the international framework were being carried under the GATT Tokyo Round (1973-1979). Finally, on April 12 1979, the GATT Agreement on Government Procurement (AGP) was concluded and became part of the Community's legal order by virtue of Article 228(2) EC and Council Decision 80/271.[104]

The primary aims of the AGP were similar to those of Supplies Directive 77/62, *viz*, transparency of laws and procedures on government procurement and elimination of protection for domestic suppliers and discrimination between foreigner suppliers.[105] However, the AGP provisions went further than those of Directive 77/62 by introducing more favourable conditions for tenders from outside the Community; the AGP was envisaged as the vehicle for establishing an international framework of

---

[101] See EC Council Regulation 1461/93 (O.J. 1993, L 146) and EC Council Decision 93/324 (O.J. 1993, L 125).
[102] For the concept of origin of goods and their lawful free circulation in the Common Market see Regulation 802/68, O.J.English Special Edition 1968 (1), p.165.
[103] O.J.1977 C11/1.
[104] O.J.1980 L 215/1.
[105] See F.Weiss, *Public Procurement in the EC- Public Supply Contracts*, (1988) European Law Review.

rights and obligations with respect to government procurement with a view to achieving liberalisation and expansion of world trade. As a consequence, third countries / signatories to the AGP are under obligation to provide the same opportunities for access to Community tenderers in their respective public markets, as those provided for by EC Member States to undertakings from these countries.

Due to the above modifications, Directive 77/62 was amended. The result of this amendment is that the AGP rules are now incorporated in the Supplies regime,[106] which is the only regime in the Public Procurement sector, the application of which produces extra-territorial effects.

The situation under the AGP (Tokyo Round) rules, which have been incorporated in Directive 88/295 is the following: foreign undertakings (from third countries) which have subsidiaries within the Common Market will have the same access to public supplies contracts as European undertakings and can invoke and enforce Community law both at Community and (mainly) at national level. Obviously, it is required that undertakings from outside the Community must have an economic presence in it. Subsidiaries should take the form of a corporate personality subject to tax laws of the Member State within which they operate. It should also be noted that under all Public Procurement Directives, contracting authorities have the right to impose an obligation on one or more undertakings awarded a contract, that the latter take a specific legal form. Suppliers, signatories to the GATT, but not established in the Community, will still be subject to the GATT Agreement on Government Procurement, although they cannot invoke and enforce Community law. They cannot even enforce GATT rules, unless the competent forum (EC Member State or third state-GATT signatory) provides for the appropriate remedies. The AGP lays down a rather inoffensive dispute settlement and enforcement procedure, where consultation and conciliation between the aggrieved contractor and the contracting authority play the dominant role. With respect to enforcement of the AGP rules, the Committee on Government Procurement (composed of representatives from each of the Parties), as the body responsible for consultation on matters relating to the operation of the AGP or the furtherance of its objectives has the right to authorise any measure adopted by a Party aiming at suspending the reciprocity principle, between that Party and a Party that refuses access to public markets for undertakings of the former. State retreat represents a

---

[106] Directives 80/767 and 88/295, supra.

very interesting compliance method of international trade, which, however, may result in unsatisfactory consequences, as it represents a complex interrelation of private and public law rights. Undertakings which are non-signatories to GATT may face trade restrictions by Member States according to Article 115 EC, which governs the Community's Common external policy.

Despite its promising aims and purposes,[107] the AGP-EC regime on public supplies contracts has had a rather limited application as i) it embraced only its signatories, ii) it covers only the supply of products and services that are incidental to the supply contract and not services contracts per se and iii) it applied only to centrally-controlled authorities, thus leaving local or regional authorities outside its scope.

The above-mentioned regime has left large areas of procurement activity unregulated by the GATT or by EC secondary legislation. Works and utilities contracts and supply of services have been excluded. Both Community and global public procurement markets are very promising business fields. The Council in its 1977 Resolution[108] noted that the opening up of the public procurement market in respect of non-Community countries could only be accomplished through reciprocity in treatment and mutual balance of advantages. The reciprocity doctrine or the "mirror principle" requires that non-member states provide in their domestic markets similar opportunities to those provided by the European Member States to undertakings coming from those countries. This means that the element of reciprocity should occur between all European Member States and the third country in question. This is a rather unlikely situation, so the Commission in its statement in 1977 concerning Article 115 EC[109] was prepared to permit a limited and controlled use of it by individual Member States, which have established economic and commercial relations with non-member countries in the field of Public Procurement. During the Tokyo Round negotiations, the Council noted also that Community undertakings were participating in contracts awarded in third countries. This reveals that reciprocity was a bilateral phenomenon in economic activities between a Member State and a third country. At first sight, this appears contradictory with the centralised policy that Community

---

[107] See the FIDE Congress on *The Application in the Member States of the EC Directives on Public Procurement*, Madrid 1990.
[108] O.J.1977 C 11/1.
[109] O.J.1977 C 11/2.

Institutions seek to apply in the Public Procurement sector. In this regard, the Commission stated that, in order to prevent deflection of trade between a Member State and a third country, it would authorise the former, under Article 115 EC, to exclude from public contracts certain products, originating in third countries, which are in free circulation in another Member State, where similar arrangements (reciprocity effects) have been made for products imported directly. In other words, it was thought that the use of Article 115 EC might eliminate the "free rider" phenomenon and "protect" the benefits gained through a bilateral trade flow between a Member State and a third country. From an economic point of view, this tactic may prevent deflection and diversification of trade, but on the other hand, it creates what is sometimes more serious: non-tariff barriers to intra-Community trade. It is difficult, in the framework of an economic union such as the EC, to strike the balance between a common external tariff and individual commercial policies pursued by one or more Member States.

One could question the reason that the AGP did not extend its scope to cover works contracts also. It should be recalled that supplies and works contracts were the only regimes covered by Public Procurement Community legislation during the GATT Tokyo Round (1979). A possible answer could be that supply of products was the maximum that could be agreed, at least at the first stage in the cumbersome and laborious negotiations between the European Communities and GATT signatories. Like the EC Treaty, GATT does not prohibit discrimination by government purchasing agencies in favour of national products. Under the EC regime, discrimination based on economic reasons is justified. National authorities may justify their discriminatory purchasing practices invoking concerns for employment and social equity, under the broader goal of promoting greater economic efficiency and industrial adjustment. Under the GATT regime, Article III 8(a) excludes government procurement from the principle of national treatment regarding its regulation. Thus, free movement of goods was considered, with respect to public procurement, to be the first step under the framework of the Multilateral Agreements between the EC and GATT signatories with a view to liberalising trade and preventing non-tariff barriers arising from national procurement policies.

Another possible justification of the limitation of the AGP rules to supplies of goods only could have been that works and construction contracts involve further aspects that must be taken into account in an attempt to liberalise their regime. They involve social and regional policy, short and long term employment considerations, peripheral development of the EC regions, etc. Liberalising the public works regime between the Community and third countries will not only bring into play free trade area considerations (free movement of goods), but will also go further, trespassing on the field of economic union, where labour, capital, payments and services need also to circulate freely.[110]

The Utilities Directive 90/531 intends to open up procurement practices in the four previously excluded sectors- water, energy, telecommunications and transport- mainly to EC-wide competition. With regard to goods (and services) originating in third countries, things are more complicated. A product outside the Community, in order to be subject to a public contract regulated by one of the EC Public Procurement Directives, must lawfully be put in free circulation in at least one Member State.[111] Except where there has been an international agreement which grants comparable and effective access for Community undertakings to public markets of a third country (reciprocity principle), Article 29 of Directive 90/531 renders it possible for EC contracting authorities in the utilities sector to reject offers from outside the Community and requires Community preference where Community offers are equivalent to offers from third countries (where the price difference does not exceed 3%). With reference to an international agreement granting access to public markets, Directive 90/531 opens the door for the application of the GATT Agreement on Government Procurement in the utilities sector, concluded between the European Community and 11 GATT signatories during the GATT Tokyo Round in 1979. The AGP embraces only supplies contracts, which are currently the only public sector regime open to international competition. The European Union's commitment towards international liberalisation of public markets has been demonstrated by its offer to the GATT AGP signatories during the Uruguay Round, to eliminate all discrimination regarding contracts in urban transport, ports, airports, heavy electrical and telecommunications equipment.[112]

---

[110] See L.Gormley, *Some reflections on Public Procurement in the EC*, (Nov.1990) European Business Law Review.

[111] For the concept of origin of goods and their lawful free circulation in the Common Market see Regulation 802/68, O.J.English Special Edition 1968 (1), p.165.

[112] See Council Regulation 1461/93, O.J. 1993, L 146, on access to public contracts for tenderers from the United States; Council Decision 93/323, O..J. 1993, L 125, on the conclusion of agreement between the EC and USA on government procurement.

Expansion of the AGP framework to embrace supplies and works contracts in the utilities sector and services contracts has being pursued during the GATT Uruguay Round.[113] The new regime introduced substantial changes in the application of the AGP with respect to types of contracts and coverage of contracting authorities as well as remedies. Works and services contracts are now covered and the list of contracting authorities embraces not only central government departments and their agencies but regional and local authorities and some utilities in the form of public authorities or public undertakings. Certain exemptions between the signatories do apply, but based on bilateral agreements, the new regime promises a significant expansion of the existing European procurement legislation.[114]

With respect to EFTA countries, the EC reached an agreement on October 22 1991 with the seven states (European Economic Area) to participate in the Single Market from January 1 1993. This will change the so far existing framework under the preferential agreement regime existing until 1991[115] to a free trade area, as the EFTA states will be required to implement Community law, and of course EC Public Procurement Directives in their national legal orders. The regime applies also to Hungary and Poland, by virtue of their Association Agreements.[116]

## The new WTO Government Procurement Agreement

The Government Procurement Agreement (GPA) is based on a number of general principles, which depict the principles of the old AGP regime. The most important of them is the principle of *national treatment*. Under this principle, the parties to the GPA must give the same treatment afforded to national providers and products to providers and products of other signatory states. Reinforcing the principle of national treatment, the *most favoured nation* (MFN) principle guarantees treatment no less favourable than that afforded to other parties. In addition to the above principles, the

---

[113] Article XXIV 1 AGP, signed on April 15, 1994 by all the previous signatories except Hong Kong and Singapore.

[114] The applicability of the new GPA by its signatories is subject to its ratification before January 1, 1996.

[115] See F.Weiss, *The law of Public Procurement in EFTA and the EC; The legal framework and its implementation,* Yearbook of European Law 1987.

[116] O.J. 1993, L 347/36 and O.J. 1993, L 348/36.

principle of *non-discrimination* prohibits discrimination against local firms on grounds of the degree of their foreign affiliation or ownership, or on the grounds of origin of the goods or services where these have been produced in one of the states which is party to the Agreement.

The GPA stipulates a set of procedures for contracting authorities in the signatory parties which must be followed when awarding contracts within its scope. These procedures aim to ensure transparency and openness as well as objectivity and legitimacy in the award of public contracts and to facilitate cross-border trade between the signatories. The influence of the European Community on the GPA regime is apparent, an indication of the maturity and validity of the regulatory process of the European public markets integration. The procedures are, however, less strict than those applicable for the award of public sector contracts under the Community regime, and depict the integral flexibility envisaged by the regulatory regime for utilities procurement.

The GPA intends to regulate access specifically to the government procurement markets. General market access between the signatories is in principle dealt with under other agreements, notably the GATT (on the import of goods) and the GATS (on access to services markets). The detailed scope and coverage of the GPA with regard to the entities covered, the type of procurement and monetary thresholds is set out in Appendix I of the Agreement. The Agreement applies in principle to all bodies which are deemed as "contracting authorities" for the purposes of the European public sector Directives. With reference to utilities, the GPA applies to entities which carry out one or more of certain listed "utility" activities, where these entities are either "public authorities" or "public undertakings", in the sense of the Utilities Directive. However, the GPA does not cover entities operating in the utilities sector on the basis of *special and exclusive rights*. The utility activities which are covered include (i) activities connected with the provision of water through fixed networks; (ii) activities concerned with the provision of electricity through fixed networks; (iii) the provision of terminal facilities to carriers by sea or inland waterway; and (iv) the operation of public services in the field of transport by automated systems, tramway, trolley bus, or bus or cable. The provision of public transport services by rail is included in principle, but there is an exclusion for entities listed in Annex VI of the European Utilities Directive, designed to exclude non-urban transport services. However, the trust of the applicability of the GPA in relation to utilities activities appears short in comparison with that under the European regime. Activities connected with the distribution of gas or heat, the exploration or extraction of fuel are notable exceptions from the GPA's ambit.

The thresholds for the applicability of the GPA regime to public contracts of signatories are as follows: For supplies and services it is SDR 130,000 for central government; 200,000 for local government; and 400,000 for all contracts in the utilities sectors (including those awarded by central and local government). For works contracts, the threshold is SDR 5 m, for all entities.

Although in principle the GPA regime represents a significant improvement in relation to the old AGP regime in terms of coverage and thrust, certain important derogations from its applicability would result in diluting the principal aims and objectives envisaged by the signatories. As far as central or federal government works and supply contracts are concerned, the Agreement is expected to facilitate market access and enhance cross-border trade patterns in public contracts. However, for contracts relating to services and for certain contracts in the utilities sector, as well as for contracts awarded by local, municipal or regional authorities, the effect of the Agreement appears considerably moderate. A number of signatories have been unable, or unwilling, to offer for coverage all of their entities or contracts in the above categories. Political and legal particularities in the systems of the signatories have prevented similar coverage between the parties. In addition, by applying the principle of *reciprocity* in negotiating the GPA, the result would probably have been very similar to the old AGP regime in covering central or federal public contracts. The solution to this fundamental, apparently, deadlock was to be found in a rather peculiar method. Each signatory should effectively negotiate with each other signatory, to come to a satisfactory agreement on coverage based on reciprocity on a bilateral basis. This approach constitutes a significant departure from the premises of the *principle of most favoured nation* (MFN) and has resulted in some considerable divergence in the applicability of the GPA by virtue of derogations and limitations imposed by signatories on access to their public markets. Thus, for example, coverage in the utilities sector does not apply to Canada, since that country did not commit itself to opening its own markets to the European Community. When the Agreement was first concluded in December 1993 there was also no coverage for utilities with respect to the

United States, but there have since been modifications to the EC-US coverage as a result of a subsequent EC-US bilateral agreements. Also outside the coverage of the Agreement in the utilities sector are, in relation to Japan, urban transport and electricity; in relation to South Korea, urban transport and airports; and in relation to Israel, urban transport. There are also significant derogations for certain categories of services and for specified types of equipment.

The scope and coverage the GPA, as well as the structure of its applicability present a unique instrument of international law which is based on a series of bilateral agreements rather than a multilateral arrangement. This represents a significant compromise of the most favoured nation principle, which is a fundamental premise of the majority of international trade agreements. Members to the World Trade Organisation joining the GPA, at their discretion, need to reach separate agreements on the scope of coverage with all existing parties to the Agreement. The GPA thus, has acquired a *plurilaterality* status, a fact that weakens its thrust and complicates its applicability.

# 4 The Mechanism of Integration of the European Public Markets

The internal structure of the public procurement law intends to embrace all the phases of the purchasing behaviour of the demand side of the equation (the contracting authorities) in an attempt to introduce the envisaged regulatory system. Of paramount importance to the internal structure of the EC public procurement Directives, is the comprehensive and clear definition of the term *contracting authorities*, a factor which would determine the applicability of the relevant rules. The term contracting authorities for the purposes of public purchasing regulation should not pose considerable conceptual difficulties; it should cover authorities which disperse public funds in pursuit of or on behalf of public interest. EC public procurement law characterises as contracting authorities the state and its organs interpreted in functional terms. The term *state* covers central, regional, municipal and local government departments. The above contracting authorities are primarily responsible for the core procurement requirements of supplies, works and services in a society. The public procurement Directives include detailed lists of all central and regional government departments that fall under their ambit.[1] However, the state in its function as a procurer of goods, works and services does not contain a range of purchasing operations which are attributed to its *organs*. By the term organs, procurement law has envisaged all entities which somehow

---

[1] See the Annexes attached to the EC Public Procurement Directives.

deliver public interest functions and has described them as *bodies governed by public law*. The latter category is subject to a set of cumulative criteria[2] in order to be classified as contracting authorities for the purposes of the Directives. *Bodies governed by public law* must be established for the specific purpose of meeting needs in the general public interest. Although they must have legal personality, their operations should not have industrial or commercial character. These entities must be financed, for the most part, by either the central government, or regional or local authorities, as well as be under their management and supervision control.

Contracting authorities for the purposes of public procurement law also include entities which are considered part of the state and its organs *in functional terms*. The definition of *authorities awarding contracts* under the Public Works regime was sought through reference procedures by a Dutch court.[3] In particular, the European Court of Justice was requested to clarify whether a *local land consolidation committee* could fall within the framework of Art. 1(b) of Directive 71/305. Pursuant to that provision, the state, regional or local authorities and legal persons governed by public law are to be regarded as *authorities awarding contracts*. The consolidation committee in question had no legal personality, but its functions and compositions were specifically governed by legislation. The Court interpreted the term *state* in functional terms and considered the local consolidation committee, which depended on the relevant public authorities for the appointment of its members, was subject to their supervision of its operations and it had as its main task the financing and award of public works contracts, as falling within the notion of state for the purpose of the above-mentioned provision [art. 1(b)], even though it was not part of the state administration in *formal terms*.[4] The Court held that the aim of the Public Works Directive 71/305, which was to ensure the effective attainment of freedom of establishment and freedom to provide services in respect of public works contracts, would be jeopardised if the provisions of the Directive were to be held to be inapplicable, solely because a public works contract is awarded by a body, which although it was set up to carry out tasks entrusted to it by legislation, was not formally part of the State's administration.

---

[2] Article 1(b) of Directive 93/36 and Article 1(b) of Directive 93/37.
[3] Case 31/87, *Gebroeders Beentjes B.V. v. State of Netherlands* [1988] ECR 4635.
[4] See Case 249/81, *Commission v. Ireland*, [1982]ECR 4005.

The enactment of the Utilities Directive brought an end to the exclusion of procurement of entities operating in the water, energy, transport and telecommunications sectors of the Member States. A wide range of these entities are covered by the term *bodies governed by public law*, which is used by the Utilities Directives for the contracting entities operating in the relevant sectors.[5] Interestingly, another category of contracting authorities under the Utilities Directives includes *public undertakings*.[6] The term indicates any undertaking over which the state may exercise direct or indirect dominant influence by means of ownership, or by means of financial participation, or by means of laws and regulations which govern the public undertaking's operation. Dominant influence can be exercised in the form of majority holding of the undertaking's subscribed capital, in the form of majority controlling of the undertaking's issued shares, or, finally in the form of the right to appoint the majority of the undertaking's management board. Public undertakings cover utilities operators which have been granted exclusive rights of exploitation of a service. Irrespective of their ownership, they are subject to the Utilities Directive in as much as the *exclusivity* of their operation precludes other entities from entering the relevant market under substantially the same competitive conditions. Privatised utilities could be, in principle, excluded from the procurement rules when a genuinely competitive regime[7] within the relevant oligopsonistic market structure would rule out purchasing patterns based on non-economic considerations.

Under the Tokyo Round GATT Agreement on Government Procurement, the term public authorities confined itself to central governments and their agencies only.[8] The new World Trade Organisation Government Procurement Agreement applies in principle to all bodies which are deemed as "contracting authorities" for the purposes of the Public Supplies and Public Works Directives. As far as utilities are concerned, the GPA applies to entities which carry out one or more of

---

[5] Article 1(1) of Directive 93/38.

[6] Article 1(2) of Directive 93/38.

[7] The determination of a genuinely competitive regime is left to the utilities operators themselves. See case, C 392/93, *The Queen and H.M. Treasury, ex parte British Telecommunications PLC*, O.J. 1993, C 287/6. This is perhaps a first step towards self-regulation which could lead to the disengagement of the relevant contracting authorities from the public procurement regime.

[8] Council Decision 87/565, O.J. 1987, L 345.

certain listed "utility" activities,[9] where these entities are either "public authorities" or "public undertakings", in the sense of the Utilities Directive. However, the GPA does not cover entities operating in the utilities sector on the basis of *special and exclusive rights*.

## The principle mandatory advertisement and publication of public contracts

One of the most important principles of the Public Procurement Directives is the principle of transparency. The principle of transparency serves two main objectives: the first is to introduce a system of openness in public purchasing of the Member States, so a greater degree of accountability should be established and potential direct discrimination on grounds of nationality should be eliminated. The second objective aims at ensuring that transparency in public procurement represents a substantial basis for a system of best practice for both parts of the equation, but in particular relevant to the supply side, to the extent that the latter has a more *proactive* role in determining the needs of the demand side. Transparency in public procurement is achieved through community-wide publicity and advertisement of public procurement contracts over certain thresholds by means of publication of three kind of notices in the Official Journal of the European Communities:

i) Periodic Indicative Notices (PIN). Every contracting authority must notify its intentions for public procurement contracts within the forthcoming financial year.[10] By doing so, it provides for an estimate intention of its purchasing and gives the supply side the necessary time for planning and response to future contract opportunities. The publication of Periodic Indicative Notices, if properly observed, also serves as a useful indicator in determining the relevant market size for the supply side, as well as the relevant procurement magnitude for a type of contracting

---

[9] The listed utility activities which are covered under the new GPA include (i) activities connected with the provision of water through fixed networks; (ii) activities concerned with the provision of electricity through fixed networks; (iii) the provision of terminal facilities to carriers by sea or inland waterway; and (iv) the operation of public services in the field of transport by automated systems, tramway, trolley bus, or cable bus.

[10] Article 9(1) of Directive 93/36; Article 11(1) to (3) of Directive 93/37; Article 22(1)(a) to (c) of Directive 93/38; Article 15(1) of Directive 92/50.

authorities on an annual basis. The fact that through PIN notices contracting authorities produce only an estimated figure for forthcoming contracts they intend to award, does not absolve them from their responsibilities in strictly adhering to their publication. The Commission brought the Italian State before the European Court of Justice[11] for a declaration that, by failing to communicate for publication in the Official Journal, an indicative notice summarising all the contracts which the Italian Ministry of Finance planned to award during that year, and then by failing to publish a notice inviting tenders for the concession of the system for the computerisation of the lottery.

ii) Invitations to tender. All contracts above the relevant thresholds should be tendered and the notice containing the invitation to tender must include the award procedures and the award criteria for the contract in question.[12] The Invitation to tender is the most important publicity and advertisement requirement for the creating of transparent and open public markets in the European Community. The publication of the invitation to tender refers only to a particular contract, or a range of similar contracts of repetitive nature and provides the supply side with the opportunity to respond and make an offer in order to meet the needs and requirements of the demand side. The invitation to tender is part of the contractual nexus in the public procurement process between the relevant contracting authority and the tenderers/candidates competing for the award of the contract in question. It is through the invitation to tender that the supply side has a clear view as to the award procedures and the award criteria contracting authorities intend to utilise, thus being able to respond accordingly. The invitation to tender represents the first step towards the award of public contracts and failure by contracting authorities to adhere to the minimum requirements specified in the Directives could invalidate the whole process.[13]

iii) Contract Award Notices (CAN). This is a form of notification after the award of the contract of the successful tenderer and the price of its offer,

---

[11] See case 272/91R, *Commission v. Italian Republic*, order of June 12, 1992

[12] Article 9(2) of Directive 93/36; Article 11(2) of Directive 93/37; Article 21 of Directive 93/38; Article 15(2) of Directive 92/50.

[13] For more details see Chapter 5 and the remedies available to interested parties under European Law and the Public Procurement Compliance Directives.

as well as the reasons for its selection by the contracting authority.[14] In principle, Contract Award Notices publicise the reasoning of contracting authorities during the selection and award stages of the process, but quite often price information of the successful tenderers and other candidates is withheld for reasons of commercial confidentiality. The publication of CAN notices can be used as an effective indicator in monitoring the purchasing patterns of contracting authorities, as well as in providing a picture relevant to the tradability of public contracts.

All types of notices are published by the Publications Office of the European Communities. Within twelve days (or five days in the case of the accelerated form of restricted or negotiated procedures), the Publications Office publishes the notices in the Supplement to the Official Journal and via the TED (Tenders Electronic Daily) database. Two notices are published in full in their original language only and in summary form in the other Community languages. The Publications Office takes responsibility for the necessary translations and summaries. The cost of publishing notices in the Supplement to the Official Journal are borne by the Community.

## The monetary applicability of the Public Procurement Directives

The European rules of public procurement and all the requirements and procedures laid down therein are triggered only if certain value thresholds are met. The application of the Directives is subject to monetary considerations in relation to the value of the relevant contracts. There is a clear-cut distinction of coverage of the public procurement rules upon contracts representing transactions between the public sector and the industry of a certain economic substance and volume. Contracts below the required thresholds are not subject to the rigorous regime envisaged by the Directives. However, contracting authorities are under the explicit obligation to avoid discrimination on nationality grounds and apply all the provisions related to the fundamental principles of the Treaties of Rome and Maastricht. The thresholds laid down are as follows:

---

[14] Article 9(3) of Directive 93/36; Article 11(5) of Directive 93/37; Article 24 of Directive 93/38; Article 16(1) of Directive 92/50.

- ECU 5 m for all work and construction projects[15]
- ECU 200,000 for supplies contracts within the European Union[16] and ECU 136,000 for supplies contracts from third countries[17] which participate in the WTO Government Procurement Agreement.
- ECU 600,000 for supplies of telecommunication equipment under the Utilities Directive[18] and ECU 400,000 for all other supplies contracts awarded by public utilities.[19]
- ECU 200,000 for services contracts.[20]

One could question the reason behind the separation of public procurement regulation into dimensional and sub-dimensional nature as a results of the relevant thresholds. Interestingly enough, it was thought that contracts above the thresholds laid down by the Directives could embrace the majority of the public procurement requirements in the Member States, thus eliminating the danger of discriminatory public purchasing for those contracts left outside the ambit of the Directives. However, a careful monitoring of procurement systems in the Member States have revealed that sub-dimensional procurement appears at least three times the size of dimensional public purchasing,[21] a fact that renders the application of the Directives only partly responsible for the integration of public markets in the European Community.

The way in which the value of a contract is calculated is crucial for the application of the relevant Directive. To ensure that identical calculation methods are used throughout the Member States of the European Community and to prevent intentional avoidance of the procurement Directives by artificially low contract valuations, the Directives lay down specific rules.[22] Where the contract is to be concluded in the form of a lease, rental or hire-purchase agreement, the calculation, method varies according to the duration of the contract. The estimated value is to be calculated on the basis of the following requirements:

---

[15] Article 3(1) of Directive 93/37; Article 14(c) of Directive 93/38.
[16] Article 5(1)(a) of Directive 93/36.
[17] Article 5(1)(c) of Directive 93/36.
[18] Article 14(b) of Directive 93/38.
[19] Article 14(a) of Directive 93/38.
[20] Article 7(1) of Directive 92/50.
[21] See, European Commission, *The Use of Negotiated Procedures as a Non-Tariff Barrier in Public Procurement*, Brussels, CC 9364, 1995.
[22] Article 5(2) to (6) of Directive 93/36; Article 6(1) to (5) of Directive 93/37; Article 14(4) to (13) of Directive 93/38; Article 7(2) to (8) of Directive 92/50.

- where its term is 12 months or less, the total value for the contract's duration;
- where its term exceeds 12 months, the total value for the contract's duration, including the estimated residual value of the products;
- where the contract is concluded for an indefinite period or where its term cannot be defined, the monthly value multiplied by 48.
- where contracts are of a regular nature or are to be renewed over a given period, the following must be taken into account:

- either the actual aggregate value of similar successive contracts awarded over the previous 12 months or accounting period, adjusted where possible for anticipated changes in quantity or value over the subsequent 12 months;
- or the estimated aggregate value of the successive contracts concluded during the 12 months following the initial delivery or accounting periods where this exceeds 12 months. In any event, the choice between these two valuation methods must not be made with the intention of keeping contracts outside the scope of the Directive.

If a proposed procurement of supplies of the same type may lead to contracts being awarded at the same time in separate lots, the estimated value of all the lots must be taken into account. If it reaches the relevant threshold, all the lots must be awarded in compliance with the Directive. The same rules apply when estimating the value of leasing, rental or hire-purchase contracts. Where provision is explicitly made for options, the basis for calculating the estimated contract value must be the highest possible total permitted for the purchase, lease, rental or hire options included.

When calculating the value of a public works contract, account has to be taken of the estimated value of the works and of the estimated value of the supplies needed to carry out the works, even if these supplies are made available to the contractor by the contracting authorities. The estimated value of work which the contracting authority intends to have carried out later by the contractor awarded the current contract and which consists in a repetition of the work to be carried out under the current contract, must be included in the contract value.

The Works Directive provides for special rules when a contract is subdivided into several lots. When the aggregate value of the lots is over five million ECU, the provisions of the Directive apply to all lots. A work or a contract may not be split up with the intention of avoiding the applicability of the Directive. However, lots of a value, net of VAT, less than one million ECU may be exempted from the scope of the Directive, provided that the total estimated value of all the lots exempted does not exceed 20 per cent of the total estimated value of all lots.

**Selection and Qualification Criteria**

After the advertisement and publicity requirements the next phase in the public procurement process is the selection and qualification of the tenderers. At this stage, contracting authorities vet all the responses received and determine the suitability of the candidates according to objectively defined criteria which aim at eliminating arbitrariness and discrimination. The selection criteria are determined through two major categories of qualification requirements; i) legal, and ii) technical / economic. Contracting authorities must strictly follow the homogeneously specified selection criteria for enterprises participating in the award procedures of public procurement contracts in an attempt to abolish potential grounds for discrimination on grounds of nationality and exclude technical specifications which are capable of favouring national undertakings.

The relevant provisions of the procurement Directives relating to the criteria of a tenderer's good standing and qualification are directly effective.[23] These criteria comprise of grounds for exclusion from participation in the award of public contracts, such as bankruptcy, professional misconduct, failure to fulfil social security obligations and obligations relating to taxes. They also refer to the technical ability and knowledge of the contractor, where proof of them may be furnished by educational or professional qualifications, previous experience in performing public contracts and statements on the contractor's expertise. In construction projects, the references which the contractor may be required to produce must be specified in the notice or invitation to tender.[24] They include: the contractor's educational and professional qualifications or those of the firm's managerial staff, and, in particular, those of the person or persons responsible for carrying out the works; a list of the works carried out over

---

[23] Case 76/81, *SA Transporoute et Travaux v. Minister of Public Works*, [1982] ECR 457.

[24] Article 27 of Directive 93/37 and Article 31 of Directive 93/38.

the past five years, accompanied by certificates of satisfactory execution for the most important works. These certificates shall indicate the value, date and site of the works and shall specify whether they were carried out according to the rules of the trade and properly completed. Where necessary, the competent authority shall submit these certificates direct to the authority awarding the contracts; a statement of the tools, plant and technical equipment available to the contractor for carrying out the work; a statement of the firm's average annual manpower and number of managerial staff for the last three years; a statement of the technicians or technical divisions which the contractor can call upon for carrying out the work; whether or not they belong to the firm.

On the other hand, in supplies contracts, the references which may be requested[25] must be mentioned in the invitation to tender and are the following: a list of the principal deliveries effected in the past three years, with the sums, dates and recipients, public or private, involved in the form of certificates issued or countersigned by the competent authority; a description of the undertaking's technical facilities, its measures for ensuring quality and its study and research facilities; indication of the technicians or technical bodies involved, whether or not belonging directly to the undertaking, especially those responsible for quality control; samples, descriptions or photographs of the products to be supplied, the authenticity of which must be certified if the contracting authority so requests; certificates drawn up by official quality-control institutes or agencies of recognised competence attesting conformity to certain specifications or standards of goods clearly identified by references to specifications or standards; where the goods to be supplied are complex or, exceptionally, are required for a special purpose, a check carried out by the contracting authorities (or on their behalf by a competent official body of the country in which the supplier is established, subject to that body's agreement) on the production capacities of the supplier and, if necessary, on his study and research facilities and quality control measures. The provisions covering the contractors' eligibility and technical capacity constitute an exhaustive list.

In principle, there are automatic grounds for exclusion,[26] when a contractor, supplier or service provider; i) is bankrupt or is being wound

---

[25] Article 22 of Directive 93/36.
[26] Article 20 of Directive 93/36; Article 24 of Directive 93/37; Article 31 of Directive 93/38; Article 29 of Directive 92/50.

up; ii) is the subject of proceedings for a declaration of bankruptcy or for an order for compulsory winding up; iii) has been convicted for an offence concerning his professional conduct; iv) has been guilty of grave professional misconduct; v) has not fulfilled obligations relating to social security contributions; and vi) has not fulfilled obligations relating to the payment of taxes.

However, for the purposes of assessing the financial and economic standing of contractors, an exception to the exhaustive list covering the contractors' eligibility and technical capacity is provided for,[27] where, in particular, contracting entities may request references other than those expressly mentioned therein. Evidence of financial and economic standing may be provided[28] by means of references including: i) appropriate statements from bankers; ii) the presentation of the firm's balance sheets or extracts from the balance sheets where these are published under company law provisions; and iii) a statement of the firm's annual turnover and the turnover on construction works for the three previous financial years. The non-exhaustive character of the list of references in relation to the contractors' economic and financial standing was recognised by the European Court of Justice,[29] where the value of the works which may be carried out at one time may constitute a proof of the contractors' economic and financial standing. The contracting authorities are allowed to fix such a limit, as the provisions of the public procurement Directives do not aim at delimiting the powers of Member States, but at determining the references or evidence which may be furnished in order to establish the contractors' financial and economic standing. The Court in another case referred to the European Court by a Dutch court[30] maintained that the examination of a contractor's suitability based on its good standing and qualifications and its financial and economic standing may take place simultaneously with the award procedures of a contract.[31] However, the two procedures (the

---

[27] Article 25 of Directive 71/305.

[28] Article 22 of Directive 93/36; Article 26 of Directive 93/37; Article 31(b) of Directive 93/38; Article 31 of Directive 92/50.

[29] Cases 27/86, 28/86, 29/86. Case 27/86, *Constructions et Enterprises Indusrtielles S.A (CEI) v. Association Intercommunale pour les Autoroutes des Ardennes*; Case 28/86, *Ing.A. Bellini & Co. S.p.A. v. Regie de Betiments*; Case 29/86, *Ing.A. Bellini & Co. S.p.A. v. Belgian State*, [1987] ECR 3347.

[30] Case 31/87, *Gebroeders Beentjes B.V. v. State of Netherlands* [1988] ECR 4635.

[31] See *Bellini* Case 28/86, [1987] ECR 3347, op.cit.

suitability evaluation and bid evaluation) are totally distinct processes which shall not be confused.[32]

*Legal requirements for the qualification of contractors*

The definition of a contractor wishing to submit a tender for the award of a public contract comprises any legal or natural person involved in supplies, construction or services activities. It also includes private consortia, as well as joint ventures or groupings. Contracting authorities may impose a requirement as to the form and legal status of the contractor that wins the award.[33] This requirement focuses only on the post selection stage, after the award of the contract and indicates the need for legal certainty. Specific legal form and status required by contracting entities facilitates monitoring of the performance of the contract and allows better access to justice in case of a dispute between the contracting entity and the undertaking in question. The successful contractor should also fulfil certain qualitative requirements concerning his eligibility and technical capacity[34] and his financial and economic standing. An opportunity to elaborate on consortia participation under public procurement Directives occurred in 1992 when the Belgian *Raad van Staat* asked the European Court of Justice for a preliminary ruling on the interpretation of the relevant provisions the Works Directives, which were in dispute in a case before the former.[35] The national litigation concerned with the dispute of a holding company against the Belgian State for failure to include the former in an official list of recognised contractors for future public works contracts on the grounds that the holding company did not posses any technical expertise in relation to construction projects. The Works Directives require specific qualitative technical criteria for selection of tenderers (Articles 23 to 26 of the Works Directive 71/305) and the official list of recognised contractors refers to these criteria (Article 28 of the Works Directive 71/305). The Court proceeded by endorsing the wide interpretation of the definition of works contracts under the original Works

---

[32] See case C-71/92, *Commission v. Spain*, judgment of June 30, 1993.
[33] Article 21 of Directive 71/305 as amended by Directive 89/440 and Article 18 of Directive 77/62 as amended by Directive 88/295. The same regime is followed in the Utilities Directive 90/531, Article 26, and the Services Directive 92/50, Article 26.
[34] Articles 20-23 of Directive 77/62; Articles 23 et seq of Directive 71/305; Articles 29 et seq of Directive 90/531; Articles 29 et seq of Directive 92/50.
[35] Case C 389/92, *Ballast Nedam Groep NV v. Belgische Staat*, [1994] 2 CMLR.

Directive 71/304 and under the amending Works Directive 88/295 and declared that even when an undertaking does not possess the relevant expertise to perform the actual works, contracting authorities by no means should exclude it from tendering procedures. The Court also made reference to the explicit provision of group tendering through consortia and the obligation of contracting authorities to require specific legal personality from the group only after the award of the contract to that group.

*The list of recognised contractors*

Registration in lists of recognised contractors that exist in various Member States may be used by contractors as an alternative means of proving their suitability, also before contracting authorities of other Member States.[36] Information deduced from registration in an official list may not be questioned by contracting authorities. Nonetheless, the actual level of financial and economic standing and technical knowledge or ability required of contractors is determined by the contracting authorities. Consequently, contracting authorities are required to accept that a contractor's financial and economic standing and technical knowledge and ability are sufficient for works corresponding to his classification only in so far as that classification is based on equivalent criteria with respect to the capacities required.

A reference for a preliminary ruling from *Le Conseil d'Etat* of the Grand Duchy of Luxembourg was made to the European Court of Justice[37] in an attempt to clarify the relevant provisions. An establishment permit imposed by national legislation[38] on foreign undertakings seeking to participate in the award of public works and public supplies contracts was held incompatible with the relevant provisions of the Public Works Directive 71/305 and Article 59 EC (the freedom to provide services). The Court held that official registration in a list in a Member State[39] constitutes a means of proving, before the authority of another Member State awarding contracts, that the tenderer satisfies the qualitative criteria

---

[36] Article 25 of Directive 93/36; Article 29 of Directive 93/37; Article 35 of Directive 92/50.
[37] Case 76/81, *SA Transporoute et Travaux v. Minister of Public Works*, [1982] ECR 457.
[38] *Reglement Grand-Ducal du 6 Novembre 1974*.
[39] Articles 24 and 28(3) of the Public Works Directive 71/305.

referring to the technical capacity and ability specified in the Directives.[40] In another similar case referred by a national court,[41] the European Court maintained that the inclusion of a contractor in an official list of recognised contractors in a Member State may be used as an alternative means of proving, before the authority of another Member State awarding contracts, the qualitative criteria listed in the relevant Directive. However, as harmonisation of official lists of recognised contractors concerns only the references attesting to financial and economic standing and their technical knowledge and ability, the criteria for their classifications are not harmonised. In regard to evidence of contractors' economic and financial standing and good standing, and qualifications, registration in a official list of recognised contractors may replace the references laid down in the provisions relating to technical requirements and ability as well as financial and economic standing, in so far as such registration is based upon *mutually equivalent* information.[42] Thus, a request from a contractor recognised in another Member State to furnish proof that his undertaking has the minimum funds, manpower and managerial staff required by the domestic law of the contracting authority, is compatible with Directive 71/305. The possible rejection of his tender by the awarding authority, if he fails to meet these domestic provisions, would appear legitimate even if the tenderer is recognised in a class equivalent to that required by domestic law governing the conditions of the contract to be awarded.

### The Award of Public Contracts

*Tendering procedures*

Participation in tendering procedures is channelled through open, negotiated or restricted procedures.

---

[40] Articles 23 to 26 of the Public Works Directive 71/305.
[41] Cases 27/86, 28/86, 29/86. Case 27/86, *Constructions et Enterprises Indusrtielles S.A (CEI) v. Association Intercommunale pour les Autoroutes des Ardennes*; Case 28/86, *Ing.A. Bellini & Co. S.p.A. v. Regie de Betiments*; Case 29/86, *Ing.A. Bellini & Co. S.p.A. v. Belgian State*, [1987] ECR 3347.
[42] See C. Bovis, *The eligibility of enterprises to participate in tenders for the award of Public Procurement contracts*, European Business Law Review, January 1994, Vol.5, p.p. 1-36.

- Open procedures are those where every interested supplier, contractor or service provider may submit an offer.[43]
- Negotiated procedures[44] are such procedures for the award of public contracts whereby contracting authorities consult contractors of their choice and negotiate the terms of the contract with one or more of them. In most cases they follow restricted procedures and they are heavily utilised under framework agreements in the Utilities sectors.[45] There are two different kinds of negotiated procedures: i) negotiated procedures with prior notification and ii) negotiated procedures without prior notification.

    - Negotiated procedures with prior notification[46] provide for selection of candidates in two rounds. In the first round, all interested contractors may submit their tenders and the contracting authority selects, from the candidates, those who will be invited to negotiate. In the second round, negotiations with various candidates take place and the successful tender is selected. In principle, the minimum number of candidates to be selected is three, provided that there is a sufficient number of suitable candidates.

    - Negotiated procedures without prior notification[47] are the least restrictive of the various award procedures laid down in the Directive and may be conducted in one single round. Contracting authorities are allowed to choose whichever contractor they want, begin negotiations directly with this contractor and award the contract to him. The Directive provides for only a few rules with which this procedure must comply. A prior notice in the Official Journal is not required.

---

[43] Article 1(d) of Directive 93/36; Article 1(e) of Directive 93/37; Article 1(7)(a) of Directive 93/38; Article 1(d) of Directive 92/50.

[44] Article 1(f) of Directive 93/36; Article 1(g) of Directive 93/37; Article 1(7)(c) of Directive 93/38; Article 1(c) of Directive 92/50.

[45] See the section on framework agreements under *Specific Types of Contracts under the Public Procurement Directives*, op. cit.

[46] Article 6(2) of Directive 93/36; Article 7(2) of Directive 93/37; Article 20(1) of Directive 93/38; Article 11(2) of Directive 92/50.

[47] Article 6(3) of Directive 93/36; Article 7(3) of Directive 93/37; Article 20(3) of Directive 93/38; Article 11(3) of Directive 92/50.

- Finally, Restricted procedures[48] are those procedures for the award of public contracts whereby only those contractors invited by the contracting authority may submit tenders. The selection of the winning tender usually takes place in two rounds. In the first round, all interested contractors may submit their interest and the contracting authority selects, from the candidates, those who will be invited to tender. In principle, the minimum number of candidates to be selected is five. In the second round, bids are submitted and the successful tender is selected.

An accelerated form of restricted or negotiated procedure may be used[49] where, for reasons of urgency, the periods normally required under the normal procedures cannot be met. In such cases, contracting authorities are required to indicate in the tender notice published in the Official Journal the grounds for using the accelerated form of the procedure. The use of an accelerated procedure must be limited to the types and quantities of products or services which it can be shown are urgently required. Other products or services must be supplied or provided under open or restricted procedures.

The Directives stipulate that open procedures, where possible should constitute the norm. Open procedures increase competition without doubt and can achieve better prices for the contracting authorities when purchasing goods in large volumes. Price reduction based on economies of scale can bring about substantial cost savings for the public sector. Open procedures are mostly utilised when the procurement process is relatively straightforward and are combined with the lowest price award criterion. On the other hand, competition in tendering procedures is limited by using the restricted and negotiated procedures. By definition, the number of candidates that are allowed to tender is limited (5 in restricted 3 in negotiated procedures respectively), therefore the Directives have attached a number of conditions for the contracting authorities to justify when they intend to award their contracts through restricted or negotiated procedure. Restricted and negotiated procedures are utilised in relation with the most economically advantageous offer award criterion and suited for more complex procurement schemes. Although contracting authorities can freely

---

[48] Article 1(e) of Directive 93/36; Article 1(f) of Directive 93/37; Article 1(7)(b) of Directive 93/38; Article 1(d) of Directive 92/50.

[49] Article 12 of Directive 93/36; Article 13 of Directive 93/37; Article 26(2) of Directive 93/38; Article 19(4) of Directive 92/50.

opt for open or restricted procedures, the latter should be justified by reference to the nature of the products or services to be procured and the balance between contract value and administrative costs associated with tender evaluation. A more rigorous set of conditions apply for the use of negotiated procedures. When negotiated procedures with prior notification are used, they must be justified on grounds of irregular or unacceptable tenders received as a result of a previous call. Negotiated procedures without prior notification are restrictively permitted in absence of tenders, when the procurement involves manufactured products or construction works purely for research and development, when for technical or artistic reasons or reasons connected with the protection of exclusive rights a particular supplier or contractor is selected, in cases of extreme urgency brought by unforseeable events not attributable to the contracting authorities, when additional deliveries and supplies or works would cause disproportionate technical operational and maintenance difficulties.

All negotiations with candidates or tenderers on fundamental aspects of contracts, in particular on prices, are prohibited in open and restricted procedures; discussions with candidates or tenderers may be held, but only for the purpose of clarifying or supplementing the content of their tenders or the requirements of the contracting authorities and provided this does not involve discriminatory practices.[50] The need for such a prohibition is clear, since the possibility to negotiate may allow the contracting authority to introduce subjective appraisal criteria. A Declaration on the above subject has been made by the European Council and the Commission of the European Communities.[51] Also the European Court of Justice has condemned post tender negotiations as in case 243/89, *Commission v. Denmark.*[52]

It should be clear that the selection process must be completely distinguished from the award process. Quite often, contracting authorities appear to fuse the two basic processes of the award of public procurement contracts. This runs contrary to legal precedence of the European Court of Justice and in particular case 31/87 *Gebroeders Beentjes v. Netherlands.*[53] The Court stated expressly that suitability evaluation and bid evaluation

---

[50] Article 24 of Directive 93/36.
[51] See O.J. [1994] L 111/114
[52] Judgment of 22 June 1993.
[53] See [1988] ECR 4635

are distinct processes which shall not be confused. The same line was adopted by the Court in case C-71/9? *Commission v. Spain*.[54]

*The Award Criteria*

In principle, there are two criteria laid down in the Public Procurement Directives for awarding public contracts:
- the lowest price
- the most economically advantageous offer

The lowest price criterion is self-explanatory.[55] The tenderer who submits the cheapest offer must be awarded the contract. Subject to the qualitative criteria and financial and economic standing, contracting authorities do not rely on any other factor than the price quoted to complete the contract. The reasons for utilising the lowest price criterion are: simplicity, speed, less qualitative consideration during the evaluation of tenders.

The appreciation of what is the most economically advantageous tender offer[56] is to be made on a series of factors and determinants chosen by the contracting entity for the particular contract in question. These factors include: price, delivery or completion date, running costs, cost-effectiveness, profitability, technical merit, product or work quality, aesthetic and functional characteristics, after-sales service and technical assistance, commitments with regard to spare parts and components and maintenance costs, security of supplies. The above list is not exhaustive and the factors listed therein serve as a guideline for contracting authorities in the weighted evaluation process of the contract award. The order of appearance of these factors in the invitation to tender or in the contract documents is of paramount importance for the whole process of evaluation of the tenders and award of the contract. The most economically advantageous factors must be in hierarchical or descending sequence so tenderers and interested parties can clearly ascertain the relative weight of factors other than price for the evaluation process. However, factors which have no strict relevance to the particular contract in question or factors

---

[54] Judgment of June 30, 1993.
[55] Article 26(1)(a) of Directive 93/36; Article 30(1)(a) of Directive 93/37; Article 34(1)(b) of Directive 93/38; Article 36(1)(b) of Directive 92/50.
[56] Article 26(1)(b) of Directive 93/36; Article 30(1)(b) of Directive 93/37; Article 34(1)(a) of Directive 93/38; Article 36(1)(a) of Directive 92/50.

which are irrelevant in economic terms are classified as subjective. It is clearly stated in the *European Commission's Guide to the Community rules on open government procurement*[57] that ".....only objective criteria which are strictly relevant to the particular project may be used...". Along the same lines, the European Court of Justice has established a precedence in case 31/87 *Gebroeders Beentjes v. Netherlands*,[58] where the award criteria concern only the qualities of the service the provider can offer.

Along the same lines, in 1993 a reference to the European Court of Justice was made by the High Court (Queen's Bench Division) on, *inter alia*, the utilisation of public procurement Directives for the purchasing of pharmaceutical products (narcotic drugs previously being supplied under licence) by the competent health authorities.[59] The national court requested a preliminary ruling on the interpretation of Article 25 of the Supplies Directive 77/62, particularly the meaning of the "most economically advantageous offer". The national court asked whether factors concerning continuity and reliability as well as security of supplies fall under the framework of the most economically advantageous offer, when the latter is being evaluated. The Court of Justice, following previous case law,[60] reiterated the flexible and wide interpretation of the relevant award criterion and had no difficulty in declaring that contracting authorities may use the most economically advantageous offer as award criterion by choosing the factors which they want to apply in evaluating tenders, provided these factors are mentioned, in hierarchical order in the invitation to tender and or the contract documents. Two Member States intervened in the case and submitted that a restricted system of supply of potentially dangerous substances could be justified by having recourse to Article 6(1) and (4) of the Supplies Directive, which permits the use of negotiated procedures when, for technical reasons, the supply of goods in question can be guaranteed by only a particular supplier [Article 6(1)], or when, for security reasons, the supply of goods in question is declared secret, or when their delivery must be accompanied by the application of administrative laws or regulations that guarantee the secrecy of the delivery [Article [6(4)].

---

[57] [1987] O.J. C 385/1 at 36.
[58] [1988] ECR 463.
[59] Case C 324/93, *R. v. The Secretary of State for the Home Department, ex.p . Evans Medical Ltd and Macfarlan Smith Ltd.*
[60] Case 31/87, *Gebroeders Beenjes v. The Netherlands*, [1988] ECR 4635, op.cit.

*Framework Agreements*

The Utilities Directives have introduced a new selection and tendering procedure, namely framework agreements which is influenced to a large extent by the benefits of chain supply management and partnership schemes. The Supplies, Works and Services Directives do not refer to framework agreements. A framework agreement is an agreement between a contracting authority and one or more suppliers, contractors or service-providers the purpose of which is to establish the terms, in particular with regard to prices and, where appropriate, the quantity envisaged, governing the contracts to be awarded during a given period. A framework agreement does not possess binding character and should not be considered as a contract between the relevant parties.[61] In practical terms it represents a sort of a standing offer which remains valid during its time-span. Within the provisions of the Utilities Directive, when a contracting authority awards a framework agreement under the relevant procedures which are common to other public contracts covered therein, subsequent individual contracts concluded under the framework agreement may be awarded without having recourse to a call for competition. Individual contracts which have been awarded under a framework agreement are subject to the requirement of the publication of a contract-award notice in the Official Journal. The Directive specifically stipulates that misuse of framework agreements may distort competition and trigger the application of the relevant rules, particularly with reference to concerted practices which lead to collusive tendering.

*In-house Contracts and Contracts to Affiliated Undertakings*

Article 6 of the Services Directive provide for the inapplicability of the Directive to service contracts which are awarded to an entity which is itself a contracting authority within the meaning of the Directive on the basis of an exclusive right which is granted to the contracting authority by a law, regulation or administrative provision of the Member State in

---

[61] Framework agreements should not be confused with framework contracts, the latter producing binding effects; see P.Armin- Trepte, *Public Procurement in the EC,* 1993, CCH Europe, p. 93.

question.[62] Article 13 of the Utilities Directive provides for the exclusion of certain contracts between contracting authorities and affiliated undertakings. An affiliated undertaking, for the purposes of Art. 1(3) of the Utilities Directive, is one the annual accounts of which are consolidated with those of the contracting entity in accordance with the requirements of the seventh company law Directive [Council Directive 83/349 (OJ 1983 L193/1)]. These are service contracts which are awarded to a service-provider which is affiliated to the contracting entity and service contracts which are awarded to a service-provider which is affiliated to a contracting entity participating in a joint venture formed for the purpose of carrying out an activity covered by the Directive. The explanatory memorandum accompanying the text amending the Utilities Directive (COM (91) 347-SYN 36 1) states that this provision relates, in particular, to three types of service provision within groups. These categories, which may or may not be distinct, are: the provision of common services such as accounting, recruitment and management; the provision of specialised services embodying the know how of the group; the provision of a specialised service to a joint venture. The exclusion from the provisions of the Directive is subject, however, to two conditions: the service-provider must be an undertaking affiliated to the contracting authority and, at least 80 per cent of its average turnover arising within the European Community for the preceding three years, derives from the provision of the same or similar services to undertakings with which it is affiliated. The Commission is empowered to monitor the application of this Article and require the notification of the names of the undertakings concerned and the nature and value of the service contracts involved.

*Design Contests*

Under the Services Directive, provision has been made for a fourth type of award procedure, namely *design contests*, with particular reference to planning projects. According to the Services Directive, *design contests* are those national procedures which enable the contracting authority to acquire in the fields of area planning, town planning, architecture and civil

---

[62] This practice resembles the market testing process often employed in the United Kingdom between a contracting authority and an in-house team; see I. Harden, *Defining the range of application of the public sector procurement Directives in the United Kingdom*, Public procurement Law Review 1992, Vol.1 p.362.

engineering, a plan or a design selected by a jury, after being put out to competition with or without the award of prizes. The award of *design contests*, according to the Services Directive must follow specific rules. The admission of participants to the contest shall not be limited either by reference to the territory or part of a Member State, or on the grounds that under the law of the Member State in which the contest is organised, participants would have been required to be either natural or legal persons. Furthermore, where design contests are restricted to a limited number of participants, the contracting authorities must lay down clear and non-discriminatory selection criteria which ensure sufficient and genuine competition among the participants. The jury shall be composed exclusively of natural persons who are independent. The award criteria for design contests remain the same with other public contracts (the lowest price or the most economically advantageous offer)

*Concession Contracts*

The Public Works Directive has adopted a special, mitigated regime for the award of concession contracts the value of which is 5 million ECU or more. There are no specific rules as to the way the value of the contract must be calculated or rules referring to aggregation. For the award of concession contracts, contracting authorities are obliged to follow the advertising rules concerning open and restricted procedures for the award of ordinary works contracts. Also, the provisions on technical standards and on criteria for qualitative selection of candidates and tenderers do apply. However, the Works Directive does not prescribe the use of specific award procedures for concession contracts. The Directive presupposes the concession contracts are awarded in two rounds, such as in the case of restricted procedures or negotiated procedures for works contracts. Nothing, however, prevents contracting authorities from applying a - one round - open procedure. The Directive contains no rules on the minimum number of candidates which have to be invited to negotiate or to submit a tender. It would seem that a contracting authority may limit itself to selecting only one single candidate, provided the intention to award a concession contract has been adequately published. A contracting authority may under no circumstances refrain from publishing a notice.

*Additional award criteria*

*Sub-contracting and public procurement.* Sub-contracting plays a major role in the opening up of public markets as it is the most effective way of small and medium sized enterprises' participation in public procurement. All Directives on Public Procurement, influenced by Commission's Communications on sub-contracting and small and medium enterprises encourage the use of sub-contracting in the award of public contracts. Particularly, in public supplies contracts, the contracting entity in the invitation to tender may ask the tenderers on their intention to sub-contract to third parties part of the contract. This reveals the importance of sub-contracting for regional development in public procurement. In public works contracts, contracting authorities awarding the principal contract to a concessionaire may require him to subcontract to third parties at least 30% of the total work provided for by the principal contract.

*Local labour employment and Public Procurement.* Contracting authorities are often faced with the dilemma of utilising public procurement contracts, particularly in construction projects, as a tool for combating long-term unemployment within their region. Although at first instance, local labour clauses appear to fall foul of the relevant Treaty provisions on non-discrimination (Art. 7) and right of establishment (Art. 52), the European Court of Justice in a seemingly important case[63] on public procurement pronounced that the utilisation of local labour clauses could be included in the non-exhaustive list of factors determining award criteria, especially the most economically advantageous offer, if they did not have discriminatory effects. The Court apparently rejected the possible utilisation of local labour clauses as a selection criterion, a decision which runs in consistency with previous case law, recognising the exhaustive character of selection criteria stipulated by the Public Procurement Directives.

*The award of Public Housing Schemes.* The award of public housing contracts[64] may deviate from the normal regime of the Directive for the purpose of selecting a contractor who meets the requirements specified by the public authority. The design and construction of a public housing

---

[63] Case 31/87, Gebroeders Beentjes B.V. v. State of Netherlands [1988] ECR 4635.
[64] Article 9 of Directive 93/37.

scheme, as well as the size and complexity of the project, as well as the estimated duration of the work involved, require that planning be based from the outset on close collaboration within a team comprising representatives of the contracting authorities, experts and the contractor to be responsible for carrying out the works. In these cases, the contracting authorities have to apply the advertising rules and the criteria for qualitative selection relating to the restricted procedure. Moreover, the contracting authorities have to include in the contract notice as accurately as possible, a description of the works to be carried out. With respect to quantitative selection, no restrictions apply. Hence, there is no obligation for the contracting authorities to select more that one single contractor to negotiate admission to the building team.

# 5 Enforcement of and Compliance with Public Procurement Law: A Critique of the System

The implementation of public procurement Directives by Member States through the enactment of national legislation or the employment of administrative practices has been subject to a double regime of judicial control at Community and at national levels. Both the centralised and decentralised orientation of judicial control relating to the enforcement of and compliance with public procurement rules reveal the *horizontal* and *vertical* effects of the public procurement legislation on the demand and the supply sides respectively. The centralised control (at Community level) is directed to the demand side (contracting authorities) of the public procurement equation and includes the supervision, monitoring and evaluation of the application and appropriate implementation of the relevant Directives at domestic legal orders. It focuses primarily on compliance procedures (Article 169 EC) before the European Court of Justice, where the European Commission asks the Court to condemn a Member State's failure to comply with European Community Law, although in a number of occasions the Commission has availed itself of the proceedings relating to interim measures which are ordered by the European Court of Justice (Article 185 EC).

On the other hand, the decentralised control has a vertical nature, to the extent that it encompasses litigation between the demand and the supply sides. The verticality of the litigation reveals disputes arising from the operation of public procurement legislation at domestic level, after their incorporation to the national legal systems. However, it should be mentioned that the decentralised (at national level) judicial control often ends with a reference by the national court to the European Court of Justice (Article 177 EC) for a preliminary ruling in relation to the interpretation of the Directives' provisions or in relation to the compatibility with Community law of national laws implementing them. Apparently, for the enforcement of and compliance with public procurement law Community control plays a crucial role, although the public procurement sector is dominated by national sensibilities requiring the utilisation of a system of decentralised control.

The centralised and decentralised judicial control of public procurement law has also revealed the formulation of two patterns which address the impact of public procurement legislation on the demand and supply sides. The first pattern is associated with compliance proceedings against defaulting Member States that failed to implement correctly public procurement Directives and often occurs during the early stages of implementation of public procurement legislation into domestic legal orders. It reveals the impact of the new regime on existing national systems, although it is not surprising that well after the completion of the internal market compliance proceedings are still being brought before the European Court of Justice. The second pattern relates to the utilisation of the Court's rulings as a guide for the direct effectiveness and/or the interpretation of provisions of the relevant Directives. This pattern can be identified in case law related to Article 177 EC proceedings and occurs in cases where clarification and interpretation of provisions of the relevant Directives is needed; it can be associated with the post implementation era, where the Directives have been digested into the domestic legal orders.

**Judicial control at centralised level**

Since the forms and methods of incorporation of secondary Community legislation into national provisions rely mainly on the discretion of Member States[1], the EC Treaty primarily envisaged a centralised judicial

---

[1] Article 189 EEC.

control at Community in order to ensure that Member States fulfil their obligations. This type of judicial control involves proceedings under Articles 169, 170, 171 EC Treaty, which include actions against a Member State for failure to fulfil Treaty obligations. Under Article 169 EC, it is the European Commission that brings a Member State before the European Court of Justice. Other Member States may avail themselves of the provisions laid down in Article 170 EC to have the Court condemn a Member State's infringement of the Treaty.[2] Interestingly, both proceedings lack an enforcement mechanism and the Court's judgment has only a declaratory character. Even under Article 171 EC, where the Court may continue to condemn a Member State's failure to comply with a previous judgment, enforcement proceedings are not present. The completion of the internal market has witnessed fifteen compliance cases under Article 169 EC,[3] the majority of which were attributable to the relevant States' failure to implement or comply with provisions of public procurement Directives. Interestingly, during the same period, the European Court of Justice, after an application by the European Commission, considered the award of interim measures under Article 185 EC in three cases, one against Ireland and the other two against Italy, in which the award of the contract in question was suspended.

It has been suggested[4] that Community Institutions may take sanctions against a Member State that has failed to fulfil its obligations under the Treaty and to comply with a Court's judgment. There is a parallel under the European Coal and Steel Community Treaty,[5] but in fact, such action has never been used. It should be mentioned here that in the area of public procurement, non-compliance with the European Directives may lead to withdraw of Community funds allocated to the defaulting Member State. This appears an effective from of sanction, initiated by the European Commission, after a decision of the European Court of Justice pronouncing on the non-compliance issue.[6] Centralised judicial control also covers proceedings under Article 177 EC, where

---

[2] It is not common to see an action under Article 170 EEC, as Member States wish to maintain good relations amongst themselves.
[3] Nine out of fifteen 169 cases have been brought against Italy; two against Greece and one against Ireland, Spain, Portugal and Denmark respectively.
[4] See Kapteyn and Verloren van Themaat, *Introduction to the law of the European Communities*, 2rd.ed. 1989, Kluwer, Deventer, p.35.
[5] Article 88 paras 3 and 4.
[6] See European Commission, *Public Procurement and Community Financing*, O.J. C 22, 1989.

national courts make references to the Court of Justice asking for a preliminary ruling on the interpretation of EC legislation and the compatibility of national laws with the former, but this type of review lies in the borderline between Community and national jurisdictions.

The European Commission, by virtue of Article 169 EC may initiate proceedings, on its own initiative[7] or in response to a complaint, against a defaulting Member State for failure to fulfil its obligations under the Treaty. Existence of specific legal interest is not required[8] as a condition of the admissibility of the action, since it is in the general interest of the Commission to observe, supervise and ensure the correct application of Community law. Even in cases where the national litigation (*Farmaindusrtia v. Consejeria de salud de la Junta de Andalucia*)[9] was withdrawn, the Commission proceeded in launching an action against Spain for failure to comply with the provisions of the Public Supplies Directive 77/62, on the basis of the incompatibility with the principles and provisions of public procurement law of a framework agreement entered into by Spanish public authorities and the national association of pharmaceutical companies *(Farmaindustria)*, in which the prices and other terms and conditions governing the direct purchase of pharmaceutical products destined for social security institutions and the indirect purchase of such products for institutions non-related to social security.

The enactment of the Compliance Directives[10] has introduced a special procedure of centralised nature, the so-called *correction procedure*. Under the Compliance Directives, there is the possibility for the European Commission to intervene in cases where it feels there has been a breach of the procurement rules, under the provisions laid out in Article 3 of the Public Sector Compliance Directive and Article 8 of the Utilities Compliance Directive. However, as far as the Public Sector Compliance Directive is concerned, the relevant provision applies only where there appears to have been a breach of the rules relating to contracts covered by the Works Directive (93/37/EC) and the Supplies Directive

---

[7] Individuals cannot force the Commission to bring a State before the Court under Article 169 EEC procedure, case 48/65 *Alfons Luttucke GmbH v. Commission*, [1966] ECR 19.
[8] Case 167/73 *Commission v. France*, [1974] ECR 359.
[9] Case 179/89, *Farmaindusrtia v. Consejeria de salud de la Junta de Andalucia*, [1989] O.J. C 160/10.
[10] See the Public Works and Public Supplies Compliance Directive 89/665, O.J. 1989 L 395, and the Utilities Compliance Directive 92/13, O.J. 1992 L 76/7.

(93/36/EC). There seems to be nothing in the Services Directive to make a particular provision applicable to services, although the rest of the Compliance Directive applies to award procedures under the Services Directive, as well as to those covered by Works and Supplies. This was, apparently, due to an oversight in the drafting stages and was not intentional. The oversight in relation to public sector services is not, however, important, since the provision adds nothing to the powers which the Commission has already had under Article 169 EC. Basically, the corrective procedure may be invoked whenever the Commission considers that there has been a *clear and manifest* breach of the public procurement law. When the procedure is invoked, the Commission must notify both the relevant state and the contracting authority of the reasons which have led it to this conclusion, and request that the infringement be corrected [Article 3 (2)]. The State must reply within 21 days of receipt of notification, and must either confirm that the infringement has been corrected or give an explanation as to why no correction has been made (unless the award procedure has already been suspended in which case it is simply required to notify the Commission of this). Failure by a Member State to give a reply which is to the satisfaction of the Commission does not attract any specific sanctions under Article 3, nor does the Commission enjoy any special powers where this "corrective mechanism" is invoked. It was originally proposed that the Commission should be able to suspend the relevant award procedure on its own initiative, but the proposal was dropped because of opposition from the member states. Thus, if a satisfactory reply is not received, the Commission may initiate proceedings under Article 169 EC in the usual way. It is the Commission's practice to treat a notification of a breach given under the Article 3 procedure as a "letter of infringement" for the purpose of the Article 169 EC procedure. If the state does not give a satisfactory reply within the 21 day period stated in Article 3, a reasoned opinion will be issued on expiry of that period. It is submitted that 21 days is a "reasonable" period for a state to prepare a response, and that the Commission's practice in this respect is consistent with the requirements of Article 169 EC. The effect of the corrective procedure under the Compliance Directives appears to demonstrate in an official manner that a State is in breach of the law, if it does provide a satisfactory reply or does not provide a reply at all. The corrective procedure does not in practice facilitate the powers of the Commission to effectively enforce public procurement law.

## Proceedings before the European Court of Justice

The European Commission has an important role to play in ensuring that the public procurement rules are enforced, and positively encourages complaints from aggrieved firms. In practice, the Commission follows all genuine complaints with the state concerned, in an attempt to negotiate an amicable satisfactory solution. A complaint to the Commission is, thus, always a potentially useful avenue of redress for an aggrieved contractor. In those cases where no satisfactory solution can be reached, the Commission may, as a last resort, consider bringing compliance proceedings before the Court of Justice of the European Communities, under the provisions of Article 169 EC. Proceedings are brought against Member States as such, and not against the particular contracting authorities which are responsible for the breach. Thus, States are not held responsible only for breaches of Community law committed by the central or local government but also for breaches by other public authorities and bodies over which States exercise a certain degree of control. Based on previous case-law, it appears likely that the state will be held responsible under Article 169 EC for the award procedures of bodies which are defined as "contracting authorities" for the purposes of the public procurement Directives, since these are all bodies which have sufficient connection with central authority for that authority to be held accountable for all their activities.

However, it may be that the State will not be held accountable for all those bodies which are caught as "contracting authorities" under the Utilities Directive.[11] In particular, in the United Kingdom those entities operating in the telecommunications, energy, water and transport sectors, which have been privatised, may have insufficient connection with the State. A leading case which has defined the ambit of the state from a functional perspective is *Foster v British Gas*[12], in which the European Court of Justice ruled that a Directive capable of having direct effect could be invoked against a body which is subject to the *control* of the State and has been delegated special powers. The House of Lords then held that this applied to *the British Gas Corporation* (publicly controlled entity), the predecessor of *British Gas* (privatised utility). However, it is not clear

---

[11] Directive 93/38/EEC
[12] *Foster v British Gas* [1990] ECR-1313

that the privatised utilities could be covered by the *Foster* principle[13], thus state accountability under the compliance proceedings of Article 169 EC could not embrace privatised enterprises.[14] It may be pointed out, nevertheless, that in those cases where the State is not generally held responsible for a contracting authority's activities, however, accountability might still arise where the state exercises some specific control (e.g. auditing, regulation) over the contractual activities of the entity concerned.

*The consequences of a judgment by the Court of Justice*

Compliance procedures before the European Court of Justice lack an enforcement character to the extent that the Court only pronounces on the failure of the defaulting State to comply with European Community Law. The nature of the Court's judgment is to give the State in question the opportunity to take all the necessary measures to avoid future violations, rather than penalise it for the particular breach. Unfortunately, the compliance procedure under Article 169 EC represents a rather soft approach to monitoring the correct application of and adherence to Community Law, when it comes to Member States' infringement of the spirit and the letter of the Treaties. A solemn declaration of the State's inability to comply with its obligations apparently does not create the right level of confidence in the centralised judicial control system of the Community nor does it reflect the degree of commitment of European Institutions in the European Integration process. Failure by a Member State to take into account the outcome of compliance procedures may bring an action under Article 171 EC, where the State comes under an obligation to take all the necessary measures to comply with the judgment. Again here the Court decision has declaratory character and no specific enforcement measures are attached to it.

In public procurement cases, the European Commission has instigated compliance procedures in order to have the Court declare the failure of a Member State to align general legal measures or specific administrative practices with primary and secondary Community Law relevant to public procurement. It follows that after the Court's judgment, and under Article 171, there is a concrete obligation imposed upon the

---

[13] See P. Trepte, *Public Procurement in the EC*, 1993, pp. 197-198

[14] This was the view of Advocate General Lenz in case 247/89, *Commission v. Portugal*, [1991] ECR I 3659.

State in question to repeal any legislation and to abandon any unlawful practices that might contravene the Court's judgment. If this is not done, the State concerned may be brought before the Court in a further Article 169 EC action, based this time on a breach of Article 171.

An issue which is less clear, however, and which deserves careful consideration, is whether there is an obligation imposed on a Member State to set aside any contract which has actually been concluded and which has not yet been finally performed. This assumption would imply that the relevant award procedure would be reopened and conducted in a lawful manner, if the case relates to an individual award procedure, rather than that the challenge of general implementing measures. The main argument in favour of setting aside a public contract is the confidence in the legal system in observing and enforcing Community procurement law. On the other hand, the main argument against is the unfairness which this may cause to the successful tenderer or to the public interest as a result of the delay. It should be mentioned here that under the Compliance Directives, the question of whether national courts or review bodies should be allowed to set aside a contract which has already been awarded or concluded is expressly left to the discretion of Member States.

It is suggested, however, that where the Court pronounces the failure of a Member State to implement public procurement law in an appropriate manner under Article 169 EC, the duty of the Member State under Article 171 EC to comply with the judgment reflects an obligation to set aside a contract which is affected by the judgment. This argument is substantiated by virtue of the *Lottomatica* case, where the Court exercised its powers under Articles 185, 186 EC to *suspend* a concluded contract. The same line of argumentation is found in the opinion of Advocate-General Lenz in case *Commission v Italy*.[15] This case concerned an alleged breach of the procurement rules relating to a contract for the construction of a waste recycling plant. The crucial question which was raised was whether the State in question had complied with the reasoned opinion issued by the Commission. Apparently it had not, thus the Advocate-General suggested that compliance with the reasoned opinion presupposed the setting aside of the contract. Although the substantial case before the Court was compliance procedures under Article 169 EC, the requirements of an action for failure to act under Article 171 EC do not preclude the conclusion that the content of the obligation to comply with a

---

[15] Case 199/85, *Commission v Italy* [1987] ECR 1039.

reasoned opinion is the same as that under Article 171 EC. In both cases the knowledge of the successful tenderer of any illegality or its complicity in a particular breach were not considered to be relevant factors in determining whether the contract should be set aside.

*Interim measures*

The postponement of a particular procurement procedure leading to the award of a public contract or the postponement of the performance of the contract after an award is made can be sought by obtaining an order through interim measures, until the substantial or the procedural disputes have been finally settled. Interim measures refer to the case where aggrieved tenderers challenge the legality of the selection or the award stages of public procurement and wish to delay the process in order to avoid damages. Interim measures are very important legal remedies in public procurement cases. Where contracting authorities refuse to delay the award procedure and no interim relief is available, by the time the matter is finally determined by the Court it is likely that the contract will have been finalised. If this is the case, then in practice it would not be possible to reopen the procedure, and an action for damages would generally be the only remedy available to those who have been prejudiced by the breach.[16] Perhaps even more important than the outcome in a particular case, the availability of interim relief is also likely to act as an important deterrent to a breach of the rules, possibly much more so than any award of damages or any financial penalty. Although interim measures may be more important in this respect in the context of national review procedures than in the context of procedures before the European Court of Justice, since the prospect of an action under Article 169 EC would seem much more remote a possibility than a national review action, the thrust of interim measures at centralised level appear as a more effective *modus* of judicial control in public procurement.

On an application by the European Commission the Court may grant interim measures in relation to procurement cases under a general power which is found in Article 186 EC. The detailed rules governing the

---

[16] This is certainly likely to happen in the context of proceedings before the Court of Justice, where the average length of proceedings for cases decided in 1991 was 24.2 months. See Proceedings of the Court of Justice and of the Court of First Instance of the European Communities No. 23191, 30 January 1992.

application are set out in Articles 83-88 of the Rules of Procedure of the Court of Justice. Applications are made to the President of the Court, who may hear the matter himself or refer it to the Court. However, it is not possible for the Commission to apply for interim relief until Article 169 EC proceedings have actually been instituted before the Court. This is arguably implicit in Article 186 EC, and is stated in Article 83 (2) of the Rules of Procedure which permits an application only if made by a party to a case before the European Court. It was explained earlier that the Commission must follow certain formal requirements before compliance proceedings under Article 169 EC can be instituted, which are concerned notably with providing an opportunity for the state concerned to dispute the allegations made and to redress any breach. There might be some delay between observation of the breach, and commencement of proceedings and the opportunity to obtain interim relief.

It was once thought that this delay might cause considerable problems, to the extent that contracting authorities might rush to conclude a contract before interim relief could be sought to suspend the award procedure, and in this way make it difficult for the Court to affect the outcome of the procedure. It was partly in response to this fear that a proposal was originally made in the Compliance Directive to allow the Commission to suspend the procedure of its own motion when a breach appeared to be *clear* and *manifest*; but the suggestion was eventually dropped. The fear was based on the assumption that the Court might not consider itself to have the power to prevent the performance of a contract once it had actually been concluded. It now seems, however, that this fear was groundless, since the Court does indeed have a power to suspend the implementation and the performance of a concluded contract. This was accepted by the Court in the *Lottmatica* case.[17] This case concerned the award by the Italian government of a concession contract for the establishment and operation of a computerised lottery system. Participation in the competition was limited to firms (or groups of firms) which had the majority of their shares in Italian public ownership, which condition the Commission contended contravened Articles 52 and 59 EC. It was also alleged that there had been a breach of Article 30 EC, and of some of the provisions of the Supplies Directive. Article 169 EC proceedings were instituted, and interim relief sought under Article 186 EC. At the relevant time the award decision by the contracting authorities had already been

---

[17] Case C-272/91R, orders of 31 January 1992 and 12 June 1992

made, and it seems that the contract might actually have been entered into. The application for interim relief thus requested not simply the suspension of the award procedure, but also suspension of i) the legal effects of the Ministerial Decree awarding the contract and also ii) the legal effects of *any contract actually concluded*. This relief was granted by the President in the order of 31 January (a later application to have the order discharged was rejected on 12 June 1992). Thus the Court was prepared to order the parties to suspend the execution of an actual contract. It is suggested that this decision also seems to indicate that a public contract would be required to be set aside if the action is successful at the final hearing concerning the substantive requirements of the alleged breach (the hearing under Article 169 EC). If this appears to be the case, the inevitable delay between the opening of negotiations over an alleged breach (initiation of compliance procedures) and any application to suspend the award procedure (interim measures) would not be of much practical importance, if the power to set aside an illegally awarded public contract, either at the interim relief stage or at the substantive stage is vested in the Court of Justice.

However, interim relief is not given automatically in every case. There are a number of conditions which must be met. First, the applicant must establish a *prima facie* case, which means that the application should not be *"manifestly without foundation"*. It must then be shown that the need for measures is "urgent". A second condition will be satisfied when it can be shown that interim measures are needed to prevent *"serious and irreparable"* damage to the applicant. There is some doubt over whether, in the case of actions brought by the Commission, it is necessary in order to meet this requirement to show some specific and concrete damage to Community interests, or whether it is sufficient that there is a *prima-facie* breach of Community law, the effects of which are irreversible. In public procurement cases it will often be difficult to show any concrete effect on the competitive market structure brought about by a breach of the law which relates merely to an isolated award procedure. However, specific and concrete damage to Community interests can be demonstrated by serious and irreparable injury to tenderers interested in the particular contract. Although third party interests cannot, in principle, be taken into account in applications for interim measures, this is permissible where the European Commission is the applicant, as it represents all affected interests in the Community.[18] This approach, however, raises the question of whether the damage to interested parties is indeed irreparable, given the availability of remedies for the award of damages before national courts. In the three cases concerning interim measures before it, the Court did not make clear the basis for its decision in this respect - whether it relied on damage to individual contractors, or simply took the view that it is appropriate to award interim measures in order to prevent any irreversible breach of Community law.[19]

Another important consideration for the award of interim measures is the *"balance of interests"* of the relevant parties. This condition requires the Court to examine the merits of the case against any injury which would be caused by an award of interim measures and in particular the possible harm to the public interest which would be caused by the delay to the procurement of goods, works or services in question. Balancing the interests of the relevant parties in a public procurement case appears to be a difficult exercise, as the hierarchical classification of the interests in question would determine the outcome of the interim relief proceedings.

On the one hand, the economic interests of a tenderer or a number of tenderers which might be prejudiced by the unlawful behaviour of a contracting authority could be protected by recourse to decentralised judicial control, in the sense that aggrieved contractors may generally obtain damages in actions before national courts or some sort of interim relief, as the case may be. On this side of the balance, the adverse effects arising from the violation of Community Law should be also added. On the other hand, every public procurement project serves the public interest and the possible suspension of its award or the set aside of the particular contract could cause unnecessary delays which may inevitably have an effect upon public interest aspects such as public health, public safety, the protection of the environment.

Balancing on the one hand, individual economic interest damaged by breaches of Community Law against the general public interest potentially harmed by delays in the dispersement of public service has revealed the priorities of European Institutions, particularly the European Court of Justice in the process of the integration of the Community. The

---

[18] See case *61/77R, Commission v Ireland* [1977] ECR 1411.
[19] See case 45/87R, *Commission v Ireland* [1987] ECR 1369; and case 194/88R, *Commission v Italy* [1988] ECR 5647

reluctance of some Member States to recognise the relative importance of individual interests harmed through violations of European Law was reflected in the early case of law of the European Court of Justice. In the *Dundalk* pipeline case[20] which concerned the award of a contract for the construction of a water pipeline, although interim relief was initially granted in order to assess the situation, at a later stage, the Court refused the suspension of the contract on the basis of a possible threat to public health and safety caused by the shortage of water and the potential delay of the project. Along the same lines, in an earlier case[21], the Court was also reluctant to delay the award of a construction project on the grounds of public interest. The case concerned an Ethiopian government contract for the construction of a hydro-electric dam, which was subject to the supervision of the Commission under the terms of the Lome Convention. One of the aggrieved tenderers sought interim measures against the Commission in an attempt to secure the suspension of the procedure. Interim relief was refused by the Court on the basis that delays in the award procedures would inevitably reflect upon the conclusion of the contract and the public interest would be prejudiced as a result. In both cases where interim measures were refused, the Court emphasised the potential damage to the public interest which would be caused by delays in public procurement and counterbalanced any adverse effects of Community Law violations on individual economic interests and the principles stipulated in the Treaties.

However, the balancing exercise between individual economic interests and public interest at large revealed a completely different dimension in two recent cases, where a refusal of interim relief on the grounds of public interest is likely to be the exception rather than the rule. The first case is *Commission v. Italy (La Spezia)*,[22] which concerned a contract for the renovation of a waste disposal plant. The Court awarded interim measures despite acceptance of the fact that damage to both public health and the environment might result from the delay. The differentiating factor which distinguishes this case from *Dundalk* was that the urgency of the renovations was due to the fault of the contracting authorities themselves in not acting earlier on the matter, although it might be that the

---

[20] Case 45/87, *Commission v. Ireland*, [1988] ECR 4929.
[21] 118/83R, *CMC Co-operativa Muratori e Cementisti v Commission* [1983] ECR 2583.
[22] Case 194/88R, *Commission v. Italy* [1988] ECR 4547.

Court would normally refuse interim measures in cases where this is no fault by contracting authorities and there is an immediate and serious threat to public health. However, in this case the Court prioritised the individual economic interests and the violation of Community procurement law over the possible prejudice to the public interest as a result of delays in the procurement process. The Court is not only the guardian of the public interest of the subjects of European Law, but also, and more importantly, it is the guarantor of the success in the European Integration process. *La Spezia* certainly showed the commitment of European Institutions to the principles and rule of the public sector integration and could be seen to pave the way for interim relief where the prejudice to public interest is less serious, even when there is no fault on the part of the contracting authority. As was noted above, relief has now also been given in the case Commission v. Italy (*Lottomatica*)[23] *case*. In this case Italy argued that the measures requested should be refused on the balance of interests because of, first, the loss of revenue which the government would suffer and, second, the fact that delay to the computerised lottery system would delay the governments fight against illegal gambling schemes. However, these arguments were quickly dismissed by the Court on the basis that the interests of the Community should prevail over those of Member States. *Lottomatica* seems to have redefined the concept of public interest in applications for interim measures relating to public procurement projects to an extent that the concept should be narrowly construed.

The spirit of *Dundalk* returned in interim measures litigation in the *Wallonia* case, interestingly after the completion of the internal market. The Commission initiated interim measures against Belgium[24] under Article 185 ECT in order to suspend the award of a contract relating to the purchase of buses for public transport in Wallonia. The Commission had already opened proceedings under Article 169 EC against Belgium for infringement of the Utilities Directive 90/531, particularly the selection of tender offers and their evaluation. The Commission argued that interim measures with suspension of the award procedures were justified by conditions of manifested urgency dictated by the possibility of serious and irreparable damage and to an aggrieved tenderer. The Court in balancing the interest of the parties in question, ruled that the performance and completion of the contract should take precedence over potential economic

---

[23] Case 272/91R, *Commission v. Italy*, order of June 12, 1992.
[24] Case C 87/94R, *Commission v. Belgium*, order of April 22, 1994.

damage, on the grounds of public interest. The contract concerned with the purchase and operation of new buses by a transport authority and delays in its execution could seriously harm the lives of individuals-commuters who rely on the modernisation of the transport fleet. The President of the Court refused the interim measures requested.

**Judicial control at domestic level**

National courts can claim jurisdiction for a Member State's failure to fulfil Treaty obligations, when primary and secondary Community legislation is directly applicable and directly effective. Direct applicability of Community law means that there is no need for implementing measures to be taken by Member States,[25] whereas direct effectiveness implies the reliance of individuals upon Community law before national courts.[26] Individuals may avail themselves of legal remedies before national courts relying on provisions of Community law armed with direct effectiveness. With respect to Public Procurement Directives, actions may be launched by individuals against the State, central government, local government and other contracting authorities, provided that the particular provisions of the Directives upon which individuals rely produce *vertical direct effect*. The verticality of direct effectiveness implies the responsibility of the State vis-à-vis individuals, arising from obligations stipulated in the particular Directive in question and assimilates the direct effect of the Directives with the direct applicability of Regulations. Direct effectivity in its vertical dimension provides for access to justice for individuals against the State in situations where judicial review is otherwise unattainable, due to the fact that Directives are addressed to Member States only, thus requiring legislative incorporation into domestic legal systems in order to confer rights and duties upon individuals. On the other hand, *horizontal direct effectiveness* may allow individuals to rely on Community law in actions against other individuals.[27] Interestingly the Court rejected the argument

---

[25] See H.Winter, *Direct applicability and direct effective of EC law*, [1972] 9 CMLRev 425.

[26] See the Court's judgement in case 26/62 *NV Algemene Transport-en Expeditie Onderneming Van Gend en Loos v. Nederlandse Administrtie der Belastigen*, [1963] ECR 1. Also cases 57/65 *Alfons Luttucke GmbH v. Haupzollampt Saarlouis*, [1966] ECR 205, and 28/67 *Firma Molkerei Zentrale Westfalen/Lippe GmbH v. Haupzollampt Paderborn*, [1968] ECR 143.

[27] The concept of horizontal direct effect has been defined by the Court of Justice in

that Directives may produce horizontal direct effect[28] on the grounds that their binding nature exists only in relation to the Member States to which they are addressed.

The legal nature of Directives precludes them from being directly applicable, as Member States are required to introduce implementing measures, and the direct effectiveness of their provisions depends on three cumulative conditions, as defined by the European Court of Justice[29]: i) the sufficient clearness and precision of their provisions, ii) their unconditionality and finally, iii) the lack of discretion on the part of Member States when implementing them. The concept of direct effectiveness is closely linked with the normative character of Community law. However, access to justice before national *fora* based upon reliance of directly effective Community law requires judicial precedence set by the European Court of Justice. Judicial control at domestic level relies heavily on the utilisation of the Court's rulings as a guide for the direct effectiveness and/or the interpretation of provisions of the relevant Directives through Article 177 EC proceedings. In cases, where there is no clear precedence, clarification and interpretation of provisions of the relevant Directives is needed, thus the national court embarks upon a reference procedure asking the assistance of the Court of Justice.

Public procurement litigation which has been the subject of domestic judicial control is based on the doctrine of vertical direct effectiveness of Procurement Directives' provisions and focuses particularly at the *post* implementation era[30], where the Directives have been digested into the domestic legal orders. Individuals claim the existence of direct effectiveness requesting the court to apply the provision of the Directive in question directly, irrespective of any implementing measure adopted by the State. In almost all cases, even if the case is

---

case 13/61 *Kledingverkoopbedrijf de Geus en Uitdenbogerd v .Robert Bosch GmbH*, [1962] ECR 45.
[28] Case 152/84 *Marshal v. Southampton and South West Hampshire Area Health Authority*, [1986] ECR 723.
[29] See cases 6/64 Costa v. ENEL, [1964] ECR 585; 27/67 *Firma Fink-Frucht GmbH v. Haupzollamt Munchen Landsbergerstrasse*, [1968] ECR 223; 13/68 *SpA Salgoil v. Italian Ministry for Foreign Trade*, [1968] ECR 453; 41/74 *Van Duyn v. Home Office*, [1974] ECR 1337.
[30] Most Directives provide for a period between their enactment and their coming into force in order to give Member States the time necessary to adjust their national systems to Community standards and also gear their legislative machinery with a view to introducing laws implementing the Directives. See R. Lauwaars, *Lawfulness and legal force of Community Decisions*, A.W.Sijthoff, Leiden 1973, pp.28-37.

obviously clear or has already been covered by a Court's previous materially identical reference,[31] national courts feel safer to ask the Court of Justice for a reference regarding the direct effect of the relevant provision. The majority of litigation initiated before national courts and later referred to the European Court of Justice focus on the application of selection and award criteria defined in the public procurement Directives. Until the completion of the internal market, there have been nine cases before national courts relying on Public Procurement Directives' provisions, which have been referred to the Court of Justice for a preliminary ruling under Article 177 EC. In five other cases before national courts,[32] the latter dealt with them without having recourse to 177 proceedings. The post internal market era has witnessed litigation which was mainly concerned with the interpretation and clarification of provisions of European legislation on public procurement.

The decentralised judicial control in public procurement cases has revealed the perpetuation by some Member States of preferential and discriminatory procurement as the major persisting obstacle to public market integration in the European Community. Failure to comply with the provisions of the relevant Directives as well as incorrect and illegal application of them by contracting authorities constitute the most important non-tariff barrier in the European Integration Process. While technical standards and specifications have been harmonised to a considerable degree to eliminate any potential ground for discrimination based on nationality, the movement of goods and services related to public markets is not undistorted, or it appears more distorted than the movement of good and services destined for private markets.

*The award of damages under Community law*

In the absence of specific remedies available to individuals before national courts in order to rectify infringements of Community Law, two questions arise with respect to the award of damages suffered by individuals as a result of the State's violation of European Community Law. The first

---

[31] Case 283/81, *Srl CILFIT v. Minisrty of Health*, [1982] ECR 3415. The theories of *acte eclaire* and *acte claire*.
[32] Case No.10475 *SA.SHV Belgium v. La Maison Ideale et Societe Nationale du Longement*; judgment of 24/6/86 of the Belgian *Conseil d'Etat*; case 194/84 P.Steinhauser v.Ville de Biaritz, before the *Tribunal Administratif du Pau;* judgment of 24/12/87 before the District Court of Maastricht and finally, an arbitration award of the Raad van Arbitrage of 31/3/87.

question is whether an infringement of a directly effective primary or secondary Community provision may be used by individuals before national courts as grounds for an action for damages against the State. The second question approaches the problem from a different perspective; if the infringed provision does not produce direct effect, is, then, the State liable to compensate individuals who have suffered as a result of its infringement or its wrongful implementation of Community law?

In public procurement cases, Article 30 EC Treaty establishing the free movement of goods and Article 52 concerning the right of establishment, both have direct effect.[33] Also, the Court of Justice has recognised that specific (substantive) provisions of the relevant Directives produce direct effect.[34] There are also cases in which national courts have awarded compensation to individuals who suffered damages due to a mere breach of Community law.[35] More intriguing are those cases before national courts where infringement of Community law has already been pronounced directly by the Court of Justice through a proceeding under Article 169 EC. In these cases, national courts are confronted with State legislation, the incompatibility of which with Community law has been unequivocally and authoritatively declared by the Court. Is the existence of incompatible State legislation a ground for an action for damages before national courts?

The whole matter goes further to the question as to whether the Court can require the courts of the Member States to make declarations of invalidity in respect of national legislation found to infringe Community law or to make declaration of awards of damages to the victims. By virtue of Article 171 EC Treaty, the Court said in the *Waterkeyn* case[36] that national courts are bound to draw the *"necessary inferences"* from judgments under Article 169 EC. What is meant by this term is not clear. In the *Waterkeyn* case, the Court did not expressly require national courts to declare invalid a national law or administrative rule that violates a

---

[33] This occured at the end of the transitional period (31/12/69); see also cases 2/74 *Reyners v.Belgian State*, [1974] ECR 631 and 33/74 *Van Bisbergen v.Bestuur van de Bedrijfsvereninging voor de Metaalinijverheid*, [1974] ECR 1299.
[34] See the case law analysis in Chapter 3 below.
[35] Case 213/89, *The Queen v.Minister of Agriculture Fisheries and Food* [1990] ECR I-2433; also case 14/68 *Wilhem v.Bundeskartellampt* [1969] ECR 1 at 27; case 78/70 *Deutche Grammophon GmbH v.Metro-SB Grossmarkte GmbH* [1971] ECR 1 at 31; case 44/84 *Hurd v. Jones* [1986] ECR 29.
[36] Cases 314-316/81&82 *Procureur de la Republique et al. v.Waterkeyn*, [1982] ECR 4337.

directly effective primary or secondary Community legislation. On the other hand, there is a strong suggestion, in the same case, that such measures should be considered as invalid.

The assertion of a national rule that violates Community law as valid, probably justified by public interest, would leave individuals with the possibility of being compensated only through judicial review based on the system of non-fault liability, where a wrongful act is not required. This appears contrary to the principles of good faith and legitimate expectation and far beyond the spirit of the Treaty.[37] On the other hand, if national courts recognise the unlawful nature of an infringement of Community law as such, they should, normally, open the door for compensation on the basis of fault.

With respect to the second question, that of the possibility of relying upon a provision of Community law that does not have direct effect, as ground for an action for damages against the State before national courts, the Court in one of its most important recent judgments[38] answered it in the affirmative. The cases referred to it concerned the non-implementation by Italy of an EC Directive on the protection of employees in the event of the insolvency of their employer and reached the Court through a reference under Article 177 EC. The questions the Court faced, at the request of national courts, were i) whether provisions of the Directive in question were capable of producing direct effect, thus being relied upon by individuals and ii) the above being answered in the negative, whether individuals had a right to receive compensation from the Member State for the negative effects of its failure to implement the Directive. The Court found that the provisions of the Directive were not sufficiently clear, precise and unconditional to produce direct effect, thus answering the first question in the negative. In considering whether an individual has a right to be compensated by a State that has failed to implement a Directive, the Court held that in principle, an individual is entitled to compensation in such circumstances.[39] In order to found State liability, it relied on Article 5 of the EC Treaty, the principle of Community loyalty and solidarity, which provides that Member States are under an obligation to take all the

---

[37] All the above-mentioned principles, legal certainty, legitimate expectation, Community loyalty and Community solidarity are inherent in the fundamental provision of Article 5 EEC.
[38] Judgment on the joint cases 6/90 and 9/90 (*Francovich and Bonifaci v. Italian Republic*)
[39] See also case 213/89 *The Queen v.Minister of Agriculture Fisheries and Food* [1990] ECR I-2433.

necessary measures to ensure that Community law is properly applied. It has been held by the Court[40] that Article 5 EC (especially its negative obligation) is capable of producing direct effect, but only in conjunction with other substantive Treaty provisions or in circumstances in which this obligation is further developed in implementing legislation or through case-law. Based on the above considerations, as well as on the doctrine of the useful effect (*effet utile*) of Community rules and the rights being acknowledged therein, and which would be weakened if individuals were not provided with the possibility of compensation in the case of their rights being affected by a violation of Community law by a Member State, the Court proceeded further and examined the specific conditions that should be met in order for an individual suffering damages to be entitled to compensation by the defaulting State.

Three conditions should be fulfilled: firstly, the result required by the Directive must involve the granting of rights to individuals; secondly, these rights must be identifiable on the basis of the provisions of the Directive and thirdly, there must be a clear causal link between the breach of its obligations by the Member State and the damage suffered by the individual concerned. The above conditions being met, then an individual may benefit from a right to compensation at national level based on Community law which is not directly effective. The amount of compensation payable should be determined by national courts in accordance with relevant domestic legislation. The *Francovich* judgment was a landmark decision with respect to State liability under Community law. Individuals may rely upon Community law which does not produce direct effect before their national courts. The Court of Justice laid down the required conditions for the admissibility of an action for damages before national courts submitted by an individual claiming damages against a Member State which has failed to implement a Directive, hereby injuring a right conferred therein. How strict the national courts will be when confronted with such actions remains to be seen in due course. Obviously, harmonisation of domestic provisions on award of compensation will be required.

What appears to be the most important element is the importance that is given to the interest of individuals. According to the judgment of the

---

[40] Case 14/68 Wilhem v.Bundeskartellampt [1969] ECR 1 at 27; case 78/70 *Deutche Grammophon GmbH v.Metro-SB Grossmarkte GmbH* [1971] ECR 1 at 31; case 44/84 *Hurdv. Jones* [1986] ECR 29.

Court in the *Francovich* case,[41] the individual must be granted rights conferred by the Directive itself. This means that Member States and their competent national authorities must not have any discretion in determining the content and extent of such rights. Here, it should be recalled that lack of discretion in the hands of a Member State is perhaps the most fundamental condition for the direct effect of provisions of Directives. Thus, the relevant provisions of the Directive should be close to producing direct effect, being deprived of it due to their conditionality or to their insufficient clarity and precision.

The whole issue came to test in 1993, when the Divisional Court of the Queen's Bench Division of the Supreme Court of England and Wales made a reference to the European Court of Justice on the interpretation of Directive 90/531 concerning procurement in public utilities. The national case[42] concerned with the definition of the relevant provision of the Directive relating to the application of procurement rules to entities operating in the telecommunication sector. Also request was made for clarification of the possibility of award of damages to individuals in case of wrongful implementation of the relevant provision by Member States. In the preliminary ruling, the European Court of Justice elucidated the Member States' obligation to award damages to individuals who suffered from wrongful implementation of Directives. The Court held that the conditions laid down in the *Brasserie du Pecheur* and *Factortame* cases[43] concerning state liability applied where a Member State had incorrectly implemented a Directive; however, in this case the breach of Community law was not sufficiently serious, as the relevant provision of the Utilities Directive [Article 8(1)] was imprecisely worded and reasonably capable of bearing the interpretation given to it by the UK government in good faith, no guidance had been available from previous case law as to the interpretation of the relevant provision, and the Commission had not raised the matter when the national relevant legislation was adopted. The Court therefore held that no liability could be attributed to the state in question.

As many provisions of Community legislation concerning public procurement (Directives) are deemed to produce direct effect, the question

---

[41] See joint cases 6/90 and 9/90 *Francovich and Bonifaci v. Italian Republic*, [1993] ECR 61.
[42] Case C 392/93, *The Queen and H.M. Treasury, ex parte British Telecommunications PLC*, O.J. 1993, C 287/6.
[43] *Brasserie du Pecheur SA v. Germany, Regina v. Secretary of State for Transport, ex parte Factortame LTD* (C 46 & 48/93), 5 March 1996: [1996] 1 CMLR 889.

of whether an infringement of them can be considered as sufficient ground for an action for damages at national level, combines with the duty of national courts to afford an effective protection mechanism (remedies) of the rights conferred on individuals by directly effective Community law.

## The judicial structure of Member States with reference to public procurement litigation

Access to justice for individuals before domestic *fora* in public procurement cases is of paramount importance as it constitutes the mechanism for judicial control at national level. Existing national legal systems channel public procurement disputes through either public law review proceedings or through civil law review proceedings as a result of their conceptual predisposition of public market transactions. In principle, and to a certain degree in practice, arbitration through the operation of non-judicial *fora* and alternative dispute resolution systems appears in many jurisdictions. Although a detailed investigation of domestic procedural and substantive legal regimes of Member States is beyond the thrust of this work, the following brief analysis intends to expose the main difference between national legal systems when dealing with public procurement disputes. The level and degree of access to justice for interested parties is exposed by reference to the remedies and actions available to them for review procedures, interim measure and finally actions for the award of damages. For the sake of consistency with previous analyses concerning the procurement markets of the Member States, the legal systems of the new members of the European Union (Sweden, Austria and Finland) are not included in the following analysis.

French law regards public procurement contracts as subject to the exclusive jurisdiction of Administrative courts.[44] There are two types of action available: an action for annulment and an action for damages. Both can be lodged at the same time, provided the time limits required have been met. Interim measures may be ordered in cases of urgency. An action for annulment may be brought before the competent administrative court within two months from the issue of the administrative act in question.

---

[44] For a detailed analysis of the French legal order with respect to Public Procurement regulation see the report of C.Brechon-Moulenes in the 14th FIDE Congress *on Application in the Member States of the Directives on Public Procurement*, Madrid 1990.

French courts apply the *theorie de l'act detachable* and separate the act awarding the contract or the act calling for tender or the act that approves the award, or preparatory acts before the award of the contract in question, from the contract itself. Thus, they focus on the administrative part of the public procurement contract. The most common ground on which to base an action for annulment is *exces de pouvoir*, a concept which hardly coincides with misuse of powers found in English law. *Exces de pouvoir* means the grave disregard of the limits by the authority in question, which would have acted in a manner beyond the competence and the powers attributed to it. In addition to the above-mentioned ground, the plaintiff may plead the direct effect of a provision of a Directive. Although the *Conseil d'Etat* has recognised the supremacy of Community law over national law, sometimes it is reluctant to pronounce on the direct effectiveness of Directives, thus following a restrictive interpretation of Article 189 EC. On the merits, the plaintiff may attack the external legality of the administrative act, as well as its internal legality. The former provides for the following grounds: i) incompetence of the awarding authority, ii) irregularities as to its composition and function, iii) any violation of a rule relating to the award of the contract in question (this should be a substantial one capable of nullifying the act). As to the internal legality, four grounds may be invoked against the authority: i) material inaccuracy of the act, ii) non respect of the principle of equality among the candidates, iii) *detournement de pouvoir* (misuse of powers attributed to the authority) and iv) manifestly wrong exercise of its discretion. Under those grounds the plaintiff may achieve the annulment of the detachable act (awarding act, or the act calling for tender etc.), but not the annulment of the contract itself. An action for damages should also be addressed to the Administrative courts. To award compensation, they look for a *faute de service* (a wrongful act of the administration). With respect to public procurement such a *faute* includes: i) the illegal selection of a candidate and ii) the illegal award of a contract. The plaintiff must prove the existence of actual damages, in particular damages resulting from the preparation for the bid, expecting profits had the contract been awarded to him and finally, damages for the bad reputation attaching to his undertakings in a case that the authority illegally rejected its offer and revealed the reasons for that rejection. Needless to say, the causal link between the damage and the *faute* must be proved by the plaintiff.

In Belgium, the incorporation of the provisions of Public

Procurement Directives through *Arretes Royaux* has created a nexus of rights and duties which are enforceable before the *Conseil d'Etat*, in case of an action for annulment, and before tribunals and ordinary courts in case of an action for damages.[45] The Belgian administrative law accepts the theory of detachable acts. Under this doctrine, the courts are allowed to separate the defaulting part of an act, seeking to save the remaining legitimate part(s). (To some extent, this doctrine is also recognised in common law jurisdictions, known as the doctrine of severance). Under *la theorie de l'acte detachable*, the decision of the administration awarding a public procurement contract constitutes an act separable from the contract itself. In fact, only those administrative acts that award contracts fall under the jurisdiction of the *Conseil d'Etat*, which may annul them on the grounds of excess or misuse of powers (*exces ou detournement de pouvoir*), or order their suspension in the form of interim measure, as the case may be. On the other hand, the contract itself falls under the jurisdiction of private law in a case where disputes and grievances concerning damages may arise between the parties. It should be mentioned that in both cases (before the *Conseil d'Etat* and tribunals or ordinary courts) third parties may also avail themselves of the appropriate remedies provided they can show and prove the existence of a legal-legitimate interest. This means that third parties (mainly unsuccessful tenderers) must prove not only a personal link with the dispute in question, but also the legal consequences arising from this personal link. In respect of public law jurisdiction, the *Conseil d'Etat* may annul the decision awarding a public procurement contract either because of substantial irregularities that derogate from the framework of powers attributed to the contracting authority, or because of non-substantial irregularities due to arbitrary exercise of its margin of appreciation. A successful request for annulment of the act awarding the contract will normally open the door for an action for damages under private law, as the *Conseil d'Etat* will pronounce on the illegality of that act. Before the tribunals and ordinary courts the plaintiff should prove, apart from the existence of a legal interest, the wrongful act of the contracting authority (*faut de service*), the actual damage caused by that act and the existence of a causal link between the wrongful act and the damage suffered.

Both public and private law regulate the settlement of public

---

[45] See the report of Yvon Hannequart and Andre Delvaux in 14th FIDE Congress, op.cit.

procurement disputes in Luxembourg. The control of the award of public contracts (the act awarding them) relies on the jurisdiction of the *Conseil d'Etat*, which may annul on grounds of want of authority, infringement of essential procedural requirement, *ultra vires* and misuse of powers, the act or decision awarding a contract or any unilateral administrative act carried out under the award procedure. In principle, the *Conseil d'Etat* may suspend the execution of the contract or order any other appropriate interim measure. Damages resulting from a breach of the rules governing public procurement are under the jurisdiction of ordinary courts. Private law regulates state liability in public procurement as a quasi-tort[46] and action for damages before ordinary courts normally requires the prior annulment of the act awarding the contract by the *Conseil d'Etat*.

Under Greek law, all administrative disputes (disputes where one party is the State, legal or regional authorities and bodies governed by public law) fall under the jurisdiction of administrative tribunals and of the *Conseil d'Etat*. The latter has also unlimited jurisdiction to examine the legality of the act awarding the contracts. Thus, applying *la theorie de l'act detachable* the *Conseil d'Etat* may annul the awarding (administrative) act of a contract, as it considers it an act separable from the contract itself. In such a case, an aggrieved participant in the tender may sue for damages before the administrative courts. He may also sue directly before ordinary (civil) courts[47] seeking compensation and contesting the legality of the award at the same time, but in that case he will not be able to ask for the suspension of the latter. It should be noted that the power to annul the act awarding the contract is exclusively vested in the hands of the *Conseil d'Etat*.[48]

In Spain, review procedures for public procurement contracts are channelled through administrative and judicial routes. Under the former, the *Bureau of Supervision of Projects* is vested with the power to examine technical aspects in the award of the contract in question and to adjudicate of possible disputes arising therein; in addition, the Intervention of the State, another administrative organ, deals with aspects concerning the financial control of the award, the formal legality of the contract and the

---

[46] Article 1382 of the Civil Code.
[47] In both cases the action will be based on Article 105 of the Introductory law to the Civil Code, which lays down State liability (non-fault liability) for illegal actions performed by its organs in pursuit of the exercise of official authority.
[48] For a general introduction to the Hellenic Administrative Law see the report of P. Stathopoulos in the FIDE Congress, op.cit.

decision awarding it. Furthermore, under the adjudication stage within the administrative review procedures, the *Mesa de Contratacio*, (also an administrative organ) is empowered, upon request from one of the parties concerned, to pronounce on the validity of the offers, on the conditions for participation in the tender competition, and on the qualitative criteria for the selection of the tenderer to whom the contract has been awarded. It also has the power to make provisional award of contracts based on the criterion of the best (lowest) price, and it may modify the conditions of the award in case of infringement of the law or in case of an abnormally low or disproportional price with regard to the project. The lengthy administrative review proceedings constitute a requirement of admissibility in order to pursue judicial review at a later stage.[49] Judicial review denotes the involvement of Administrative Tribunals, in the case that the dispute has not been settled through the administrative stage or in case of a claim for damages. Under the former, the Tribunals have competence to declare the act awarding a public contract void, mainly on grounds of want of authority, failure to comply with procedural or substantive requirements, *ultra vires* and misuse of powers. What is interesting is that such a declaration results in rendering the contract itself void. An action for damages must fulfil very strict requirements, as Spanish Courts are very stringent in awarding compensation for damages which can be attributed to the State. Interim measures are available on request of the applicant in accordance with a separate procedure before the same forum.

In Portugal, administrative courts have jurisdiction on matters concerning the validity, interpretation and annulment of the act which awards a public procurement contract. Portuguese law follows to a large extent the notion of *administrative act* which emanates form the French *droit administratif*. The relative importance of the awarding act is reflected also in the fact that it constitutes the most crucial stage in the public procurement process. The plaintiff may submit before administrative courts an application for annulment of the act awarding the contract, which is subject to an appeal before the same courts. It is also possible to lodge an action for damages before administrative courts, after the administrative law review process has been exhausted and the act awarding the relevant public contract has been found unlawful. Damages are in most cases nominal, to the extent that the courts award compensation only with respect to the exact amount the plaintiff has

---

[49] The latter must be lodged within two months of dismissal of the former.

suffered as a result of the unlawful behaviour of the contracting authority. The substantive disputes arising out of a public contract between the successful tenderer and the contracting authority, are the subject of the civil law jurisdiction. Interim relief in relation to the award of public contracts is in theory available to affected parties, although the administrative courts are often reluctant to award measures which have a suspensive effect upon the awarding act. The reason for such reluctance is probably attributed to the relatively slow process of judicial review of the administrative act which awards a public contract and the need to avoid the prejudice of the public interest.

In the Italian legal system, apart from administrative redress available to · aggrieved contractors, where the hierarchical superior authority is entitled to review the act awarding a public contract, reviewing both its legality and its substance, there are legal remedies available to them before administrative and ordinary courts. The Italian system is interesting, as in cases where an injury caused by an administrative act relates to a right of the contractor or a third party, ordinary courts have jurisdiction; where, on the other hand, the dispute concerns the legality of the administrative act awarding the contract, then ordinary courts take over. Administrative courts have not only the power to suspend the award of the contract, by means of interim measure, but also to set aside it or any other administrative act performed in the course of the awarding procedure. Action for damages brought by the contractor or a third party against the contracting authority before ordinary courts, is admissible only when a "subjective" right is in breach. State responsibility embraces contractual and pre-contractual liability, but it is only for the successful tenderer who has been awarded the contract to seek remuneration. Unsuccessful tenderers are not entitled to pursue an action for damages as they have only a "lawful interest" and not a "subjective right". Actions for damages before ordinary courts are allowed to proceed on condition of a previous delivery of judgment concerning the annulment of the act awarding the contract by an administrative court.

Under Danish law, there is no distinction between administrative and civil disputes in a public procurement contract. There are no administrative courts. The decision awarding a public procurement contract may be reviewed by a higher administrative authority. This sort of review is not a judicial one, but rather seeks the adjudication and conciliation of the dispute. The offended party or third parties (unsuccessful tenderers) may resort to ordinary courts seeking compensation from damages caused by a wrongful act of the authority awarding contracts. There is no statutory rules governed state liability but well established judicial precedence regulates the issue. The plaintiff has the burden of proof as regards the wrongful act of the administration, the actual damage suffered and the causal link between the wrongful act and the damage. Compensation covers any economic loss caused by the fault of the contracting authorities, but the plaintiff's contribution (negligence) to that loss may reduce or exempt the State from an obligation to compensate.

To ensure the application of Public Procurement Directives both at *"Bund"* and at *"Länder"* levels, Germany has enacted administrative instructions[50] that are legally binding by means of and through pertinent budgetary laws. Under the principle of legality of administration,[51] the State, and local authorities are entitled to act on their own initiative in case that a violation of provisions of public Procurement Directives occurs. Nationals and non-nationals (from other EC Member States or non-EC Member States) enjoy the same treatment, as a consequence of the principle of equal treatment laid down in the German Basic Law. Disputes concerning the award of public contracts fall under the jurisdiction of administrative control. The power of supervision over acts and decisions of the contracting authorities is based on similar principles at the "Bund" and "Länder" levels.[52] The organs finally responsible for the administration, the State and the Länder, exert their supervision over inferior authorities controlling the legality of acts awarding public contracts. In particular, they have powers to suspend the act awarding a public contract, to order new tendering procedures, to rescind the act that invites tenders for a public contract, even to invite tenders on their own initiative in cases where the inferior (contracting) authority does not comply with the instructions given within a certain time. What is interesting is the fact that once the contract has been awarded, administrative control is no longer applicable. The award is considered to be the acceptance of the contractor's or the supplier's offer and according to principles of German Law, the contractor must not be burdened with the uncertainty of a

---

[50] *"Verdingungsordnung fur Leistungen- ausgenommen Bauleistungen"* for public works and *"Verdingungsordnung fur Bauleistungen"* for public supplies contracts.
[51] Article 20, para.3 of the German Basic Law.
[52] The constitutionally established right of organization, Article 65, sentence 2 of the German Basic Law.

potential cancellation of the contract due to the violation of rules by the contracting authority. Thus, aggrieved contractors may only apply before ordinary courts against public authorities seeking damages. Their claim requires a fault on the part of the contracting authority in concluding the contract or in its preparation- *culpa in contrahendo*.[53] The claim is based on the relationship of confidence, which resembles that of contract, arising between the contracting authority and the contractor by virtue of the invitation to tender. The amount of damages depends on the actual damage which the contractor can prove. The damage may be limited to the cost of taking part in the tendering process. This might be the case when the supervisory administrative authority cancels an illegitimate invitation for tender. On the other hand, if the contractor can prove that the contracting authority has illegally discriminated against him in awarding the contract to another one, then he is entitled to damages to the amount of his lost profits, on condition that he can substantiate that he would have been awarded the contract, had the contracting authority not discriminated. If the contracting authority holds a monopoly or a dominant position, the applicant which has been denied the award of the contract may base his claims for damages against the former also on the provisions of the "Statute against Distortions of Trade" or on the "Statute against Unfair Competition". He may suspend the award process by requesting the court for an injunction.

In the Netherlands, the judicial review of the award of public contracts is subject to the control of civil courts and also to arbitration. Supplies and services contracts are under the jurisdiction of ordinary courts, whereas public works contract are channelled through a special institution (*Raad van Arbitrage*).[54] The appropriate forum for judicial control of public procurement is determined by virtue of the laws implementing the relevant Directives. In practice, the legal *forum* which handles the majority of public procurement disputes is the *Raad van Arbitrage*, as the laws implementing the Directives contain arbitral clauses under which the jurisdiction of civil courts is secondary. Both the civil courts and the *Raad van Arbitrage* are competent in awarding damages to aggrieved tenderers, on condition that the applicant can prove that he would have won the contract.

---

[53] Paragraph 242 of the Civil Codebook.
[54] See the report of P.Glazener, E.H.Pijnacker Hordijk and E.M.A van der Riet in the FIDE Congress, op.cit.

The situation in the United Kingdom is that an aggrieved contractor could initiate judicial review proceedings against a contracting authority under public law or seek redress through private actions, in a case where there has been a breach of a statutory duty. In addition to the remedies which have been created under the Statutory Instruments implementing the Directives specifically for enforcing the procurement rules,[55] an aggrieved contractor may also make use of the more general remedies which may be used in order to ensure that public bodies act lawfully.[56] The right of damages under judicial review is not an independent remedy. What is peculiar in comparison with continental legal systems, is that the High Court or the Court of Appeal must be satisfied that the claim for damages before it fulfils all the conditions in order to be successful under private law; that means the breach of a statutory duty. The award of damages is in the discretion of the court and when the applicant (aggrieved contractor) claims damages alternatively (in a case where the application for annulment of the act awarding the contract is dismissed), the court may order the continuation of proceedings as if they had begun by writ. Action for damages in tort represents the private way of judicial redress of public procurement cases in the United Kingdom. Such actions can be based on breach of statutory duty or negligence. The plaintiff is entitled to compensation for the loss he suffered, on condition that he can prove that

---

[55] Remedies which are required to be available under the Compliance Directive in the United Kingdom include: i) provision for the court to "set aside" a decision or action which is in breach of the Regulations. The effect of an order of set aside will be that the decision or action has no legal effect and cannot be acted upon. For example, if the government makes an award decision in breach of the Regulations, and that award decision is set aside, the government may not go ahead and conclude a contract with the selected firm , but must take the award decision again in a lawful manner. ii) provision that the court may order the contracting authority to amend any document. Thus if a contract document contains unlawful specifications, for example, the court may order the authority to amend them. This is a useful power: it allows a firm effectively to ensure documents are amended without the need to strike down the whole call for tenders. iii) finally, provision that a remedy in damages must be available to disappointed contractors who suffer loss.

[56] Among the main remedies available in an action for judicial review are *certiorari*, *prohibition* and *mandamus*. The first will annul with retrospective effect, an order or decision of a person or a body of persons having legal authority to determine questions affecting the rights of subjects; the second has a prospective effect, prohibiting an administrative authority from acting either at all or in the way it proposes; the latter is an order requiring a public body to do something on condition that the applicant has first called on it unsuccessfully to do its duty.

the tort has caused his loss.

In Ireland, the appropriate *forum* for the review of public procurement cases is the High Court, which has general jurisdiction over administrative, civil or criminal cases. The Irish legal system does not provide for an administrative law *forum*, however, a number of *ad hoc* administrative tribunals have been established and are under the supervision of the High Court. Judicial remedies available to aggrieved contractors in public procurement cases before the High Court include the general public law remedies in the form of *certiorari, prohibition* and *mandamus*. Through these remedies the Court has the power to quash unlawful administrative decisions (practically the same results with setting aside a decision under the Compliance Directive), to prevent an unlawful decision being made, and to order a decision to be taken in a lawful manner. The general remedies of *declaration*, where the Court simply declares the legal position in the case before it, and *injunction* are also available. The challenge of an unlawful administrative act through the above public law remedies requires prior application for judicial review. However, declarations and injunctions are also available in plenary proceedings. Damages may be sought by the applicant on grounds of deliberate breach of public law rules by virtue of the tort of misfeasance in public office.[57]

**A critique of the national judicial structures in relation to public procurement cases**

The possibility for setting aside the act awarding the contract is provided in most Member States. In some jurisdictions, administrative courts have power to set aside unlawful administrative acts and deal with claims concerning the act awarding the contract. With respect to the contract itself, they follow the theory of detachable acts, whereby the validity of administrative acts leading to the conclusion of a public contract may be viewed in isolation from the contract itself and challenged on grounds of their unlawfulness, without the validity of the contract necessarily being affected. However, in other jurisdictions the validity of the contract may be automatically affected if the award decision is set aside.

The theory of detachable act, which in operation in French-

---

[57] See the report of Mary Robinson in the FIDE Congress, op.cit.

influenced continental jurisdictions presents considerable weaknesses when applied to public procurement cases. Under that theory, the public procurement process is subject to both public and private law jurisdiction. The above jurisdictional separation lies in the fact that the decision of a contracting authority under which a particular public contract is awarded is considered an administrative act which is subject to the jurisdiction of public law and as such is separated from the contract itself, which falls under civil law jurisdiction. However, it is undisputed that the administrative act awarding the contract constitutes an integral part of the whole procurement process and forms the legal justification for the conclusion of the contract between the contracting authority and the successful tenderer. By the separation, both jurisdictional and actual, of the act of awarding the contract and the contract itself, there is the possibility that the whole procurement process could be thrown to legal uncertainty in the event that the legality of the awarding act is contested. If the contract itself has not yet been concluded, its suspension represents the most logical solution and, in principle, falls under the same jurisdiction with the action to annul the awarding decision. If the act is annulled, then the contract remains without legal basis. In case that the contract itself has not yet been concluded, this does not represent a major problem. The administrative act will be re-issued by the contracting authority without defaults this time. However, a question remains as to whether the contracting authority has liability to compensate the previously successful contractor in the award stage of the procurement process, when the re-issued act awards the contract to a different tenderer. If for example, the act awarding the contract is declared illegal and the contracting authority is ordered to re-open the tendering procedures for its award, the contracting authority should compensate the existing contractor for losses of profits, should the contract be finally awarded to another tenderer. The issue remains unclear, although the European Court of Justice in proceedings concerning interim measures before it did not consider the successful contractor's knowledge of the illegality of the awarding act and was not considered to be a relevant factor in determining whether the contract should be set aside.[58]

Problems arise when the parties have concluded the agreement (by signing the relevant contract) or even when the contract is in its

---

[58] See case 199/85, *Commission v Italy* [1987] ECR 1039. Also, case 272/91R, *Commission v. Italy*, order of June 12, 1992.

performance stage. An action to annul the administrative act which awarded the contract would probably shake the entire legal foundation of the latter. Two elements deserve attention here: firstly, if the administrative act is annulled, the legal basis of the concluded contract or the contract under performance disappears. This means that the contract, as a private law covenant, cannot be executed; therefore it should be suspended. Even in the event of the re-issued act awarding the contract to the same contractor, this new administrative act cannot *stricto sensu* be the legal foundation of the contract already awarded by the first one. The second element refers to the prejudice or the harm of the public interest as a result of the amount of legal uncertainty which covers the period during which the case concerning the legality of the awarding act is pending, as well as the period during which the performance of the contract is suspended.

On the other hand, the *doctrine of severance* utilised in common law jurisdictions may have more balanced results. In contrast with the theory of detachable acts, the doctrine of severance allows the courts, in principle, to separate the defaulting parts of a contract, thus saving the legitimate ones. If the contract is viable only with the latter then it could be legally executed, otherwise it should be declared null and void. The viability, in legal terms, of a public procurement contract after severance of any unlawful or illegal parts of the procurement process may insert an element of *qualitative evaluation* of the stages under which public contracts are awarded. Such evaluation, perhaps, would classify in hierarchical order the relative importance of violation of procurement law. For example, a breach over the time limits for the receipt of tenders under open procedures could not in itself be a sufficient reason to nullify the award of a public contract. However, violations of rules concerning the qualification of tenderers or the selection and award criteria cannot be severed by other legitimate parts of a public contract, as they considerably affect its substantive validity. The doctrine of severance cannot be applied in legal systems where public law and private law jurisdiction co-exist. In such a case the doctrine could hardly give an answer.

## The Compliance Directives

The public procurement sector is by nature decentralised and requires a decentralised control. In some Member States there are already remedies for breach of public procurement laws, and it is the responsibility of all the Member States to provide legal remedies to the parties concerned capable of enforcing the provisions of the public procurement Directives. The aim of the European Institutions should be to provide for the possibility of having uniform remedies in all Member States, of harmonising procedures or at least of co-ordinating national laws and administrative provisions relating to the application of procedures for reviewing public procurement contracts.[59] Uniformity of application, as far as legal remedies are concerned, is a desirable situation but it is an ideal which is difficult to achieve, since there are different ways, already established, for solving public procurement disputes. It is almost impossible to have one law applicable in all Member States due to separate legal traditions and procedures. Any attempt to abolish existing national systems would be extremely difficult, useless and a waste of time. Similarly, harmonisation of national procedures concerning the availability of legal remedies for breach of public procurement contracts is neither possible nor necessary. In order to achieve harmonisation, that is approximation of national legal orders, one should start from a common point; in other words, the national legal orders to be harmonised should be homogeneous.

In the case of public procurement, the existing national remedies are addressed to civil or administrative courts or administrative bodies or arbitrators. Furthermore, the national law applicable in each Member State varies from civil to public administrative law. Finally, the cost of initiating proceedings differs from Member State to Member State, depending on the cost of living or the judicial cost in each country. Under those conditions, it is hardly possible to achieve harmonisation. What remains is to co-ordinate these national legal remedies with a view to ensuring a procedure and a sanction for the application of the underlying public procurement Directives.

In an attempt to give an answer to these questions, the Council enacted a Directive on the harmonisation of laws, regulations and administrative provisions relating to the application of review procedures to the award of public works and public supply contracts (Directive 89/665 EC).[60] In addition, Directive 92/13[61] extends the remedies and review procedures covered by Directive 89/665 to the water, energy,

---

[59] This is the aim of Article 100 EC and to a certain point of Article 100A EC.
[60] O.J.1989 L 395.
[61] O.J.1992 L 76/7.

transport and telecommunication sectors. According to the Compliance Directives, Member States should be left to implement procedures consistent with their own judicial practices to achieve effective and rapid review rules. This approach is consistent with the provisions in Article 189 EC, that a directive shall be binding as to the result to be achieved, leaving the form and the methods to the discretion of the Member States. In some Member States, highly developed systems of monitoring public procurement procedures already exist. Both Directives aim at co-ordinating existing procedures and procedures to be introduced with a view to a uniform application of the underlying Directives concerning public supplies, public works, and utilities. It seems that neither Directive produces direct effect.

According to Article 1 of Directive 89/665 and Article 1 of Directive 93/13, Member States shall ensure effective and rapid review of decisions taken by contracting authorities which infringe public procurement provisions. Undertakings seeking relief from damages in the context of a procedure for the award of a contract, should not be treated differently under national rules implementing European public procurement laws and under other national rules. This means that the measures to be taken concerning the review procedures should be similar to national review proceedings, without any discriminatory character.

Any person having or having had an interest in obtaining a particular public supply or public works contract and who has been or risks being harmed by an alleged infringement of public procurement provision shall be entitled to seek review before national courts. This is laid down in the third paragraph of Article 1 of Directive 89/665 and Article 3 of Directive 92/13 and in both cases is followed by a stand-still provision concerning the prior notification by the person seeking review to the contracting authority of the alleged infringement and of his intention to seek review. However, with respect to admissibility aspects, there is no qualitative or quantitative definition of the interest of a person in obtaining a public contract. As to the element of potential harm by an infringement of public procurement provisions, it should be cumulative with the first element, that of interest. The prior notification should intend to exhaust any possibility of amicable settlement before the parties have recourse to national courts.

However, by virtue of Article 2 of Directive 89/665 and Article 2 of Directive 92/13, the measures concerning the review procedures shall include interim measures, by way of interlocutory procedures, with the aim of correcting the alleged infringement or preventing further damages. Provision shall be made for measures to suspend or to ensure the suspension of the procedure for the award of a public contract or the implementation of any decision taken by the contracting authority. In most of the Member States, suspension would be effected by an injunction. National courts have the power to grant an injunction to restrain unlawful acts. It should be borne in mind that suspension of the whole procedure or of the implementation of any decision will create some problems.

Firstly, review procedures should not have an automatic suspensive character. Indeed, Article 2(3) in both Directives reads so. Secondly, in practical terms, a disappointed tender would ask the court to order the procuring authority to reconsider its bid and not to enter into a contract in the meantime. Many times, this will cause disproportionate hardship. Therefore, the national courts or administrative bodies should take into account the probable consequences to all interests likely to be harmed as well as the public interest. In fact, Article 2(4) in both instruments introduces a proportionality principle, reading that where any grant of a review measure causes negative consequences, such consequences shall not exceed the benefits. For the sake of history, it is worth mentioning that Article 3 of the draft Directive 89/665[62] gave the Commission the right to suspend a contract award procedure for a period of up to three months. Since this would have led to legal uncertainty, as at the same time national courts have suspensive powers, it has been deleted from the final text.

In addition to interim measures correcting the alleged infringement or suspending the award procedure, Article 2(1)(b) provides for measures to set aside unlawfully taken decisions by the contracting authority, including the removal of discriminatory technical, economic or financial specifications in the invitation to tender, the contract document or any other document relating to the award procedure. The present texts of the Directives are not sufficiently clear in respect to the execution of the contract itself. It could be argued that contracts might be set aside, even after having been awarded. The effect of annulling contracts would be to render uncertain for several years the basis for proceeding with important public works and could cause damages extending well beyond the authority under challenge. The Commission has made clear its intention that contracts once awarded should not be at the risk of being overturned. However, the fact of setting aside a decision leaving the contract

---

[62] COM(88) 733 fin.

unaffected causes serious doubts as to the validity of the contract. In some continental legal orders, the theory of detachable acts has been developed and permits the validity of administrative acts leading to the making of a contract to be considered distinct from the contract itself and for them to be open to challenge on grounds of their illegality, without affecting the validity of the contract. In these legal orders, the attack of the unlawful decision is a pre-requisite to an action for damages. In other jurisdictions, the setting aside of the decision without touching the contract will create problems, as the legal basis of the contract has been removed.

It is the discretion of the national court to decide whether it should set aside the decision to enter into a contract or simply to declare illegalities in the award procedure and therefore grant damages. Directive 92/13 recognises explicitly the theory of detachable acts and provides in Article 2(d), that prior to an award of damages, the contested decision must first be set aside or declared illegal. The power to order the removal of discriminatory specifications in the contract documents is a different matter. Such an order should not be made in a way which would hinder the procurement process and it should ensure that the procedure is in accordance with the Community principle of non-discrimination.

*The Award of Damages under the Compliance Directives*

Article 2(1)(c) in both Directives provides for award of damages to persons harmed by an infringement of public procurement law. The purpose behind this provision is to mobilise the interested contractors in order to supervise the application of public procurement Directives. In addition, damages as financial consequences control in a very immediate way contract officers, their superiors and their financial control authorities.

As already mentioned above, European law does not require the provision of a remedy for the award of damages when there is a breach of a directly effective rule. The reasons for that absence vary: in some cases the national court has held that the authority in breach of Community Law did not owe any obligation directly to the plaintiff or that the plaintiff's losses were the results of foreseeable economic risk; in others, the award of damages has been seen as an unacceptable fetter on the freedom of authorities to enact legislative measures or administrative rules in good faith, pursuant to their general duty to safeguard public interest, such as human health. Damages may be available as a consequence of provisions of national law which make a national authority liable to compensate for breach of its obligations. Procuring authorities are subject to a duty to observe European rules and are liable for damages in breach of those rules. In the context of the Compliance Directives, a question arises as to whether an aspiring contractor seeking damages should prove that he would have been accepted as a tender or he would have won the contract, if not for the infringement.

Under the restrictive procedures, a limited number of contractors or suppliers are invited to tender pursuant to Article 22 of the public works Directive or Article 19 of the public supplies Directive. Where a contractor or a supplier has applied as a candidate, but he has not been invited to tender and the contracting authority has infringed the Directive, the assessment of loss would be difficult since tender costs have not been incurred and the contractor or supplier might not, in any case, have been awarded the contract.

In the case that he has submitted a tender, it may be easier to show that he has suffered a quantifiable loss in respect of which he should be indemnified, at least so far as the expenses of tendering are concerned. Any additional loss would be more difficult to prove. Under the Utilities Compliance Directive, the undertaking claiming damages must prove the infringement of public procurement law and the effect of this infringement on his chance of being awarded the contract. He does not have to prove that, in the absence of the infringement he would have been awarded it.[63]

Where the complaint is that the procuring authority has failed to accept the most economically advantageous tender, as required by the Procurement Directives, there is probably no alternative; the procuring authority will be required to advise unsuccessful tenders of the reason for their failure. Then, it is for the unsuccessful tenders to assess whether these reasons are so defective as to justify legal proceedings for compensation. It should be recalled that the criteria laid down in the Procurement Directives are wide-ranging, leaving a great deal of discretion to the contracting authority. The burden of proof will be on the unsuccessful tender to persuade the court that his tender was more economically advantageous than that of the winning tender. On the other hand, where the potential tender complains of unlawful exclusion from the tendering process, he should be entitled, on proof, to recovery of costs actually incurred, which will usually not be substantial. Under the draft

---

[63] Recital 11 of Directive 92/13.

Compliance Directive on Utilities sectors, the amount of damages refunded should be deemed to be one per cent of the value of the contract, in a case where a contractor is preparing a bid or participating in an award procedure, unless he proves that his costs were greater. This provision has been deleted from the final text of Directive 92/13. It should be noted that the draft Directive 89/665 mentioned three grounds of action for damages: the cost of unnecessary studies, forgone profits and lost opportunities. The final text of the Directive, interestingly, remains silent and refers only to award of damages generally [Article 2(1)(c)]. There have been fears that the inclusion of forgone profits and lost opportunities could have lead to speculative and wasteful litigation.

There are two observations relating to damages litigation in public procurement. First, as it is generally admitted, undertakings will be hesitant to bring a contracting authority before a court, since they want to maintain good relations in the future. Litigation between a supplier and a contracting authority often results in an irrevocable break of their relation. Secondly, if damages are too greatly and too readily awarded, contracting authorities would find themselves proceeding so extremely carefully as to seriously impede any public work or supplies contract. It remains to be seen how, in practice, national courts will deal with the matter. Since there is a number of different jurisdictions throughout the Community, it also follows that there would be great differences in the amounts awarded as compensation by national courts. This could prevent some undertakings from taking any proceedings in Member States that provide for low sanctions. In this case, the Member State is obliged to introduce more effective procedures, similar though not necessarily identical to those of the rest of the Member States of the Community. The Commission should launch an action under Article 169 EC to have the Court declare that a Member State has not conformed with the Compliance Directive.

The Directives provide that Member States should establish judicial or administrative bodies responsible for their enforcement. Member States, therefore, have a choice as to the forum and procedures provided for hearing disputes or otherwise achieving the required result. In addition, they require that all decisions taken by bodies responsible for review procedures shall be effectively enforced.

As explained above, since contracting authorities are involved in a public contract, in many continental jurisdictions public law will be applied and the dispute is to be addressed before administrative courts. In other cases, civil law applies in public procurement litigation, whereas in the Netherlands, for example, there is a remarkably swift arbitration system for construction contracts. Consequently, the question of enforcement of the decisions is relevant to the choice of the forum. Normally, national courts have the power, the prerogative and the means to enforce their decisions. An administrative body, without judicial powers to order discovery or injunctions, could not ensure effective enforcement of its decisions. In case of arbitration, the winning party, in order to have the arbitration award enforced, has to go before national courts and exhaust the relevant proceedings. Moreover, there are some doubts as to the consistency of tribunals' decisions. National courts are skilled at construing contracts and statutory provisions, knowledgeable about the principles of damages and staffed by judges. On the other hand, an administrative body or a tribunal, normally staffed by lawyers and laymen experienced in public procurement, is a swift, flexible and rapid institution with simple proceedings to resolve disputes, since it will deal exclusively with this matter.

Where the Compliance Directive in the Utilities sectors[64] is really novel is in Chapter 2. Member States are required to give the contracting entities the possibility of having their purchasing procedures and practices *attested* by persons authorised by law to exercise this function. Indeed, this attestation mechanism, may investigate in advance possible irregularities identified in the award of a public contract and allow the contracting authorities to correct them. The latter may include the attestation statement in the notice inviting tenders published in the Official Journal. The system appears flexible and cost-efficient and may prevent wasteful litigation. Quite promisingly, the attestation procedure under Directive 92/13 will be the essential requirement for the development of European standards of attestation.[65]

*The Role of the European Commission under the Compliance Directives*

As mentioned above, under the draft Directive 89/665, the Commission had extensive powers, namely to intervene in an administrative or judicial procedure and to suspend unilaterally the procedure for award of a public procurement contract. Those powers were indeed far beyond the provision

---

[64] Directive 92/13, O.J. 1992, L 76/7.
[65] See Article 7 of EEC Directive 92/13.

of Article 100A EC Treaty and could only be justified under Article 235 EC. The Commission's intervention was a novel provision since it has no power to be a party or to intervene in a trial before national courts. The *vires* of this provision was questioned, since the draft Directive was unclear at that particular point; it did not specify whether the Commission would have had a certain right to intervene or whether its intervention was subject to invitation or the permission of the court. In the latter case, it would have been considered as an *amicus curiae*, advising the court upon the right interpretation of European Community law. On the other hand, it could be argued that the Commission's intervention would have been desirable, since it can only be heard in a case of interim measures before the Court of Justice or under the proceedings of Article 169 EC. Interim measures may be taken by the Court only if the case in question is pending before it, and an Article 169 EC action is a heavy, cumbersome and time-consuming procedure, as far as public procurement cases are concerned.

The Commission's suspension power could lead to legal uncertainty and undermine the independence of the courts. Control by both court and the Commission simultaneously is not desirable. In the final text of Directive 89/665, all these powers have been deleted and the Commission has been left with the right to invoke the procedure of Article 3 by way of notification of an infringement of Community law provisions to a Member State requiring its correction. The same regime is provided for in Directive 92/13 (Article 8). Interestingly, the Commission's action is limited. It can only notify a clear and manifest infringement of Community law provisions in the field of public procurement, before a contract has been concluded. The former requirement introduces a kind of qualitative test. Clear and manifest infringement probably means an outspoken breach of a relevant provision. Unclear and ambiguous situations will fall outside the scope of the notification procedure. The latter requirement serves the principle of legal certainty, since after the contract has been concluded, it is extremely costly and undesirable to start investigating it, probably with a view to suspending it.

After 21 days in the case of Directive 89/665 and 30 days in the case of Directive 92/13 from the Commission's notification to a Member State, the latter is obliged to communicate to the former: i) its confirmation that an infringement has been corrected or ii) a justification as to why no correction has been made or iii) a notice that a suspension of the award procedure has been ordered. When the suspension is lifted, the Member

State is obliged to inform the Commission. It is apparent that the Commission's role has been limited on the insistence of Member States and from a power to intervene or to suspend award procedures, it has been left with the mere possibility of notification.

There have been two cases[66] so far where the Commission utilised the procedure provided in Article 3 of Directive 89/665. The Court had the opportunity to declare that the special procedure of Article 3 is a preliminary measure which can neither derogate from nor replace the powers of the Commission to initiate proceedings under Article 169 EC. In both cases, the communication of the Commission's position under Article 3 of Directive 89/665 served as the reasoned opinion for the subsequent compliance proceedings under Article 169 EC.

Where the Commission's role is really novel is under Directive 92/13, where provision has been made for a conciliation procedure, apart from the attempt to achieve an amicable settlement laid down in Article 1(3), as an endeavour to avoid any litigation between the parties. The conciliation procedure shall be distinguished from the judicial/administrative procedures at national level. Interestingly, there is no provision concerning the relationship between the two proceedings, and in a case that the same person were to initiate conciliation and judicial review proceedings under the Directive simultaneously, the relation between them is unclear. Article 11(2)(a) of the Directive stipulates that conciliation proceedings shall be without prejudice to proceedings under Articles 169 or 170 EC and the rights of the parties or any other person under national laws (Article 11(2)(b). Any person having an interest and feeling that a breach of relevant public procurement law rules occurs, may notify the Commission or the competent authorities of a Member State. The possibility of the interested person choosing either the Commission or a Member State's authorities creates some uncertainty, since it is admitted that the whole public procurement problem is decentralised. The Commission or the national authorities may refer the case to the Advisory Committee for Public Contracts[67] or the Advisory Committee on Telecommunications.[68] These Committees will set up working groups with

---

[66] Case C 359/93, *Commission v. The Netherlands*, judgment of January 24, 1995; case 79/94, *Commission v. Greece*, judgment of May 4, 1995.

[67] This Committee has been set up by EC Council Decision 71/306 (O.J.1971 L 185) as amended by EC Council Decision 77/63 (O.J.1977 L 152).

[68] See Article 31 of EEC Dir 90/531.

a view to reaching an agreement between the parties.

The degree of compliance with public procurement Directives is in close relation to the degree of enforcement of their provisions at national level. Enforcement concerns legal remedies available to individuals before national courts, in particular actions for damages. Judicial review concerning the administrative part of a public procurement contract, in almost all Member States[69] is subject to public law. The award of damages to an aggrieved contractor reflects the approach of each national legal system vis-à-vis state liability.

## Compliance with and enforcement of the rules under the WTO Government Procurement Agreement

The extra-territoriality of the legal regime regulating the public procurement of the Member States of the Community has been achieved by virtue of the special inter-governmental agreements concluded between the European Community and member / signatories to the GATT Agreement. It was initially the GATT Agreement on Government Procurement (AGP), which was concluded during the Tokyo Round of negotiations that provided third-country contractors access to European public markets. The AGP was amended by virtue of the WTO Government Procurement Agreement (GPA) during the Uruguay Round. In principle, access to the public sector markets of the Member States has been guaranteed, as far as the framework of provisions in relation to procedural and substantive stages of public procurement is concerned. However, even the most comprehensive set of rules would be ineffective, if its enforcement appeared not sufficient. Access to justice for third-country providers under the GATT / WTO agreements is thus equally important with the principles of access to the public markets of the Member States of the Community.

Both the WTO Government Procurement Agreement and its predecessor (the GATT AGP) are considered inter-governmental instruments which are addressed to States and do not intend to confer rights and duties upon individuals as such. Irrespective of the clearness and precision, the unconditionality of their provision and the lack of

---

[69] The notable exception is Denmark, where there is no distiction between administrative and civil disputes in a public contract.

discretion reserved to States for their implementation, international agreements are not deemed to produce direct effect,[70] thus depriving individuals from taking advantage of directly effective provisions in litigation before national courts. The Decision of the European Council which incorporates the WTO GPA into Community law specifically stipulates that the provisions under the GPA do not have direct effect. However, there is apparently a contradiction between the difficulties arising from applying the theory of direct effectiveness to the GPA provisions and the spirit and wording of the agreement. Express provision of remedies for aggrieved providers is made under Article XX of the GPA, where the remedies provided should be as favourable as those conferred upon Community contractors. Also, Article III of the GPA stipulates that signatories to the agreement should not be treated in a less favourable manner than national providers or providers from other parties. How in practice these provisions concerning access to justice at national level for third-party providers will operate remains to be seen.[71]

As with its predecessor, the WTO Government Procurement Agreement has created an inter-governmental mechanism for settling disputes arising from its application. The mechanism is referred to as the *Understanding on Rules and Procedures Governing the Settlement of Disputes* (DSU) and is attached to the Annex II of the Agreement. The mechanism provides for a dispute settlement procedure between parties to the Agreement, that is states and not individuals. The DSU apparently elevates the pre-contractual or the contractual dispute between a third-party provider and a contracting authority to a grievance of an inter-governmental dimension. To invoke the Dispute Settlement Understanding, a state must first exhaust all possible ways of settling the dispute in an amicable manner by means of direct consultation and negotiations with the state allegedly in breach. If settlement cannot be reached, the state then may request the WTO Dispute Settlement Body for a Panel to be established in order to hear the case. The Panel is appointed in consultation with the parties and comprised of persons with experience in the area of government procurement. The Panel has as its task the

---

[70] See cases 21-24/72, *International Fruit Co NV v. Produktschap voor Groenten en Fruit*, [1972] ECR 1236. Also case C-280/93, *Germany v. Council*, judgment of 5 October 1994.
[71] For more details see M. Footer, *Remedies Under the New GATT Agreement on Government Procurement*, Public Procurement Law Review, vol 4, 1995, p.p. 80-86.

provision of a report to the parties concerned, which then is adopted by the Dispute Settlement Body. The latter would then request the state in breach to repeal all the measures which contravene the principles of the WTO Government Procurement Agreement. Failing to do so, the Dispute Settlement Body may authorise *unilateral suspension* of the application of the GPA or any other agreement under the WTO in the territory of the state affected by the violation.

# 6 An Impact Assessment of the European Public Procurement Law and Policy

The process of the liberalisation of public procurement in the European Community has two primary objectives: i) to achieve an open and competitive regime of public purchasing which would yield substantial savings to the public sector and ii) to act as a stimulant for the much needed restructuring and adjustment of the European industrial base. When compared with other advanced integrated economic or political systems, the regulation of public procurement in the European Community has no precedence. It is not only the aspiration for the creation of a genuinely integrated public sector market within the Community, but to a large extent the impact of such a regime upon the overall process of European Integration that deserves further attention. The mechanism of the public purchasing regulation has revealed a considerable range of socio-economic considerations which interact with the envisaged aims and objectives of the regime. The public purchasing sector in the Community is by no means a *tabula blanca* readily receptive to the parameters of any legislative framework. Rather, it is a *forum* of well established socio-economic and legal patterns which for a long time have served national interests.

No one should expect a dramatic and unprecedented transformation of the way public procurement has been conducted in the Member States of the European Community, for two main reasons. Firstly, what has been asked by European law and policy on public procurement represents a significant change of the *modus operandi* of contracting authorities, which quite often have regarded the European rules as a burden. The unwillingness of public authorities to change well established public purchasing patterns and practices not only does reflect their reservations over the financial implications of such an exercise, but mostly their concern over domestic policy considerations which are closely associated with public procurement. The second reason for the modest progress in adapting to the new regime can be attributed to a number of factors which may not only slow the progress of public sector integration but also hinder the delivery of the envisaged results and the accomplishment of the objectives under the relevant framework. Other things being equal, in the sense that the Member States and their contracting authorities do indeed comply with the stipulated requirements of the Public Procurement Directives, the integration the public markets in the European Community could face actual and potential problems which focus on five main areas: a) inherent constraints of the legislation, b) public monopolies and the process of their privatisation in the Member States, c) harmonisation of standards and specifications, d) the reluctance of the supply side in initiating litigation and e) the sustainability of certain industries.

**Inherent shortcomings in the Public Procurement rules**

The legislation on public procurement is far from perfect. It has envisaged the creation of a framework which will enhance competition in public markets, but the actual mechanism in delivering the objectives has revealed a number of limitations with its impact on the demand and supply sides. The most significant danger in the legislative framework of public procurement in the Community is the potential elements of non-tariff protection which might be arising from its application. Indeed, inherent shortcomings in the legislation could pose considerable obstacles to the integration of the public sector in Europe. The impact of the law and policy of public purchasing upon the demand side in particular has exposed two fundamental limitations which are integral to the legislative framework. The first limitation refers to the quantitative division of public markets in dimensional (above certain thresholds) and sub-dimensional ones (below the thresholds which trigger the applicability of the Directives). The second limitation is concerned with the potential adverse effects of the principle of transparency upon the public procurement process.

*The dimensionality of public procurement*

The main objective of the European rules on public procurement, as implemented by Member States in the form of domestic laws is the establishment of the principle of transparency in the award of public contracts. The rules stipulate that public contracts of estimated value which exceeds certain thresholds shall be advertised in the Official Journal of the European Communities.[1] The legislation on public procurement has put much faith on the principle of transparency. Transparency and openness in the public sector in Europe represent prerequisites for its integration. The principle of transparency encompasses the principle of accountability in the public sector and is materialised through the advertisement and publicity of procurement requirements of contracting authorities. However, the ambit of the law does not encapsulate all public procurement contracts awarded by contracting authorities. It rather introduces *a de minimis rule*, where certain thresholds in relation to the value of the contracts are utilised for the applicability of the Directives. The dimensional public procurement should, in principle, encompass the majority of procurement requirements of Member States and their contracting authorities. However, the legislation on public procurement has had little effect on the principle of transparency, as empirical investigation of the patterns of contracting authorities of Member States concerning their publication record in relation to their contracts reveals a rather gloomy picture. The volume of public purchasing which is advertised and tendered according to the requirements of the relevant Directives in comparison with the total volume of public procurement of the Member States appears disproportionate and beyond expectation, bearing in mind

---

[1] ECU 5 m for all work and construction projects, Article 3(1) of Directive 93/37; Article 14(c) of Directive 93/38.
ECU 200,000 for supplies contracts within the European Union [Article 5(1)(a) of Directive 93/36] and ECU 136,000 for supplies contracts from third countries [Article 5(1)(c) of Directive 93/36]
ECU 600,000 for supplies of telecommunication equipment under the Utilities Directive [Article 14(b) of Directive 93/38] and ECU 400,000 for all other supplies contracts awarded by public utilities [Article 14(a) of Directive 93/38]
ECU 200,000 for services contracts [Article 7(1) of Directive 92/50].

the vital importance that has been given to the principle of transparency for the opening-up of the public markets in the European Community. The percentages of public contracts advertised in the Official Journal by Member States[2] (Belgium 7.9, Denmark 18.1, France 14.7, Germany 16.8, Greece 8.2, Ireland 11.5, Italy 50.6, Luxembourg 7.5, The Netherlands 6.5, Portugal 15.4, Spain 8.4, United Kingdom 16.4) reveal the relatively low impact of the public procurement legislation on the principle and objectives of transparency in European public markets. Clarification of the above impact of the law upon the transparency patterns which contracting authorities have established should be sought by exploring three scenaria.

The first scenario is based on the distinction between dimensional and sub-dimensional public procurement in the Member States. The European Directives allow the division of public contracts into lots[3] without any justification from contracting authorities. This in most cases may result in intentional contravention of the Directives, as sub-dimensional (below certain thresholds) public contracts escape their applicability. As sub-dimensional public procurement escapes from the mandatory publication requirement, contracting authorities tend to divide contracts into separate lots. It should be mentioned that the Directives stipulate the prohibition of intentional division of contracts into lots with a view to avoiding the relevant thresholds, but the provision presents practical difficulties in its observance and enforcement. Until the time of writing, there is no case or complaint before national courts or before the European Court of Justice relating to the intentional division of contracts into lots with lower thresholds in order to avoid the application of the Directives. The relevant thresholds which require the mandatory publication requirement, clearly result in a segmentation of the public markets in quantitative terms by creating a *dimensional forum* which is subject to the rigorous legal regime. A *de minimis* rule applies to contracts below the thresholds, which exempts them from the provisions of the Directives. The sub-dimensional public procurement is only subject to the principle of non-discrimination at European level, whereas at domestic level, national tendering rules regulate the award of these contracts.

---

[2] Results extrapolated from the Tenders Electronic Daily and the Supplement of the Official Journal of the European Communities for the period between 1992-1995 and relate to supplies and works contracts.
[3] Articles 17 and 20 of the Public Supplies (93/36) and Public Works (93/37) Directives respectively.

The second scenario is based on the excessive utilisation of award procedures without prior publication. Indeed, the Directives allow, under certain circumstances the award of contracts through direct negotiations with a contractor. Although the European Court of Justice condemned the above practice in a number of cases before it, the actual utilisation of negotiated procedures without prior publication is widespread. Finally, the third scenario implies the blunt violation of Community Law by Member States by avoiding the publication of tender notices in the Official Journal of the European Communities.

Bearing in mind the relative absence of complaints and subsequent litigation concerning non-advertisement of public contracts before national courts or the European Court of Justice, the third scenario reflects to a large extent the underlying reason for the lack of transparency in public procurement. In fact, intentional division of contracts into lots with a view to avoiding the Directives and excessive and unjustified recourse to award procedures without prior publication amounts to a blunt violation of Member States' obligations arising from the relevant Directives and also form primary Treaty provisions.

*The effects of the principle of transparency*

Transparency, as a principle in public purchasing has an obvious trade effect, that of price competitiveness. If more interested suppliers are aware of a contracting authority's determination to procure, automatically an element of competition occurs; this sort of competitive pattern would probably be reflected in the prices received by the contracting authority, when it evaluates the offers. The fact that more suppliers are aware of a forthcoming public contract and the fact that interesting suppliers are aware that their rivals are informed about it, indicates two distinctive parameters which are relevant to savings and value for money. The first parameter focuses on value for money for the demand side of the equation of public purchasing and reveals the possibility for contracting authorities to compare prices (and quality). The second parameter has an effect on the supply side of the equation (the suppliers) which amongst other things can no longer rely on the lack of price comparisons when serving the public sector. Openness in public procurement, by definition, results in price competition and the benefits for contracting authorities appear achievable.

However, transparency and openness in public purchasing pose a question over long-term savings and value for money considerations. Price competition, as a result of the awareness of forthcoming public contracts, represents a rather static effect in the value for money process. The fact that more and more interested suppliers are aware and do submit tenders, in the long run, appears rather as a burden. If transparency and the resulting price competitiveness are based on a *win-to-win* process, the potential benefits for contracting authorities could easily be counterbalanced by the administrative costs in tender evaluation and replies to unsuccessful tenders. Furthermore, the risk management factor is much higher in a win-to-win purchasing scenario. Price competitiveness represents also some threats for contracting authorities, to the extent that quality of deliverables as well as the delivery process itself could be jeopardised, if contracting authorities deal with different and unknown contractors. It could thus be argued here that price competitiveness, as a trade effect potentially beneficial for the demand side of the public purchasing equation, has a static character. It seems that it does not take into account medium or long-term purchasing patterns, as well as counter effects of competition. Two elements deserve further analysis here:

The first raises questions over the aggregate loss of the economy through transparent competitive purchasing patterns. For example, if a large number of interested suppliers submit their offer to a particular contracting authority, two types of costs should be examined. Firstly, the cost which is attributed to the response and tendering stage of the procurement process. Human and capital resources are directed by the suppliers towards the preparation of documents and the submission of the offers. If one of these suppliers wins the contract, the remaining would have suffered an unrecoverable loss. If that aggregate loss exceeds the benefit/saving accomplished by the contracting authority by following transparent and competitive purchasing patterns, value for money has not been achieved. Secondly, along the same lines, the evaluation and selection process during tendering represents a considerable administrative cost for the contracting authorities. If the principle of transparency complements the principle of equal treatment, contracting authorities should give the same attention to all interested suppliers that have submitted a response. Downsizing the list through evaluation and assessment based on stipulated criteria is by no means an inexpensive exercise. Human and capital resources have to be directed by contracting authorities towards meeting that cost. If the latter exceeds the potential savings achieved through the competitive tendering route, then value for money is unaccomplished.

The second element that deserves attention relates to the definition of price competitiveness in public purchasing as well as its interrelation with anti-trust law and policy. A question which arises in price competitive tendering patterns is *what would be the lowest offer contracting authorities can accept*. If the maximisation of savings is the only achievable objective in the public procurement process, the transparent/competitive pattern cannot guarantee and evaluate safeguards in relation to underpriced offers. If the supply side responds to the perpetuated competitive purchasing pattern by lowering prices, contracting authorities could face a dilemma: where to stop. It should be mentioned here that the European rules provide for an automatic disqualification of an "abnormally low offer".[4] The term has not been interpreted in detail by the judiciary at European and domestic levels and serves rather as a "lower bottom limit".[5] Also, when an offer appears low, contracting authorities may request clarifications from the tenderer in question. Contracting authorities face a dilemma in evaluating and assessing low offers other than abnormal ones. It is difficult for them to identify dumping or predatory pricing disguised behind a low offer for a public contract. In addition, even if there is an indication of anti-competitive price fixing, the European public procurement rules do not provide for any kind of procedure. The suspension of the award procedures (or even the suspension of the conclusion of the contract itself) would be unlikely without a thorough and exhaustive investigation by the competent anti-trust authorities.

The following litigation before the European Court of Justice provides for a taxonomy of approaches in relation to the abnormality of low offers in public procurement contracts. Italy had to appear before the Court of Justice in 1983,[6] when it apparently failed to fulfil its obligations in implementing correctly the Public Works Directive 71/305. In particular, a provision of Italian Law No. 741 (Article 10) added a further

---

[4] Article 29(5) of Directive 71/305 as amended by Directive 89/440.
[5] Case 76/81, *SA Transporoute et Travaux v. Minister of Public Works*, [1982] ECR 457; Case No 104/75, *SA SHV Belgium v. La Maison Ideale et Societe Nationale du Longement*, before the Belgian Conseil d'Etat, judgment of 24/6/86 of the Belgian Conseil d'Etat.
[6] Case 247/83, *Commission v. Italy*, [1985] ECR 1077.

criterion (a tender which equals the average tender or is closest to it) to those laid down in Article 29 of Directive 71/305, concerning the criteria for the award of a contract. The latter Article seems to contain an exhaustive list of grounds on which a contract may be awarded: either the lowest price tender or the most economically advantageous offer. The lowest price criterion relies purely on quantitative criteria, whereas the most economically advantageous one presupposes a combination of quantitative and qualitative criteria that vary according to the contract in question (price, period of completion, running cost, profitability, technical merit). The defendant claimed to have intended to determine the correct market price by excluding extremely low tenders not corresponding to reality, without having sought explanations from the tenderer by virtue of Article 29 of Directive 71/305. The Court rejected that argument. Advocate-General Lenz concluded[7] that extremely low tenders may be considered by contracting authorities laying down minimum prices for participation in the competition for the award of a contract, although he admitted that prices may change considerably between the invitation to tender and the completion of the project due to inflation. In another case[8] the Court ruled that Article 29 of Directive 71/305, which requires the contracting authorities awarding a contract for which an obviously abnormally low tender in relation to the transaction has been submitted[9], to examine the details of the tender before deciding the award of the contract, is also directly effective.[10] The contracting authorities are under duty to seek from the tenderer an explanation of his prices or to inform him that his tender appears to be abnormally low and to allow him a reasonable time within which to submit further details, before making any decision as to the award of the contract. The case, however, did not touch the concept of "obviously", abnormally low tenders, which came into play[11] a few years later in 1988, when an Italian court sought a preliminary ruling from the Court of Justice with respect to questions arising from a case pending before it.[12] In this case the Court was requested to interpret Article 29 of

---

[7] See his Conclusions in [1985] ECR 1084.
[8] Case 76/81, *SA Transporoute et Travaux v. Minister of Public Works*, [1982] ECR 457.
[9] Article 29(5) of Directive 71/305 as amended by Directive 89/440, op.cit.
[10] Case No 104/75, *SA SHV Belgium v. La Maison Ideale et Societe Nationale du Longement*, before the Belgian Conseil d'Etat; op.cit.
[11] See Case 103/88, *Fratelli Costanzo S.p.A. v. Comune di Milano*, [1989] ECR 1839, op.cit.
[12] Case 103/88, *Fratelli Costanzo S.p.A. v. Comune di Milano*, [1989] ECR 1839.

Directive 71/305 and pronounce on its direct effect. It held that rejection of a contract based on mathematical criteria without giving the tenderer an opportunity to furnish information, is inconsistent with Article 29(5) of Directive 71/305. The interpretation of the latter provision reveals its direct effectivity[13] as it lays down a precise and detailed procedure for the examination of tenders which appear to be abnormally low. That aim would be jeopardised if Member States were able, when implementing Article 29(5) to depart from it to any material extent. The latter consideration may create interpretation problems with respect to the question whether they appear to be abnormally low and not only when they are obviously abnormally low. The Court following previous case-law,[14] ruled that the contracting authorities must give an opportunity to tenderers to furnish explanations regarding the genuine nature of their tenders, when those tenders appear to be abnormally low and not only when they are obviously abnormally low. The Court did not proceed to an analysis of the wording of "obviously". It rather seems that the term "obviously" indicates the existence of precise and concrete evidence as to the abnormally low tender. The wording "abnormally" rather implies a quantitative criterion left to the discretion of the contracting authority. It should be borne in mind that efficient and highly competitive tenderers often submit abnormally low tenders. It appears from both the wording and the aim of the Directive that in both situations, contracting authorities should seek explanation and reject unrealistic offers, informing the Advisory Committee.[15] On the other hand, if the tender is just "abnormally" low, it could be argued that it is within the discretion of the contracting authority to utilise Article 29(5) to investigate the genuine offer of a tender. Perhaps relevant information and closer examination of the tender by the contracting authority on its own motion would suffice to award the contract without further explanations from the contractor. Finally, in 1989, the Court based on its previous case-law, in a case[16] referred to it by an Italian court, condemned the rejection of a works contract based on

---

[13] See also Case 31/87, op.cit.
[14] Case 76/81 *Transporoute*, [1982] ECR 417, op.cit.
[15] The Advisory Committee for Public Procurement was set up by Decision 77/63 (O.J.1977 L 13/15) and is composed of representatives of the Member States belonging to the authorities of those States and has as its task to supervise the proper application of Public Procurement Directives by Member States.
[16] Case 296/89, *Impresa Dona Alfonso di Dona Alfonso & Figli s.n.c. v. Consorzio per lo Sviluppo Industriale del Comune di Monfalcone*, judgment of June 18, 1991.

mathematical criteria and also did not distinguish between "obviously abnormally low" and simply abnormally low offers.

*The abuse of award procedures which may restrict competition in the public markets*

The participation of the supply side of the public procurement equation in the tendering process is channelled through open, negotiated or restricted procedures. Open procedures are those where every interested supplier, contractor or service provider may submit an offer.[17] Negotiated procedures[18] are such procedures for the award of public contracts whereby contracting authorities consult contractors of their choice and negotiate the terms of the contract with one or more of them. Finally, Restricted procedures[19] are those procedures for the award of public contracts whereby only those contractors invited by the contracting authority may submit tenders. The selection of the winning tender takes place in two rounds. In the first round, all interested contractors may submit their tenders and the contracting authority selects, from the candidates, those who will be invited to tender. In principle, the minimum number of candidates to be selected is five. In the second round, bids are submitted and the successful tender is selected.

The Utilities Directives have introduced a new selection and tendering procedure, namely framework agreements, which is influenced to a large extent by the benefits of chain supply management and partnership schemes. The Supplies, Works and Services Directives do not refer to framework agreements. A framework agreement is an agreement between a contracting authority and one or more suppliers, contractors or service-providers the purpose of which is to establish the terms, in particular with regard to prices and, where appropriate, the quantity envisaged, which govern the contracts to be awarded during a given period.[20] A framework agreement does not possess a binding character and should not be considered as a contract between the relevant parties. In

---

[17] Article 1(d) of Directive 93/36; Article 1(e) of Directive 93/37; Article 1(7)(a) of Directive 93/38; Article 1(d) of Directive 92/50.

[18] Article 1(f) of Directive 93/36; Article 1(g) of Directive 93/37; Article 1(7)(c) of Directive 93/38; Article 1(c) of Directive 92/50.

[19] Article 1(e) of Directive 93/36; Article 1(f) of Directive 93/37; Article 1(7)(b) of Directive 93/38; Article 1(d) of Directive 92/50.

[20] Article 1(5) of Directive 93/38

practical terms it represents a sort of a standing offer which remains valid during its time-span. Within the provisions of the Utilities Directive, when a contracting authority awards a framework agreement under the relevant procedures which are common to other public contracts covered therein, subsequent individual contracts concluded under the framework agreement may be awarded without having recourse to a call for competition.[21] Individual contracts which have been awarded under a framework agreement are subject to the requirement of the publication of a contract-award notice in the Official Journal. The Directive specifically stipulates that misuse of framework agreements may distort competition and trigger the application of the relevant rules, particularly with reference to concerted practices which lead to collusive tendering.

Certain types of award procedures (particularly negotiated with or without prior publication in the Official Journal) are prone to abuse by contracting authorities in order to avoid the publicity requirement in advertising public contracts and in order to favour certain suppliers or contractors. Negotiated procedures[22] are such procedures for the award of public contracts whereby contracting authorities consult contractors of their choice and negotiate the terms of the contract with one or more of them. In most cases they follow restricted procedures and they are heavily utilised under framework agreements in the Utilities sectors. There are two different types of negotiated procedures: i) negotiated procedures with prior notification and ii) negotiated procedures without prior notification.

- Negotiated procedures with prior notification[23] provide for selection of candidates in two rounds. In the first round, all interested contractors may submit their tenders and the contracting authority selects, from the candidates, those who will be invited to negotiate. In the second round, negotiations with various candidates take place and the successful tender is selected. In principle, the minimum number of candidates to be selected is three, provided that there is a sufficient number of suitable candidates.

---

[21] Article 20(2)(i) of Directive 93/38
[22] Article 1(f) of Directive 93/36; Article 1(g) of Directive 93/37; Article 1(7)(c) of Directive 93/38; Article 1(c) of Directive 92/50.
[23] Article 6(2) of Directive 93/36; Article 7(2) of Directive 93/37; Article 20(1) of Directive 93/38; Article 11(2) of Directive 92/50.

- Negotiated procedures without prior notification[24] are the least restrictive of the various award procedures laid down in the Directive and may be conducted in one single round. Contracting authorities are allowed to choose whichever contractor they want, begin negotiations directly with this contractor and award the contract to him. The Directive provides for only a few rules with which this procedure must comply. A prior notice in the Official Journal is not required.

An accelerated form of negotiated procedures may be used[25] where, for reasons of urgency, the periods normally required under the normal procedures cannot be met. In such cases, contracting authorities are required to indicate in the tender notice published in the Official Journal the grounds for using the accelerated form of the procedure. The use of an accelerated procedure must be limited to the types and quantities of products or services which it can be shown are urgently required. Other products or services must be supplied or provided under open or restricted procedures.

The Public Procurement Directives stipulate that open procedures, where possible should constitute the norm. Open procedures increase competition without doubt and can achieve better prices for the contracting authorities when the latter purchase goods in large volumes. Price reduction based on economies of scale can bring about substantial cost savings for the public sector. Open procedures are mostly utilised when the procurement process is relatively straightforward and are combined with the lowest price award criterion. On the other hand, competition in tendering procedures is limited by using the restricted and negotiated procedures. By definition, the number of candidates that are allowed to tender is limited (5 in restricted 3 in negotiated procedures respectively), therefore the Directives have attached a number of conditions for the contracting authorities to justify when they intend to award their contracts through restricted or negotiated procedure. Restricted and negotiated procedures are utilised in relation with the most economically advantageous offer award criterion and suited for more complex procurement schemes. Although contracting authorities can freely opt for open or restricted procedures, the latter should be justified by reference to

---

[24] Article 6(3) of Directive 93/36; Article 7(3) of Directive 93/37; Article 20(3) of Directive 93/38; Article 11(3) of Directive 92/50.
[25] Article 12 of Directive 93/36; Article 13 of Directive 93/37; Article 26(2) of Directive 93/38; Article 19(4) of Directive 92/50.

the nature of the products or services to be procured and the balance between contract value and administrative costs associated with tender evaluation. A more rigorous set of conditions apply for the use of negotiated procedures. When negotiated procedures with prior notification are used, they must be justified on grounds of irregular or unacceptable tenders received as a result of a previous call. Negotiated procedures without prior notification are restrictively permitted in absence of tenders, when the procurement involves manufactured products or construction work purely for research and development, when for technical or artistic reasons or reasons connected with the protection of exclusive rights a particular supplier or contractor is selected, in cases of extreme urgency brought by unforeseeable events not attributable to the contracting authorities, when additional deliveries and supplies or works would cause disproportionate technical operational and maintenance difficulties.

Negotiated procedures with prior publication, since they restrict the number of tenderers may constitute an element of non-tariff protection and may encourage practices which appear to run counter to effective competition. If they are being employed as a non-tariff barrier, negotiated procedures may give rise to discrimination on grounds of nationality, preference and support of domestic uncompetitive suppliers, all of which would or could be detrimental to the position of foreign firms which will be placed at a competitive disadvantage. However, negotiated procedures may have certain positive effects in public procurement, as it may reduce the economic costs of the contracting entities, particularly in cases where product complexity which requires negotiations for the quality of procurement, or a large number of tenderers makes tender evaluation relatively expensive. Contracting authorities have also abusive recourse to award procedures without prior notification and claim a number of reasons varying from extreme urgency to the protection of industrial or commercial property rights and the need to guarantee the flow of supplies or works and award public contracts through direct negotiations with the contractor(s) of their choice. They also claim (particularly the Utilities) that the utilisation of framework agreements or list of approved vendors has resulted in cost-efficiency gains of administrative costs relating to the evaluation of tenders.

The European Court of Justice has always been very reluctant in accepting the use of negotiated procedures, particularly without prior advertisement. In a number of notable cases before it relating to improper use of the award procedures, the Court has maintained the exceptional character of negotiated procedures and the extremely onerous obligation of contracting authorities to justify them. It might be construed from the case law of the Court of Justice that the particular procedure stipulated by the rules requires some sort of clearance prior to its utilisation. This is not however the case, as the only form of official notification by contracting authorities when use negotiated procedures takes place after the award of the contract in question, where a notice containing the reasons for having recourse to negotiation should be communicated to the European Commission. This rather reinforces the exceptional character of the negotiated procedures rather than their prohibitive use. A number of cases before the European Court of Justice have clarified the position of European Institutions vis-à-vis the use of negotiated procedures.

In 1985 the Commission was informed that the Municipality of Milan had awarded a works contract without following the provisions of Directive 71/305 concerning prior publication of a notice for tender in the Official Journal. It initiated proceedings against Italy[26]. The Italian State relied on Article 9 of Directive 71/305, which stipulates an exception from the common rules on a number of occasions and particularly with respect to the case in question, when exclusive rights held by the undertaking to which the contract was awarded are involved [Article 9(b)] or the project is a matter of extreme urgency due to unforeseeable events [Article 9(d)]. The Court rejected both justifications. As for the exception laid down in Article 9(b), exclusive rights include know-how and intellectual property rights that are necessary to build a plant of the type required. For future relating cases, justification on these grounds brings into play competition law considerations, as Regulation 556/89 on know-how licensing[27], and Regulation 2349/84 on patent licences agreements[28] must be taken into account. With regard to the grounds provided for in Article 9(d), extreme urgency brought by events unforeseen by the authorities must be restrictively interpreted, as it is subject to a justification test based on the proportionality principle.

The Commission brought Italy again before the Court in a case[29] that concerned not only public supplies contracts, but also Articles 52 and 59 EC (right of establishment and freedom to provide services

---

[26] Case 199/85, *Commission v. Italy*, [1987] ECR 1039.
[27] O.J.1989 L 61/1.
[28] O.J.1984 L 219.
[29] Case 3/88, *Commission v. Italy*, [1989] ECR 4035.

respectively). The defendant, by virtue of national law, required that only companies in which all or a majority of the share capital is in public ownership are eligible to participate in and compete for the award of supplies contracts required for the establishment of data-processing systems, the design and in some cases the technical management of these systems. The Court ruled that this was contrary to Articles 52 and 59 EC which are based on the principle of equal treatment and prohibit not only overt discrimination on grounds of nationality, but also all covert forms of discrimination, which, by the application of other criteria of differentiation, lead in fact to the same result. With respect to Directive 77/62, the Court held that the establishment of a data-processing system of the type provided by the Italian legislation constituted "products" within the meaning of Article 6(1)(h) of Directive 77/95, which may be dissociated from the activities involved in the development of the data-processing system (these are to be considered services). It also rejected the argument that the award of the contract for data-processing fell under Article 2(3) of Directive 77/62, which provides for public service activities covered by special or exclusive rights to be awarded to a specific body, regardless of its legal status. The defendant's submission that the supply contracts in question were secret or their delivery must be accompanied by special security reasons, thus allowing the contracting authority to derogate from the basic principles of the Directive [publication of tender notice Article 4(1)(2)] was rejected. Although the data involved were essential in the fight against crime in areas of taxation, public health and fraud in agricultural matters, observance of confidentiality by the tenderer concerned is not dependent on public ownership. Even if the suppliers of the data-processing system in issue fell under the exception of Article 6(1)(e) of Directive 77/62, which provides for additional deliveries from a specific supplier in order for contracting authorities to avoid the purchase of equipment of different technical characteristics resulting in incompatibility or disproportionate technical difficulties, cannot justify the rule that only companies controlled by the State may be awarded such contracts.

The Commission was successful in an action against Spain[30] where the Court declared that Spain had failed to fulfil its obligations under Directive 71/305, as a result of the decision of the governing council of the *Universidad Complutense Madrid* to award contracts for works connected

---

[30] Case 24/91, *Commission v. Kingdom of Spain*, [1994] CMLR 621.

with the extension and renovation of university estates department by private contract (without publication in the Official Journal) could not be justified under the exception for reasons of urgency unforeseen to the contracting authorities.

Italy was once more brought before the Court[31] in 1992 for failure to fulfil obligations under Directive 71/305 as amended by Directive 89/440, in particular to publish in the Official Journal the tender notice in respect of the construction of an avalanche barrier in the district of *Colle Isarco/Brennero*. The case concerned the application of the award procedures by contracting authorities, particularly the negotiated procedures without prior notice. The Italian State contested the Commission's submissions that the public authority in question had awarded the construction works by virtue of a private contract on the grounds of extreme urgency and unforeseeability, as provided in Article 9 of the Works Directive. The Court, although recognised the fulfilment urgency criterion, it pronounced that the latter must be in causal link with unforeseeable events [Article 9(d)] to contracting authorities in order to deviate from the main provisions of the Directive.

In 1993 a reference to the European Court of Justice was made by the High Court (Queen's Bench Division) on, *inter alia*, the utilisation of public procurement Directives for the purchasing of pharmaceutical products (narcotic drugs previously being supplied under licence) by the competent health authorities[32]. The national court requested a preliminary ruling on the interpretation of Article 25 of the Supplies Directive 77/62, particularly the meaning of the "most economically advantageous offer". The national court asked whether factors concerning continuity and reliability as well as security of supplies fall under the framework of the most economically advantageous offer, when the latter is being evaluated. The Court of Justice, following previous case law[33], reiterated the flexible and wide interpretation of the relevant award criterion and had no difficulty in declaring that contracting authorities may use the most economically advantageous offer as award criterion by choosing the factors which they want to apply in evaluating tenders, provided these factors are mentioned, in hierarchical order in the invitation to tender and

---

[31] Case 107/92, *Commission v. Italy*, judgment of August 2, 1993.
[32] Case C 324/93, *R. v. The Secretary of State for the Home Department, ex.p . Evans Medical Ltd and Macfarlan Smith Ltd*.
[33] Case 31/87, *Gebroeders Beenjes v. The Netherlands*, [1988] ECR 4635, op.cit.

or the contract documents. Two Member States intervened in the case and submitted that a restricted system of supply of potentially dangerous substances could be justified by having recourse to Article 6(1) and (4) of the Supplies Directive, which permits the use of negotiated procedures when, for technical reasons, the supply of goods in question can be guaranteed by only a particular supplier [Article 6(1)], or when, for security reasons, the supply of goods in question is declared secret, or when their delivery must be accompanied by the application of administrative laws or regulations that guarantee the secrecy of the delivery [Article [6(4)].

In 1994 also the Commission brought two member States before the Court of Justice for infringement of procurement Directive. The first case was against Italy[34] and concerned the award of motorway construction contracts contrary to the framework of the Works Directive. The Court did not have the opportunity to pronounce on the failure of the Italian State to observe the provisions of the Works Directive in a similar case against Italy[35], which related to the same construction project, because that case was held inadmissible. In the cases before the Court, the Italian authorities justified the private award for the execution of the works contract in question on Article 9(b) and (d) of the Works Directive, which provide for deviation from the award procedures stipulated in the Directives, on the grounds of extreme urgency [9(d)] and technical reasons [9(b)]. The Court rejected both submissions based on a restrictive interpretation of Article 9 of the Works Directive.

**Public monopolies**

Public monopolies in the European Union, which in the majority are utilities, are accountable for a substantial magnitude of procurement, in terms of volume and in terms of price. Responsible for this are the expensive infrastructure and high technology products which is necessary to procure in order to deliver their services to the public. Given the fact that most of the suppliers to public utilities depend almost entirely on their procurement and that, even when some degree of privatisation has been achieved, the actual control of the utilities is still vested in the state, the

---

[34] Case C 57/94, *Commission v. Italy*, judgment of May 18, 1995.
[35] Case 296/92, *Commission v. Italy*, judgment of January 12, 1994.

first constraint in liberalising public procurement in the European Union is apparent. Utilities, in the form of public monopolies or semi-private enterprises appear prone to perpetuate long standing over dependency purchasing patterns with certain domestic suppliers. Reflecting the above observations, the reader should bear in mind that until 1991, utilities were not covered by European legislation on procurement[36]. The delay of their regulation can be attributed to the resistance from Member States in privatising their monopolies and the uncertainty of the legal regime that will follow their privatisation.

Public monopolies[37] operating in the utilities sector (energy, transport, water, telecommunications) have been the target of a sweeping process of transformation from monolithic and sub-optimal public corporations to competitive enterprises. These legal or delegated monopolies have been assigned with the exclusive exploitation of the relevant services in their respective Member States (production, distribution of water and any form of energy and the provision of telecommunications and transport) and very often possess a monopsony position. State controlled enterprises perform a different management pattern than private ones in their market activities. Profit maximisation is not their main objective and decision making responds not only to market forces but mainly to political pressure. Understandably, their purchasing behaviour follows, to a large extent, parameters reflecting current trends of the industrial policy of the government in power. It has become apparent that public monopolies in the utilities sector have sustained industries in Member States through exclusive or preferential procurement. Preferential and protectionist purchasing behaviour could not easily withstand the competitive forces under which private firms are exposed. One of the most important elements of corporate performance is sourcing and the associated costs. The private firm which is exposed to competitive forces for its deliverables would be certainly compelled to have recourse to the most cost-efficient sources. This covers not only procurement but also extends to a wide range of legal and corporate activities such as sub-contracting, research and development, maintenance services. Sustainability of "national champions", or in other terms, strategically perceived enterprises, could only be achieved through discriminatory

---

[36] Utilities were first regulated in their procurement by virtue of EC Directive 90/531, O.J. 1990, L 297.
[37] See Articles 37 and 90 EC.

purchasing patterns. The privatisation of public monopolies, which absorb, to a large extent or even entirely, the output of such industries will most probably discontinue such patterns and will result in industrial policy imbalances as it would be difficult for the "national champions" to secure new markets to replace the traditional long dependency on public monopolies and it would take time and effort to diversify their activities or to convert to alternative industrial sectors. Imbalances in social policy (unemployment) will also occur, as a result of the restructuring of the public monopoly and also the industries which are dependent on it.

The protected and preferential purchasing frameworks between monopolies and "national champions" and the output dependency patterns and secured markets of the latter have attracted considerable foreign direct investment, to the extent that Community Institutions face the dilemma of threatening to discontinue the investment flow when liberalising public procurement in the common market. However, it could be argued that the industrial restructuring following the opening-up of the procurement practices of public monopolies would possibly attract similar levels of foreign direct investment, which would be directed towards supporting the new structure.

As mentioned above, the liberalisation of public purchasing aims *inter alia* at achieving a restructuring effect in the common market, particularly in industries suffering from overcapacity and sub-optimal performance. However, the industries supplying public monopolies and utilities are themselves quite often public corporations. In such cases, procurement dependency patterns between state outfits, when disrupted can result in massive unemployment attributed to the supply side's inadequacy to secure new customers. The monopsony position when abolished could often bring about the collapse of the relevant sector.

## Standardisation and specification

National technical standards, industrial product and service specifications and their harmonisation were considered priority areas for the internal market programme. The European Commission's White Paper for the Completion of the Internal Market stipulated for a number of Directives to be adopted and implemented with a view to eliminating discrimination based on the description of national standards. The rules on technical standards and specifications have been brought in line with the new policy which is based on the mutual recognition of national requirements, where the objectives of national legislation are essentially equivalent, and on the process of legislative harmonisation of technical standards through non-governmental standardisation organisations (CEPT, CEN, CENELEC)[38]. However, persistence of contracting authorities to specify their procurement requirements by reference to national standards poses obstacles in the public sector integration[39]. The European Commission has been for some time aware of the most notable examples of circumvention of the policy on standards and specifications[40]. These include the exclusive familiarity of national suppliers with technical data existing in a particular Member State, over-specification by contracting authorities in order to exclude potential bidders and finally favouritism and discrimination by contracting authorities as a result of the availability of technical standards and specifications to certain suppliers only.

Standardisation and specification can act as a non-tariff barrier in public procurement contracts in two ways: firstly, contracting authorities may use apparently different systems of standards and specifications as an excuse for disqualification of tenderers. It should be maintained here that the description of the intended supplies, works or services to be procured is made by reference to the Common Product Classification, the NACE (General Industrial Classification of Economic Activities within the European Communities) and the Common Procurement Vocabulary (CPV), however, this type of description is of generic nature and does not cover industrial specifications and standardisation requirements. Secondly, standardisation and specification requirements can be restrictively defined in order to exclude products or services of a particular origin, or narrow the field of competition amongst tenderers. National standards are not only the subject of domestic legislation, which, of course, need to be harmonised and mutually recognised across the common market. One of the most significant aspects of standardisation and specification appears to

---

[38] Article 7 of Directive 88/295. See the White Paper on Completing the Internal Market, paras.61-79; also Council Resolution of 7 May 1985, O.J.1985, C 136, on a new approach in the field of technical harmonization and standards.

[39] See the Documents of the Advisory Committee for the Opening up of Public Procurement, *Policy Guidlines on the Obligation to refer to European Standards*, CCO/91/67 final.;

[40] See the report of the Advisory Committee for the Opening up of Public Procurement, *Standards for Procurement*, CCO/92/02.

be the operation of voluntary standards, which are mainly specified at industry level. The above category is rather difficult to harmonise, as any approximation and mutual recognition relies on the willingness of the industry in question. Voluntary standards and specifications are used quite often in the Utilities sector, where the relevant procurement requirements are complex and cannot be specified solely by reference to "statutory" standards, thus leaving a considerable margin of discretion in the hands of the contracting authorities, which may abuse it during the selection and qualification stages of the procurement process.

In a number of cases before it, the European Court of Justice seized every opportunity to condemn discriminatory use of specification requirements and standards. In the Irish *Dundalk* pipeline case[41], the Commission had received complaints that Ireland had not complied with the Public Works Directive 71/305 and in particular Article 10 of Directive 71/305. This provision prohibits Member States from introducing into the contractual clauses relating to a given contract, technical specifications, unless they are justified by the subject of the contract, which mention products of a specific make or source or a particular process which favour or eliminate certain undertakings. Such indications are only permitted if they are accompanied by the words "or equivalent" where the authorities awarding contracts are unable to give sufficiently precise and ineligible specifications of the subject of the contract. The Irish invitation to tender, contained reference to technical specifications (Irish) which were not justified by the subject of the contract. Several standards, other than that imposed by a clause in the tender invitation provided equivalent guarantees of safety, performance and reliability. If this was not the case, the Irish standards would only be permitted if the words "or equivalent" were added. Those words were not included in the relevant clause. The latter, although escaping from the framework of Directive 71/305, fell foul of Article 30 EC on the grounds that it was liable to impede imports of foreign products (pipes) into Ireland. Invocation of Article 36 and the rule of reason were rejected as unjustified. Although the Court refused the suspension of the award of the contract based on grounds of public interests, the contract was finally awarded to the contractor in question on condition that the words "or equivalent" would be included in the tender notice in the Official Journal.

---

[41] Case 45/87, *Commission v. Ireland*, [1988] ECR 4929.

In another case, the Commission brought the Netherlands before the European Court of Justice[42] for a failure to observe the Supplies Directive and in particular to specify, without discriminatory descriptions, the required goods for procurement. The *Neerlands Inkoopcentrum NV* had published a notice in the Official Journal for the procurement of a meteorological data processing system, which it specified with a particular trade mark, without using the term "equivalent". The Court following its previous case law[43], reiterated that Article 7(6) of the Supplies Directive 77/62 (as amended by Article 8 of Directive 89/295) intends to eliminate discriminatory description of supplies by utilisation of particular trade marks, unless accompanied by the words "or equivalent", and only in cases where reference to a particular trade mark is necessary for the description of the product in question. The Court of Justice also pronounced the compulsory and unconditional character of point 7 of Annex III to the Supplies Directive 77/62, which requires indication of authorised persons, date, time and place for the opening of tenders, in order to allow tenderers to identify their competitors and enable them to ensure that their offers are being evaluated in a transparent and equal manner.

**Reluctance in initiating litigation: a taxonomy of case law on public procurement**

The litigation before the European Court of Justice and national courts in relation to public procurement contracts has pointed out the areas of contention between defaulting contracting authorities and the Commission or aggrieved contractors. The most common disputes subject to centralised or decentralised judicial control include the following:
- advertisement and publicity of contracts
- selection procedures (quantitative and qualitative suitability criteria)
- technical standards (product specification and standardisation)
- award procedures
- award criteria

Interestingly, all the relevant provisions of the Directives covering the above areas are capable of producing direct effect, thus maximising the

---

[42] Case C 359/93, *Commission v. The Netherlands*, judgment of January 24, 1995.
[43] Case 45/87, *Commission v. Ireland*, [1988] ECR 4929.

opportunities for access to justice for aggrieved contractors. The impact of public procurement legislation on the demand and supply sides identified certain areas which represent obstacles to public market integration. Although the relevant legislation has provided for a great deal of flexibility, in terms of implementing methods and time, national legal systems responded slowly to the envisaged regime. The limited number of cases relating to public procurement, in contrast with its volume and the economic importance for Member States reflects a false picture. One may assume, that because of the relatively disproportionate number of cases before the European Court of Justice or before national courts, the integration of public markets is on good course and has progressed satisfactorily.

However, examination and analysis of the case-law on public procurement as the impact of the relevant legislation on the demand and supply sides reveals the nature of public procurement as a *nexus* of transaction activities between the state and its organs on the one hand and the private sector on the other. Such a nature appears to have strong *endocentric* characteristics, in terms of the reluctance in initiating litigation, the secrecy and confidentiality of the dispute itself, and finally the belief that litigation represents the *ultium refugium* in resolving the dispute. Furthermore, the contractual relation between the supply and the demand side after the litigation of a dispute between them appears to be irretrievably broken. This means that prior to having recourse to legal proceedings, parties in a public procurement dispute appear to have comprehensively exhausted all the routes in dissolving the issue in an amicable way. Therefore, the relevant litigation and its outcome serves as an epitaph in a rather unclear nexus of legal relations. The supply side appears reluctant in taking contracting authorities to court for a number of reasons: psychological, legal and financial.

The psychology behind enforcement and compliance with public procurement legislation is the key point for understanding the behaviour of the supply side. The supply side is often afraid of the vindictive behaviour of the contracting authorities. A contractor who initiates litigation (or some form of official complain) against a contracting authority would find himself on a "black list" and would not continue doing business with the latter. Even in the unlikely event that a contract is awarded to a supplier that had previously created some form of trouble for the contracting authority, the latter could make the performance of the contract intolerable, ensuring minimisation of margins of profit and delaying payments. The psychology in public procurement enforcement and compliance works against the supply side, as the latter initiates the majority of litigation against contracting authorities. Even in the case of the European Commission taking the defaulting Member State before the European Court of Justice under Article 169 EC, there is a complaint from an aggrieved contractor who has identified himself.

The supply side also appears reluctant in initiating litigation against contracting authorities because of financial reasons. If the court found that the contracting authority breached the law, the damages that could be awarded would be disproportionate to the legal costs. The extent to which compensation is awarded varies among legal orders. Compensation for loss of incurred expenses, for loss of profits and for loss of opportunity is theoretically available in all Member States, in accordance with the Compliance Directives. However, in practice the only relatively certain heading of damages an aggrieved contractor may count on is that of out-of-pocket expenses, *viz.* the cost of preparing the bid. Forgone profits and losses of opportunities would be deemed as elements of speculative litigation by the courts and would probably be rejected. It is worth mentioning that in Italy, due to the very strict requirement that only successful tenderers that have been awarded the contract may lodge an action for damages against the contracting authority, losses of profits are not easily granted; on the other hand, under the relevant arbitration proceedings for public contracts in the Netherlands, compensation is available for injury to a firm's commercial reputation. Direct compensation from administrative bodies, without judicial interference, is theoretically available in Denmark and Spain. These examples demonstrate the diversity of national systems as far as enforcement of public procurement law is concerned.

Finally, legal obstacles appear to have constrained the supply side in its attempts to enforce its rights under public procurement law. These obstacles act as non-tariff barriers, particularly in cases of cross-country litigation, where the nature of the competent *forum*, the cost of initiating a suit, legal and experts fees, translation costs and the chances of a favourable outcome deter aggrieved contractors from taking defaulting contracting authorities to court. The complexity of domestic legal regimes relating to public procurement disputes, in conjunction with the uncertainties arising from the parallel application of public and private law remedies in some Member States, appear a major deterrent for initiating litigation against contracting authorities.

## The effect of competitiveness in public procurement on the sustainability of certain industries

The low transparency levels and the low *tradability* of public contracts within the European Community have been particularly intriguing. The term *tradability*, refers to the cross-border import penetration of public procurement contracts within the common market.

| MS | t | i |
|---|---|---|
| Belgium | 7.9 | 17.7 |
| Denmark | 18.1 | 9.2 |
| France | 14.7 | 9.3 |
| Germany | 16.8 | 7.1 |
| Greece | 8.2 | 19.1 |
| Ireland | 11.5 | 20.4 |
| Italy | 50.6 | 8.6 |
| Luxembourg | 7.5 | 24.2 |
| Netherlands | 6.5 | 11.6 |
| Portugal | 15.4 | 17.6 |
| Spain | 8.4 | 15.7 |
| United Kingdom | 16.4 | 14.4 |

MS: Member State
t: transparency levels (%)
i: public procurement import penetration levels (%)

The effectiveness of the public procurement legislation relies mainly on its decentralised application by the Member States and its enforcement by the competent *fora*. The greater the regime of transparency Member States provide for their public markets, the more efficient the level of competition that occurs and the more enhanced the cross-frontier trade with the public sector that emerges, facts that will result in their full integration. Empirical results have revealed that contracting authorities award the majority of public contracts without recourse to the advertisement and publicity provisions of the relevant Directives. This finding discloses the size of dimensional and sub-dimensional procurement in Member States and brings into play questions concerning the utilisation of sub-dimensional public procurement as a tool for policy implementation in Member States. The percentages of public contracts advertised in the Official Journal by Member States justify also the concerns that the results of these efforts will not change the ingrained habits of nationalistic procurement overnight.

The above background concerning transparency and openness in the public markets brings into play questions relating to the impact of competitiveness on the public procurement markets of the Member States. Does low transparency in public markets imply low competitiveness and what is the interplay between protectionist public purchasing patterns and *national champions*? As already indicated above, the majority of public procurement contracts are awarded without prior advertisement, and if one is prepared to accept the argument of excessive bureaucracy and the implied costs in transparent public procurement procedures, the question that follows is *who is awarded those contracts*. If competitive indigenous suppliers were awarded the majority of public contracts, then the failure of the principle of transparency has had minimal effect on purchasing patterns; on the other hand if uncompetitive indigenous suppliers were awarded the majority of public contracts, then the protectionist procurement pattern would provide evidence of existing discriminatory industrial sustainability attributable to long-dependency relations between the industries concerned and the contracting authorities in question.

In order to establish the interrelation between low transparency in public procurement and industrial competitiveness in a Member State, a number of industries / sectors representing more than 80 % of the total industrial output of the Member States have been under investigation by the European Commission[44]. The investigation of these industries revealed

---

[44] Commission of the European Communities, *The Use of Negotiated Procedures as a*

a number of industrial sectors that enjoy protection by contracting authorities in the sense that the relevant public procurement import penetration ratios are relatively low. It was also revealed that the sectors in question were not internationalised, in the sense that they showed low export to production ratios and were relatively uncompetitive, in the sense that they presented low specialisation ratios.

When sectoral public procurement import penetration is low and the volume of public purchasing is met from domestic output, then the domestic industry in question would most probably be sustained through public procurement, if its competitiveness is low. It follows that public purchasing patterns, which survived the enactment of public procurement legislation may have sustained certain industries in the Member States and are responsible for perpetuating price discrepancies, attributed to factors other than quality, for public procurement within the European Community. Sectoral import penetration in public procurement denotes the amount of imports destined for the public markets. It also reveals the relative openness of the public market in question and it is useful to compare with the volume of public procurement which is met from domestic output. In theory, import penetration and public procurement met from domestic sources should cover the total volume of sectoral public procurement in a Member State.

On the other hand, the competitiveness of an industrial sector in a Member State can be determined by reference to the balance between export and production, which determines the degree of internationalisation of the sector in question as well as the production specialisation, which determines competitive and comparative advantages of the sector within the European Community. If a substantial proportion of sectoral public procurement is met from domestic output and the sectoral import penetration appears low, the sectoral public procurement market can be identified as protectionist. Moreover, when the industry in question has low export to production ratio, this might indicate its lack of internationalisation. However, the export to production ratio in itself cannot sufficiently support the argument of low competitiveness in an

---

*Non-Tariff Barrier in Public Procurement*, Brussels, 1995. The industries / sectors investigated included Chemicals & Pharmaceuticals, Heavy Steel Structures, Mechanical Engineering, Office Machinery & Electronic Data Processing Equipment, Electrical Engineering, Instrument Engineering, Motor Vehicles, Aerospace, Railway Rolling-Stock, and Food Processing.

industry. For this purpose, the specialisation index, which measures the competitive advantage of an industry within the whole European Community, indicates whether the industry in question has competitive advantages over rival industries. When an industry has low internationalisation and low specialisation levels, there is a strong indication that it is sub-optimal (uncompetitive). When the above pattern is combined with high levels of domestic public purchasing, then the picture of sustainable trends through public procurement emerges.

Apparently, the relatively uncompetitive industries (mainly national champions) have been sustained over the years through public purchasing patterns which have survived the public procurement legislation. These patterns represent the most important non-tariff barrier for the integration of the public markets in the European Community. The findings run parallel with the relevant theories which investigate public procurement as an instrument of industrial policy of Member States[45].

Table 6.1 demonstrates the public procurement import penetration ratios between 1990-1995 in the industrial sectors under investigation. The indices reveal the relative openness of the public markets of Member States in relation to the relevant sectors. A high public procurement import penetration ratio does not always mean that the relevant sector is open to competition. It might indicate low domestic production, a fact which by definition justifies high imports for the public sector. Table 6.2. indicates the amount of public procurement demand which is met from domestic production in the Member States. This index should be read in conjunction with the import penetration ratio, as the combined result reflects the total volume of sector public procurement in the Member States. Table 6.3. reflects the number of industrial sectors which appear dependent on public purchasing in the relevant Member States. If more than three quarters of the domestic sectoral industrial output is absorbed through public purchasing, dependency patterns for the industry in question emerge. However, this assumption should not be construed in a negative connotation, as dependency purchasing patterns may indicate high levels of specialisation in the industry in question. Table 6.4. shows the less export-oriented industries under examination. Where the export volume of a particular sector appears to be less than a quarter of the total production volume, there is a strong indication that the industry in question is not

---

[45] For more details on the interplay between public purchasing and industrial policy see Chapter 7 of this book and the literature cited there.

internationalised. However, in itself, the export to production ratio does not reveal much, as the domestic demand may be stronger than the demand for exports. The above indicator becomes crucial in the evaluation of preferential purchasing schemes in the public sector when it is read in conjunction with the index revealing the specialisation levels of the industrial sectors in question in Table 6.5.

The consolidation of the above indices relevant to internationalisation and specialisation levels appears in Table 6.6, where the less competitive industries in the Member States are identified. Finally, in Table 6.7 the combination of the results from Tables 6.3 and 6.6 reveal the industrial sectors that most probably have been sustained through public procurement in the relevant Member States.

Table 6.1. Public procurement import penetration ratios (i), 1990 - 1995

| Product (NACE) | Belgium & Lux | Denmark | Germany | Italy | Portugal | Spain | UK | France | Ireland | Netherlands | Greece |
|---|---|---|---|---|---|---|---|---|---|---|---|
| Chemicals & Pharmaceuticals | 17.7 | 8.4 | 2.7 | 16.1 | 32.7 | 19.6 | 3.9 | 14.2 | 15 | 2.7 | 21.2 |
| Heavy Steel Structures | 5.6 | 15.9 | 2.3 | 4.5 | 64.6 | 13.7 | 4.9 | 3.54 | 54.9 | 4.9 | 71.3 |
| Mechanical Engineering | 35.8 | 36.3 | 29.8 | 32.7 | 34.2 | 24.6 | 29.2 | 14.2 | 19 | 31.2 | 40.7 |
| Office Machinery & EDP | 85.1 | 79.8 | 74.2 | 49.5 | 96.3 | 60 | 77 | 45 | 64 | 62.7 | 76.2 |
| Electrical Engineering | 52.7 | 53.5 | 25.4 | 24.3 | 54.1 | 28.9 | 32.4 | 18.4 | 18.2 | 34.1 | 65.2 |
| Motor Vehicles | 39.7 | 95.4 | 20.3 | 19.2 | 100 | 20 | 44 | 3 | 100 | 31.7 | 100 |
| Aerospace | 79.2 | 95.6 | 33.5 | 62.4 | 100 | 90 | 75.4 | 71 | 100 | 44.2 | 100 |
| Railway Rolling-Stock | 26.7 | 95.7 | 21.2 | 8.9 | 100 | 10 | 11.2 | 2 | 100 | 19.5 | 100 |
| Instrument Engineering | 10.4 | 67.2 | 8.2 | 24.5 | 86.2 | 48 | 32.1 | 45 | 89.4 | 14.8 | 91.3 |
| Food Processing | 68.3 | 54.5 | 24 | 35.6 | 15.2 | 39 | 35 | 28 | 48.3 | 38.5 | 21.6 |

Table 6.2. Public procurement met from domestic production (d), 1990 - 1995

| Product (NACE) | Belgium & Lux | Denmark | Germany | Italy | Portugal | Spain | UK | France | Ireland | Netherlands | Greece |
|---|---|---|---|---|---|---|---|---|---|---|---|
| Chemicals & Pharmaceuticals | 81.3 | 91.6 | 97.3 | 83.9 | 67.3 | 80.4 | 96.1 | 85.8 | 85 | 97.3 | 78.8 |
| Heavy Steel Structures | 94.4 | 84.1 | 97.7 | 95.5 | 35.4 | 86.3 | 95.1 | 96.5 | 45.1 | 95.1 | 28.7 |
| Mechanical Engineering | 74.2 | 63.7 | 69.2 | 67.3 | 65.8 | 25.5 | 30.8 | 84.1 | 81 | 68.8 | 59.3 |
| Office Machinery & EDP | 14.9 | 20.2 | 15.8 | 50.5 | 3.7 | 40 | 23 | 55 | 36 | 37.3 | 23.7 |
| Electrical Engineering | 47.3 | 46.5 | 74.6 | 75.7 | 45.9 | 31.1 | 67.6 | 81.6 | 81.8 | 65.9 | 34.8 |
| Aerospace | 20.8 | 4.4 | 67.5 | 37.6 | - | 10 | 24.6 | 29 | - | 55.8 | - |
| Motor Vehicles | 60.3 | 4.6 | 79.7 | 80.8 | - | 80 | 56 | 97 | - | 69.3 | - |
| Railway Rolling-Stock | 73.3 | 4.3 | 79.8 | 91.1 | - | 90 | 90 | 98 | - | 80.5 | - |
| Instrument Engineering | 89.6 | 32.8 | 91.8 | 75.5 | 13.8 | 52 | 67.9 | 55 | 10.6 | 85.2 | 8.7 |
| Food processsing | 31.7 | 45.5 | 76 | 74.4 | 84.8 | 61 | 65 | 72 | 51.7 | 61.5 | 78.4 |

- : indicates no domestic production

Table 6.3. Domestic industries prone to be sustained through public procurement (d>75), 1990 - 1995

| Product (NACE) | Belgium & Lux | Denmark | Germany | Italy | Portugal | Spain | UK | France | Ireland | Netherlands | Greece |
|---|---|---|---|---|---|---|---|---|---|---|---|
| Chemicals & Pharmaceuticals | ■ | ■ | ■ | ■ | | ■ | ■ | ■ | ■ | ■ | ■ |
| Heavy Steel Structures | ■ | | ■ | ■ | | ■ | ■ | ■ | | ■ | |
| Mechanical Engineering | | | | | | | | | | | |
| Office Machinery & EDP | | | | | | | | | | | |
| Electrical Engineering | | | ■ | ■ | | | | ■ | ■ | | |
| Aerospace | | | | | | | | | | | |
| Motor Vehicles | | | ■ | | | ■ | ■ | ■ | | | |
| Railway Rolling-Stock | ■ | | | | | | | | | ■ | |
| Instrument Engineering | ■ | | ■ | | | | | | | ■ | |
| Food processing | | | | | ■ | | | | | | ■ |

Table 6.4. Less export-oriented industries (e<25), 1990 - 1995

| Product (NACE) | Belgium & Lux | Denmark | Germany | Italy | Portugal | Spain | UK | France | Ireland | Netherlands | Greece |
|---|---|---|---|---|---|---|---|---|---|---|---|
| Chemicals & Pharmaceuticals | 25.3 | 8.2 | 29.3 | 32 | 5.1 | 12.4 | 14.8 | 21.6 | 24 | 14.8 | 5 |
| Heavy Steel Structures | 19.8 | 3.1 | 54.2 | 45 | 1.3 | 2.4 | 8.2 | 10.3 | 40.5 | 55.4 | 1 |
| Mechanical Engineering | 2.1 | 2.7 | 8.9 | 13 | 0.9 | 3.9 | 7.3 | 27.1 | 69.6 | 6.3 | 0.2 |
| Office Machinery & EDP | 7.9 | 10.4 | 24.2 | 25.4 | - | 5.1 | 21.2 | 32.1 | 131 | 14.1 | 1 |
| Electrical Engineering | 15.1 | 9.1 | 19.4 | 36.9 | 1.2 | 7.8 | 15.4 | 35 | 41 | 21.2 | 0.2 |
| Aerospace | 0.9 | - | 32.1 | 7.4 | - | 5.6 | 27 | 48.5 | - | 21.3 | - |
| Motor Vehicles | 14.7 | - | 25.2 | 23.4 | - | 10.1 | 19 | 35.7 | - | 17.7 | 1 |
| Railway Rolling-Stock | 1.1 | 0.1 | 1.9 | 0.9 | - | 1.3 | 2.2 | 55.5 | - | 2.1 | 0.6 |
| Instrument Engineering | 2.4 | 8.7 | 19.7 | 5.2 | - | 2.1 | 24.4 | 39.9 | - | 42 | - |
| Food processing | 14.8 | 5.2 | 12.1 | 29.4 | 19.3 | 39.8 | 21.1 | 43.1 | - | | 4.5 |

- : indicates no domestic production

Table 6.5. Less Specialised industries (s<1.5), 1990 - 1995

| Product (NACE) | Belgium & Lux | Denmark | Germany | Italy | Portugal | Spain | UK | France | Ireland | Netherlands | Greece |
|---|---|---|---|---|---|---|---|---|---|---|---|
| Chemicals & Pharmaceuticals | 1.9 | 0.5 | 2.1 | 1.9 | 0.5 | 0.7 | 1.9 | 1.5 | 3.3 | 2 | 0.4 |
| Heavy Steel Structures | 2.1 | 0.4 | 1.9 | 1.5 | 0.9 | 1.2 | 1.1 | 2.1 | 0.9 | 1.7 | 0.5 |
| Mechanical Engineering | 1.5 | 0.2 | 2 | 2 | 0.7 | 1.1 | 1.3 | 1.3 | 0.1 | 1.3 | - |
| Office Machinery & EDP | 1.6 | 0.9 | 0.9 | 1.9 | 0.8 | 0.9 | 1.2 | 0.8 | 0.9 | 1.4 | - |
| Electrical Engineering | 1.2 | 0.6 | 1.5 | 1.1 | 0.9 | 1 | 1.2 | 0.9 | 1.2 | 1.2 | - |
| Aerospace | 0.9 | - | 1.9 | 1.9 | - | 0.9 | 2.8 | 1.8 | - | 2.4 | - |
| Motor Vehicles | 1.8 | - | 1.9 | 1.5 | - | 1.5 | 1.3 | 1.2 | - | 1.3 | 0.7 |
| Railway Rolling-Stock | 1.9 | - | 2.5 | 1.9 | 0.3 | 1.1 | 1.3 | 0.9 | - | 2 | 0.7 |
| Instrument Engineering | 0.9 | 0.3 | 1.5 | 2 | 0.5 | 0.9 | 1.8 | 0.7 | - | 1.8 | - |
| Food processing | 1.4 | 0.7 | 0.9 | 2.1 | 1.1 | 2 | 1.2 | 1.4 | 1.8 | 1.1 | 1.2 |

- : indicates no domestic production

Table 6.6. Less competitive industries (e<25 + s<1.5), 1990 - 1995

| Product (NACE) | Belgium & Lux | Denmark | Germany | Italy | Portugal | Spain | UK | France | Ireland | Netherlands | Greece |
|---|---|---|---|---|---|---|---|---|---|---|---|
| Chemicals & Pharmaceuticals |  |  |  |  | ✓ | ✓ | ✓ | ✓ |  |  | ✓ |
| Heavy Steel Structures |  | ✓ |  |  | ✓ | ✓ | ✓ |  |  |  | ✓ |
| Mechanical Engineering | ✓ | ✓ |  |  | ✓ | ✓ |  |  | ✓ |  | ✓ |
| Office Machinery & EDP | ✓ |  | ✓ |  |  | ✓ | ✓ |  | ✓ |  | ✓ |
| Electrical Engineering | ✓ |  |  |  |  | ✓ |  |  | ✓ |  | ✓ |
| Aerospace | ✓ |  |  | ✓ |  |  |  |  |  |  |  |
| Motor Vehicles |  |  |  |  |  | ✓ | ✓ |  | ✓ |  | ✓ |
| Railway Rolling-Stock | ✓ | ✓ |  |  |  | ✓ | ✓ |  |  |  | ✓ |
| Instrument Engineering | ✓ |  |  |  |  |  | ✓ |  |  |  |  |
| Food processing | ✓ |  |  |  |  | ✓ |  |  |  |  | ✓ |

Table 6.7. Industries sustained through public procurement, 1990 - 1995

| Product (NACE) | Belgium & Lux | Denmark | Germany | Italy | Portugal | Spain | UK | France | Ireland | Netherlands | Greece |
|---|---|---|---|---|---|---|---|---|---|---|---|
| Chemicals & Pharmaceuticals | | ▓ | | | | ▓ | ▓ | ▓ | | | ▓ |
| Heavy Steel Structures | | ▓ | | | | ▓ | ▓ | | | | |
| Mechanical Engineering | | | | | | | | | | | |
| Office Machinery & EDP | | | | | | | | | | | |
| Electrical Engineering | | | ▓ | | | | | | ▓ | | |
| Aerospace | | | | | | | | | | | |
| Motor Vehicles | | | | ▓ | | | | | | | |
| Railway Rolling-Stock | | | | | | ▓ | ▓ | | | | |
| Instrument Engineering | ▓ | | | | | | | | | | |
| Food processing | | | | | ▓ | | | | | | ▓ |

The sources used for the above analysis include a number of documents which are not publicly available as well as numerous statistical reports from Eurostat, VISA STATISTICS and the Member States' relevant statistical authorities:

- European Commission, The Cost of Non-Europe in Public Sector Procurement, 1990.
- European Commission, "Statistical Performance Indicators for Keeping Watch over Public Procurement", 1992.
- Economic and Financial Outlook, National Westminster Bank 1994; Economic Outlook, OECD, December 1994;.
- European Commission, The Effect of the Opening-up of Public Procurement to Foreign Direct Investment, 1995.
- European Commission, The Use of Negotiated Procedures as a Non-Tariff Barrier in Public Procurement, Brussels, 1995.

# 7 Policy Choices and the Regulation of Public Procurement in the Common Market

As with every form of public spending, public procurement has an impact on other government policies. The application of public purchasing as an instrument in implementing related policies has been a bone of controversy in Member States, as described in the case law of the European Court of Justice which condemned national laws and administrative practices that allowed the use of public procurement as a tool of policy. There are three main government policies that are closely related with public procurement and are the subject of the following analysis: regional development policies, social policies and finally industrial policies. These policies have been promoted through preferential or strategic public purchasing in the past, although the enactment of the public procurement legislation, theoretically speaking, leaves little margin for such perpetuation. However, provisions in the European Directives and rulings of the European Court of Justice invite further examination of the interaction of public procurement with related policies.

European Institutions seemed to have underestimated the complementarity of public procurement of the Member States with public policy choices. Having said that, there is also an inherent element of contradiction in the aims and objectives of the whole exercise of integrating the public markets in the European Union. The conceptualisation of public purchasing as a budgetary exercise appears to intentionally exclude the public policy choice element which has always been associated with it. It would be rather simplistic to assume that by the mere achievement of savings for the public sector through the application of the public procurement rules, the aims and objectives of the Treaty of Rome and the Maastricht Treaty have been realised. The achievement of "nominal savings" in public purchasing exercises leaves inevitably a large area of socio-economic policies *in limbo*. In most cases, the exercise of public purchasing through budgetary constraints (public sector savings) triggers policy choices which certainly have an economic impact. After all the attempts of European Institutions to stimulate the demand side of public procurement (the contracting authorities) in the Member States one could justifiably question the relative slow progress and the underlying reasons behind such a recalcitrant rejection of the envisaged competitive regime in public markets.[1] The answer seems pretty simple, although cynical in terms of reference to commitment to the European Integration process and the completion and functioning of a genuinely common market in Europe. By perpetuating discriminatory and preferential public purchasing, Member States pay attention to immediate needs relating to domestic / national priorities such as balance of payments, sustainability of strategic industries, employment and last but not least national pride. This exercise, in terms of the envisaged integrated public markets of the European Union represents a sub-optimal allocation of resources (human and capital) throughout the common market at the expense of the public sector, which pays more than it should for equivalent or even better products or deliveries. It is tantamount to geographical market segmentation imposed by the demand side on the supply side (the industry), with a view to determining and controlling the latter as far as its activities vis-à-vis the public sector is concerned. It should be borne in mind that the supply side is theoretically unrestricted in servicing private markets in the respective Member States.

One should never overlook the implications of public purchasing on the application of related policies in Member States and the European Union as a whole.[2] The aim and objective of the regulation of public purchasing in the common market has to a large extent acquired an "industrial policy background", which mainly focuses on the achievement

---

[1] Commission of the European Communities, *The Use of Negotiated Procedures as a Non-Tariff Barrier in Public Procurement*, Brussels, 1995.
[2] See S. Arrowsmith, *Public Procurement as an Instrument Policy and the Impact of Market Liberalisation*, op. cit.

of savings for the public sector and the much desired restructuring and adjustment of the European industrial base. However, public spending in the form of procurement is indissolubly linked with adjacent policies and agendae in all Member States of the European Union. The most important policy associated with public purchasing is social policy. Such an argument finds justification in two reasons: the first relates to the optimal utilisation of human resources in industries supplying the public sector; the second reason acquires a strategic dimension, in the sense that public purchasing serves aims and objectives stipulated in the Treaty of Rome and its amending Maastricht Treaty, such as social cohesion, combating of long-term unemployment, and finally the achievement of acceptable standards of living.[3]

The underlying objectives of the European regime on public procurement relating to enhanced competition and unobstructed market access in the public sector at first sight appear incompatible with the social dimension of European integration, particularly in an era where recession and economic stagnation has revealed unemployment as its main characteristic. All other things being equal,[4] the award of public contracts in the Member States of the European Union can only be based on two criteria: i) the lowest price or ii) the most economically advantageous offer. Contracting authorities have absolute discretion in adopting the award criterion under which they wish to award their public contracts. The lowest price award criterion is mostly utilised when the procurement process is relatively straightforward and combined with open procedures. On the other hand, restricted and negotiated procedures are utilised in relation with the most economically advantageous offer award criterion and suited for more complex procurement schemes.[5]

The lowest price criterion is self-explanatory.[6] The tenderer who submits the cheapest offer must be awarded the contract. Subject to the

---

[3] See J. Carr, *New Roads to Equality: Contract Compliance for the United Kingdom*, Fabian Society, No. 517. Also, Institute of Personnel Management, *Contract Compliance: The United Kingdom Experience*, 1987.

[4] For example in selection and prequalification of candidates and the procedures utilised for the award of public contracts (open, restricted or negotiated).

[5] See C. Bovis, *The award of public procurement contracts under the framework of EC Public Procurement Directives*, Journal of Business Law, Autumn Issue 1993, Vol.1, p.p. 56-78.

[6] Article 26(1)(a) of Directive 93/36; Article 30(1)(a) of Directive 93/37; Article 34(1)(b) of Directive 93/38; Article 36(1)(b) of Directive 92/50.

qualitative criteria and financial and economic standing, contracting authorities do not rely on any other factor than the price quoted to complete the contract. The reasons for utilising the lowest price criterion are its simplicity, its speed and finally the less qualitative considerations during the evaluation of tenders. On the other hand, the appreciation of what is the most economically advantageous tender offer[7] is to be made on a series of factors and determinants chosen by the contracting entity for the particular contract in question. These factors include: price, delivery or completion date, running costs, cost-effectiveness, profitability, technical merit, product or work quality, aesthetic and functional characteristics, after-sales service and technical assistance, commitments with regards to spare parts and components and maintenance costs, security of supplies. The Court of Justice in a recent case,[8] following its previous case law,[9] reiterated the flexible and wide interpretation of the relevant award criterion and had no difficulty in declaring that contracting authorities may use the most economically advantageous offer as award criterion by choosing the factors which they want to apply in evaluating tenders, provided these factors are mentioned, in hierarchical order in the invitation to tender and or the contract documents. The most economically advantageous offer as an award criterion represents a flexible framework for contacting authorities wishing to insert a qualitative parameter in the award process of a public contract. Needless to say, price, as a quantitative parameter plays an important role in the evaluation stage of tenders, as the meaning of "economically advantageous" could well embrace financial considerations in the long-run. So, if the qualitative criteria of a particular bid compensate for its more expensive price, potential savings in the long-run could not be precluded.[10]

It is not clear whether the choice of the two above mentioned award criteria has been intentional with a view to providing contracting authorities a margin of discretion to take into account social policy objectives when awarding their public contracts, or if it merely reflects an

---

[7] Article 26(1)(b) of Directive 93/36; Article 30(1)(b) of Directive 93/37; Article 34(1)(a) of Directive 93/38; Article 36(1)(a) of Directive 92/50.
[8] Case C 324/93, *R. v. The Secretary of State for the Home Department, ex.p . Evans Medical Ltd and Macfarlan Smith Ltd.*
[9] Case 31/87, *Gebroeders Beenjes v. The Netherlands*, [1988] ECR 4635, op.cit.
[10] The quality aspects of a tender normally indicate a longer product cycle, less frequent maintenance intervals, better prospects of residualisation and finally, less frequent replacement scenaria.

element of flexibility which is considered necessary in modern purchasing transactions. If the most economically advantageous offer represents elements relating to quality of public purchasing other than price, an argument arises here supporting the fact that the enhancement of the socio-economic fabric is a "qualitative" element which can fall into the framework of the above criterion.[11] That sort of argument would take away the assumption that the award of public contracts is a pure *economic exercise*. On the other hand, if one is to insist that public procurement should reflect only *economic choices*, the social policy considerations that may arise from the award of public contracts would certainly have an economic dimension attached to them, often in public service activities which are parallel to public procurement. To what extent contracting authorities should contemplate such elements remains unclear. The legislation remains silent in such matters and the only acceptable solution could come from the European Court of Justice, when interpreting public procurement law.

## Social policy objectives in the award of public contracts

### *The notion of contract compliance*

Social policy considerations in relation to public procurement have been associated with the term *"contract compliance"*. Contract compliance is a system of public procurement whereby, unless the supply side (the industry) complies with certain conditions relating to social policy measures,[12] contracting authorities can lawfully exclude it from selection, qualification and award procedures for public contracts. The concept is well known in North American jurisdictions and in particular in the United States,[13] as it has been in operation for some time in an attempt to reduce

---

[11] See C. Bovis, *"The eligibility of enterprises to participate in tenders for the award of Public Procurement contracts"*, European Business Law Review, January 1994, Vol.5, p.p. 1-36.

[12] For example, employment of certain percentages of ethnic minorities of religious groups, which otherwise face social exclusion and insurmountable obstacles in accessing labour markets.

[13] For a detailed analysis see P.E. Morris, *Legal Regulation of Contract Compliance:an Anglo-American Comparison*, Anglo-American Law Review, 1990, Vol.19.

racial and ethnic minority inequalities in the market. In European jurisdictions, the term *contract compliance* could be best defined as the range of secondary policies relevant to public procurement, which aim at combating discrimination on grounds of sex, race, religion or disability.[14] In North America, contract compliance focuses mainly on achieving some sort of equilibrium in the workforce market. Apparently, in both continents, the power of public purchasing as a tool capable of promoting social policy has been the subject of scepticism. Policies relevant to affirmative action or positive discrimination have caused a great deal of controversy, as they practically accomplish very little in rectifying labour markets equilibria. In addition to the practicality and effectiveness of such policies, serious reservations have been expressed with regard to their constitutionality,[15] since they could limit, actually and potentially, the principles of economic freedom and freedom of transactions.[16]

Contract compliance legislation and policy is familiar to most European Member States, although the enactment of public procurement Directives has changed dramatically the situation.[17] It should be mentioned here that the thrust of contract compliance in European jurisdictions is slightly different from the thrust of the application of similar types of policies in North American orders. The distinction lays in the fact that contract compliance in Europe originates in the need to preserve employment patterns rather than to rectify labour equilibria. In that sense, without contract compliance, there would be no labour market at all,

---

[14] See ILEA Contract Compliance Equal Opportunities Unit, *Contract Compliance: a brief history*, 1990, London.

[15] See Case 93-1841 (1995), *Adarand Constructors v. Pena*, before the United States Supreme Court. The Court questioned the constitutionality in the application of contract compliance as a potential violation of the equal protection component of the Fifth Amendment's Due Process Clause and ordered the Court of Appeal to reconsider the employment of socio-economic policy objectives in the award of federal public procurement contracts.

[16] For an overview of the Social Policy in North American systems, see C. Cnossen and C. Bovis, *The framework of social policy in federal states: An analysis of the law and policy on industrial relations in USA and Canada*, International Journal of Comparative Labour Law and Industrial Relations, vol.12, iss.2, p.p 131 - 148, June 1996.

[17] For example, in United Kingdom, every initiative relating to contract compliance has been outlawed by virtue of the 1988 Local Government Act. Contract compliance from a public law perspective has been examined by T. Daintith, in *Regulation by Contract: the new prerogative*, C.L.P, 1979, Vol. 32.

where in North America a certain degree of market existence is presupposed, as a prerequisite for the equilibrium rectification. The argument goes further to reveal that the social structure between the two continents appears rather heterogeneous, with different agendae and priorities in law and policy making. Thus, contract compliance, as a system for procurement delivery, acquires a clearly distinctive dimension. In North American jurisdictions, contract compliance may cause some constitutional questions over its compatibility with fundamental freedoms. In European legal orders, contract compliance represents a potential non-tariff barrier for the economic integration of the common market, as it may perpetuate preferential public purchasing which could distort or prevent the level of the envisaged workable and effective competition. The completion of the common market and the priorities in achieving an acceptable degree of liberalisation of the basic freedoms described in the Treaty of Rome, have, to a large extent, influenced national administrations in rethinking the whole issue of contract compliance and questions on its compatibility vis-à-vis fundamental principles of European Law.[18] It should be mentioned here that during the Uruguay Round of the GATT, the European Commission raised a number of objections to the US counterparts relating to contract compliance and its compatibility with the principles of liberalisation of pubic procurement under the Agreement on Government Procurement, which existed since the Tokyo Round.[19] Clearly, trade deflections and protected markets in public contracts emerged as a result of the application of contract compliance clauses, as the low penetration as well as the low tradability of public contracts between US and the European Community revealed.

The position of European Institutions on contract compliance has been addressed in two cases before the European Court of Justice,[20] where its possible utilisation in public procurement by contracting authorities was examined. Interestingly enough, the timing of those cases (late eighties) reflects the background approaches to public procurement by policy

---

[18] See S. Arrowsmith, *The Legality of Secondary Procurement Policies under the Treaty of Rome and the Works Directive*, Public Procurement Law Review, 1992, Vol. 1. p. 410.

[19] See C. Bovis, *Extra-territorial effects in the application of the EC Utilities Directive and the Public Procurement trade war between US and EC*, Utilities Law Review, Summer Issue 1993, Vol II, p.p. 84-87.

[20] See case 31/87, *Gebroeders Beenjes B.V v. The Netherlands*, [1989] ECR 4365. Also see case C 360/89, *Commission v. Italy*, judgment of July 3 1992,

makers and contracting authorities respectively. At the same time of the above litigation, the Community was faced with the project of completing its internal market, by abolishing any actual or potential non-tariff barrier and obstacle to intra-community trade. The European Institutions (the Commission and the Court) have restrictively interpreted the relevant provisions of the public procurement Directives, when confronted with employment policy parameters in the public procurement process. The Court of Justice maintained that contract compliance with reference to domestic or local employment cannot be used as a selection criterion in tendering procedures for the award of public contracts. The selection of tenderers is a process which is based on an exhaustive list of technical and financial requirements expressly stipulated in the relevant Directives and the insertion of contract compliance as a selection and qualification requirement would be considered *ultra vires*.

The Court also opened an interesting debate on the integral dimensions of contract compliance and differentiated between the *positive* and *negative* approaches. The concept of positive approach within contract compliance encompasses all measures and policies imposed by contracting authorities on tenderers as suitability criteria for their selection in public procurement contracts. Such positive action measures and policies intend to complement the actual objectives of public procurement which are confined in economic and financial parameters and are based on a transparent and predictable legal background. Although the complementarity of contract compliance with the actual aims and objectives of the public procurement regime was acknowledged, the Court (and the European Commission) were reluctant in accepting such an over-flexible interpretation of the Directives and based on the literal interpretation of the relevant provisions disallowed positive actions of a social policy dimension as part of the selection criteria for tendering procedures in public procurement.

However, it should be mentioned that contract compliance can incorporate not only unemployment considerations, but also promote equality of opportunities and eliminate sex or race discrimination in the relevant market. Indeed, the Directives on public procurement stipulate that the contracting authority may require tenderers to observe national provisions of employment legislation when they submit their offers. The ability to observe and conform with national employment laws in a Member State may constitute a ground of disqualification and exclusion of the defaulting firm from public procurement contracts. In fact, under such interpretation, contract compliance may be a factor of selection criteria specified in the Directives, as it contains a *negative approach* (obey otherwise excluded) to legislation and measures relating to social policy.[21]

On the other hand, in a landmark case before it,[22] the Court ruled that social policy considerations, can only be part of award criteria in public procurement, and especially in cases where the most economically advantageous offer is selected. The Court accepted that the latter award criterion contains factors and parameters that are not exhaustively defined in the Directives. It should be mentioned that contact compliance can be utilised only when it is part of a contractual obligation of the public contract and does not run contrary to the basic principles of the Treaty. The Court maintained that a contractual condition relating to the employment of long term unemployed persons is compatible with the Public Works Directive 71/305, if it has no direct or indirect discriminatory effect on tenders from other Member States.[23] Furthermore, it must be mentioned in the tender notice.[24] In other words, it must fall under Article 29(4), which provides that an award may be based on criteria of a different nature within the framework of rules whose aim is to give preference to certain tenderers by way of aid (other than that in Article 90 EC), on condition that the rules invoked are in conformity with the Treaty, in particular Article 92 et seq. Rejection of a contract on the grounds of a contractor's inability to employ long-term unemployed persons has no relation to the checking of the contractors' suitability on the basis of their economic and financial standing and their technical knowledge and ability, or to the criteria for the award of contracts referred to in Article 29 of Directive 79/305 (lowest price tender or most economically advantageous offer). Derogation from this framework is permitted only with regard to preference schemes, which by definition have a discriminatory effect on tender competition for the award of a contract. It seems peculiar, how the Court brought under the preference scheme exception [Art 29(4)] clauses

---

[21] It should be mentioned that adherence to health and safety laws have been considered by a British court as part of the technical requirements specified in the Works Directive for the process of selection of tenderers; see *General Building and Maintenance v. Greenwich Borough Council*, [1993] IRLR 535.
[22] Case 31/87, *Gebroeders Beenjes B.V v. The Netherlands*, [1989] ECR 4365.
[23] In USA it is a common practice to include such clauses in public procurement contracts. These are known as contract compliance.
[24] See *Bellini Case* 28/86, [1987] ECR 3347.

and conditions for the award of a contract, provided they have no direct or indirect discriminatory effect on contractors from other Member States. (In other cases the Court did not permit clauses reserving a percentage of public procurement contracts to undertakings established in a particular area, on the grounds that they impede intra-Community trade, thus falling foul of Article 30 and 90 EC).

It is interesting here to examine the award of public housing schemes, as a forum for the application of contract compliance clauses related primarily to employment, vocational training and other socio-economic parameters. The Public Works Directives specifically lay down provisions which cover the award procedures of contracts relating to public housing. The award of public housing contracts[25] may deviate from the normal regime of the Directive for the purpose of selecting a contractor who meets the requirements specified by the public authority. The design and construction of a public housing scheme, as well as the size and complexity of the project, as well as the estimated duration of the work involved, require that planning be based from the outset on close collaboration within a team comprising representatives of the contracting authorities, experts and the contractor to be responsible for carrying out the works.

Contract compliance in public procurement needs to be addressed at policy and law making levels, particularly in the light of the 1996 European Commission's Green Paper on Public Procurement.[26] With so much at stake, in regulating the public procurement markets of the Member States, the social policy dimensions of such an exercise should be carefully discussed at Community level and the impact of its implementation through public purchasing should be thoroughly weighted. There are arguments both for and against incorporating social policy considerations in public procurement.[27] The most important argument in favour focuses on the ability of public procurement to promote parts of the Member States' social policy, with particular reference to long-term unemployment, equal distribution of income, social exclusion and the protection of minorities. Under such a positively oriented approach, public

---

[25] Article 9 of Directive 93/37.
[26] See the *Green Paper on Public Procurement in the European Union: Exploring the way forward*, European Commission 1996.
[27] See K. Kruger, R. Nielsen, N. Brunn, *European Public Contracts in a Labour Law Perspective* DJOF Publicsing, 1997.

purchasing could be regarded as an instrument of policy in the hands of national administrations with a view to rectifying social equilibria. Contract compliance in public procurement could also cancel the stipulated aims and objectives of the liberalisation of the public sector in the European Union. The regulation of public markets focuses on economic considerations and competition. Adherence to social policy factors could derail the whole process, as the public sector will pay more for its procurement by extra or hidden cost in the implementation of contract compliance in purchasing policies.[28]

*The transfer of undertakings and employees' protection in the context of public procurement*

The Acquired Rights Directive 77/187[29] aims at protecting the interests of employees where an undertaking or a part of an undertaking is transferred from one person to another. In such cases, the transferee acquires not only the business operation but also becomes responsible for the obligations of the transferor vis-à-vis the employees of the undertaking, which arise out of their employment contracts or under legislation, and is also bound by any existing collective agreements. In simple terms, this implies that the transferee must continue to employ the existing workforce, and that the existing wages and other conditions of employment continue to apply. If employees are dismissed, the new employer will be liable to pay compensation for unfair dismissal, or for the applicable redundancy payments, as the case may be. Before any transfer of undertaking, the employees are guaranteed the right to be consulted about the transfer. Such consultation proviso is not only a procedural requirement for the transfer of an undertaking, but it is part of the substantive prerequisites for the *vires* of the transfer exercise.

The transfer of undertakings rules were adopted in 1977 and it was required by Member States to implement the relevant Directive into domestic laws. With the evolution of public procurement law and particularly the Public Services Directive, the compatibility and

---

[28] See C. Bovis, *Social Policy Considerations and The European Public Procurement regime*, International Journal of Comparative Labour Law and Industrial Relations, Summer issue, 1998.

[29] O.J. C 61/26, [1977]. The Commission's proposal for the new Aqcuired Rights Dirtective can be found in O.J. C 274 [1994]

complementarity of the two set of rules were tested at European level. The rationale behind the two Directives appears totally differentiated. Not only the legal basis for their adoption, but also the whole thrust and applicability of the regime envisaged reveals the clear *antithesis* of the policy makers in their attempts to achieve the objectives stipulated in the preambles of the Directives. The Acquired Rights Directive has as its main objective the protection of employees in cases of transfer of undertakings. This of course would embrace not only private sector transactions, where business and commercial operations are transferred between individuals, but also it could cover a substantial part of privatisation in European Member Sates. On the other hand, the Public Services Directive attempts to co-ordinate the award procedures for public contracts relating to the performance of a service, as defined in the United Nation Nomenclature of Product and Service Classification. The aim and objective of the latter Directive is to maximise savings for the public sector and enhanced competitive trends in intra-community trade of services, without discrimination on nationality grounds and preferential treatment.

The relevance of the Acquired Rights Directive with the public procurement regime became clear when contracting authorities started *testing the market* in an attempt to define whether the provision of works or services from a commercial operator could be cheaper than that from the in-house team. This is the notion of *contracting out*, an exercise which aims at achieving potential savings and efficiency gains for contracting authorities. Contracting out differs from privatisation to the extent that the former represents a transfer of undertaking only, whereas the latter denotes transfer of ownership. The application of the transfer of undertakings rules in contracting out cases has the important consequence that the external bidder must engage the authority's former employees on the same conditions as they enjoyed under the authority itself. The other consequence is that the whole contracting out exercise when filtered through the transfer of undertakings rules would render the achievement of savings by changing the conditions of the workforce virtually impossible.

The Directive proclaimed its inapplicability in cases where the undertaking was not in the nature of a commercial venture; this proviso was interpreted as exclusive of contracting out by government. The impact of the Transfer of Undertakings Directives in the context of public procurement context was felt in a recent decision of the European Court of

Justice[30] which maintained that the Directive does not permit such a limitation. Thus it became apparent that contracting out by government was covered, and a transfer of an undertaking may take place where the government contracts out to the private sector a function previously carried out in-house[31] and vice versa, viz. where the contracting authority takes back in-house a service formerly contracted out. The exact circumstances in which a transfer of an undertaking through contracting out occurs depends upon the transfer retaining its identity. This test was laid down by the European Court of Justice.[32] However, the "retention of identity" test can only be satisfied when the undertaking transferred represents *substantially the same* or *similar activities*,[33] as well as it relates to a *stable economic entity.*[34]

The application of the Transfer of Undertakings Directive in public procurement contracts poses a significant obstacle to the integration of public markets in the sense that the policy choices are painfully apparent. Contracting authorities face a critical dilemma when placing public contracts. Is it the protection of employees or the achievement of savings that is the underlying objective of the contracting out exercise? Are the two legal regimes compatible or mutually exclusive? The author admits to considerable scepticism in not only striking a balance between the apparently contradictory objectives of the legal regimes, but also in the applicability of transfer of undertakings rules to public procurement contracts. The transfer of undertakings rules explicitly rule out the realisation of savings based on measures relating to employment terms and conditions. The question that arises here is how the private sector could realistically outprice the in-house team of a contracting authority when it is bound to observe constraints imposed by the transfer of undertakings rules. Also, how could the potential savings be materialised, if labour as a factor of production (the employees of a contacting authority in a transfer of undertakings scenario) is to remain intact. Factors in the production

---

[30] Case C 29/91, *Dr Sophie Redmond Stichting v. Bartol*, IRLR 369.
[31] Case C 382/92, *Commission v. United Kingdom*, [1994] ECR 1.
[32] Case 24/85, *Spijkers v. Gebroders Benedik Abbatoir CV*, [19986] ECR 1, 1123. Case C 209/91, *Rask v. ISS Kantinservice*, [1993] ECR 1. Case C 392/92, *Schmidt v. Spar und Leihkasse der fruherer Amter Bordersholm, Kiel und Cronshagen*, [1994] ECR 1, 1320.
[33] Case C 392/92, *Schmidt v. Spar und Leihkasse der fruherer Amter Bordersholm, Kiel und Cronshagen*, [1994] ECR 1, 1320.
[34] Case C 48/94, *Rygaard v. Stro Molle Akustik*, judgment of September 19, 1995.

process other than labour, (technology, know-how) are readily available to the demand side and by no means should be deemed to be under the exclusive privilege of the supply side. If savings were to come through the application of these factors, what prohibits the demand side in introducing them in the process of delivering public service?

The Transfer of Undertakings Directive should not be conceived as a shift of employment responsibilities from the demand side to the supply side in the attempt to achieve savings for the public sector. Any transfer of undertaking presents striking similarities to industrial restructuring through the mode of outsourcing. In the private sector, such an exercise would inevitably have an impact on employment policies if it is to result in savings for the relevant organisation.

## The interrelation of Public Procurement with Regional Development Policy

A possible way of combating recession and its side effects (industrial decline, unemployment, social exclusion) is the enhancement of regionalism and the development of decentralised policies that can boost peripheral growth in the economy. A scenario like the above will need to incorporate not only the commitment of a central government towards regional economic development but also the participation of local and regional authorities in implementing the strategic plan. Regionalism and spatial economic development should focus on incentives aiming at growth, optimal allocation of resources, operating as much as possible within a regime of workable and effective competition. Regional development policies, centralised or decentralised, should have as their priority agendae small and medium sized enterprises which are often located in less favoured regions, or regions of economic decline and industrial restructuring. The idea behind the above policies is to promote and enhance the market performance and participation of small and medium firms in order to achieve economic growth within a region. The concentration of policy makers on small and medium sized firms could also be justified by the fact that in real terms they represent the vast majority of businesses within European economies. Large firms often lack flexibility in adapting their strategies to new market requirements, where industrial restructure in most cases has been materialised by taking the form of voluntary or compulsory redundancies and workforce cuts. On the other hand, small firms appear more flexible in changes as they diversify their activities more effectively than large firms, without the need to have necessary recourse to labour cuts. It has been suggested that economic recovery from the present recession will emerge from the small enterprises which will first detect the signals of growth.

The policies which aim to assist small and medium sized enterprises focus on participation incentives in the markets,[35] the latter being defined as private or public markets. These policies adopt regionalism as their objective and endeavour to promote a decentralised economic growth through the periphery.[36] Regional policies are sophisticated measures aiming at optimal allocation of resources throughout a state and equal distribution of income amongst its citizens. Small and medium sized enterprises occupy a large share in European economies[37] and should be considered as one of the most important factors of Europe's industrial policy. The economic importance of the Small and Medium Sized Enterprises in the market[38] could be attributed to their ability to:
- increase efficiency and enhance macro-economic growth
- promote industrial re-structuring and adjustment
- create the opportunity for industrial and sectoral exploitation of particular skills and advantages
- facilitate better allocation of resources and more equal income distribution

In the European Union, small and medium sized enterprises account for a remarkable 95% of the total number of enterprises (average figure throughout the European Union). Their commercial activities represent 64% of the annual turnover in the Union (average figure) and they employ 70% of the total workforce in Europe (average figure).[39]

Bearing in mind the economic magnitude of public procurement in Europe (15% of the European Union's GDP and approximately 560

---

[35] European Commission *Action Programme for SMEs* (COM(86) 445).
[36] European Commission, *Public Procurement: Regional and Social Aspects* (COM(89) 400).
[37] Commission of the European Communities, *SME TASK FORCE: SMEs and Public Procurement*, Brussels 1988.
[38] European Commission, *Promoting SME Participation in the Community* (COM(90) 166).
[39] Commission of the European Communities, *SME TASK FORCE: SMEs and Public Procurement*, Brussels 1988.

billion ECU), the participation of small and medium sized enterprises in public sector contracts accounts for 2.2% of the European Union's GDP and amounts approximately 94 billion ECU. This is translated to 15.3% of the share of the total participation of enterprises in public procurement.[40] It appears that although SMEs represent the vast majority of firms in Europe and are responsible for almost two thirds of the annual turnover, their share in public markets is limited.

Although the opening up of protected public procurement markets and the liberalisation of the public sector of the European Member States have been defined as priority objectives not only for the completion of the common market but also for the proper functioning of global markets, they pose serious obstacles and to some extent threats for small and medium sized firms[41]. Small and medium sized firms have often relied on regional preferences or other types of protectionism; they have developed long-standing dependency relations with a very limited number of buyers and their low competitiveness and quality augmented by the lack of economies of scale and the inefficient mobility of labour, capital and know-how constitute a real threat. Small and medium sized firms need extensive preparation in order to enter public markets. They need to adapt to high technical standards rather than depend on traditional relationships with established purchasers, which then will open their horizons to larger geographical markets. They have to familiarise themselves with the procedural requirements stipulated by European legislation and ensure that they meet quality assurance standards. Finally, they have to adopt and develop sophisticated marketing and management structures specifically designed for public sector contracts, a strategy which will be of substantial assistance to their future competitiveness.[42]

Policy makers at both domestic and European level face a dilemma in their attempts to promote the participation of small and medium sized firms in public procurement.[43] The dilemma lies in the choice of the most

---

[40] See C. Bovis, *Public Procurement and Small and Medium Sized Enterprises in the United Kingdom and the Republic of Ireland*, ACCA, Research Paper 17, 1996.

[41] European Commission, *SMEs participation in public procurement in the European Community* (SEC(92) 722).

[42] G. O'Brien, *Public Procurement and the Small or Medium Sized Enterprise*, Public Procurement Law Review, 1993, Vol. 2, p.82.

[43] *The Internal Market after 1992 - Meeting the Challenge.* Report to the E.C. Commission by the High Level Group on the Internal Market (Sutherland), November 1992.

appropriate method - framework for the promotion of SMEs participation in tendering procedures and the award of public contracts. The principal factors which have been claimed to inhibit small and medium sized enterprises in public procurement[44] include the relatively large size of the contracts, the difficulty in obtaining adequate information on forthcoming contracts, the shortage of language skills particularly in technical areas, the availability of time and the costs involved in preparing bids, the scare management resources, problems relating to specification of standards,[45] difficulties in certification in other Member States and obtaining quality assurance in other Member States, difficulties in achieving credibility in another Member State and finally delays in payment.[46] The most effective way to stimulate SMEs participation in public procurement and ensure for them a fair share of the awarded public contracts has been achieved through the operation of preference schemes.[47] So far, these schemes have been indissolubly linked with regional development policies, but since the completion of the Single Market (1992) they have been abolished, as they are deemed to contravene directly or indirectly the basic principle of non-discrimination on grounds of nationality stipulated in the Treaty of Rome.[48]

*Preference purchasing schemes*

Preference schemes have been indissolubly linked with regional development policies, but since the completion of the Single Market

---

[44] European Commission, *SMEs participation in public procurement in the European Community* (SEC(92) 722); European Commission *Action Programme for SMEs* (COM(86) 445); European Commission, *Public Procurement: Regional and Social Aspects* (COM(89) 400); European Commission, *Promoting SME Participation in the Community* (COM(90) 166).

[45] European Commission Recommendation (91/561/EC) of October 24, 1991, on the *standardisation of notices of public contracts* [1991] O.J. 217.

[46] Commission Staff Working Paper on the problem of the time taken to make payments in commercial transactions (SEC(92) (214).

[47] European Commission, *Public Procurement: Regional and Social Aspects* (COM(89) 400).

[48] Impact assessment studies undertaken by the European Commission (European Commission, Public Procurement: Regional and Social Aspects (COM(89) 400) showed that the operation of preference schemes had a minimal effect on the economies of the regions where they had been applied, both in terms of the volume of procurement contracts, as well as in terms of real economic growth attributed to the operation of such schemes.

(1992) they have been abolished, as they are deemed to contravene directly or indirectly the basic principle of non-discrimination on grounds of nationality stipulated in the Treaty of Rome. Preference schemes guaranteed a certain percentage of public procurement to local firms, a fact that has indicated the close interplay between public purchasing and state aids.[49] Along the above lines, preference schemes in the form of protectionist public procurement practices, when strategically exercised, have resulted in the evolution of vital industries for the state in question. The sustainability of *"national champions"* has brought about benefits for a sector or an industry, which, when protected from competition in the short-run, managed to achieve specialisation and internationalisation.

It is worth mentioning that the interpretation of preference schemes by the European Court of Justice has always been restrictive. The Commission brought Greece before the Court,[50] where the Commission brought an action under 169 EC procedure seeking the Court to declare the failure of the Greek State to fulfil its obligations under Article 30 EC and Directive 77/62. The case concerned conditions for the award of public supplies contracts, in particular, conditions of access to them. Advocate-General Mischo condemned a circular of the Minister of National Economy (Circular of 11-7-1983) which favoured domestic products in case of public supplies contracts. The circular imposed a co-efficient of 21% on prices of imported products. Italian courts sought a preliminary ruling from the Court in two cases in 1988. Both concerned supplies of pharmaceutical products to local health authorities. In the first one[51] the Court determined the effect which a preferential system reserving to undertakings established in certain regions of a national territory a proportion of public supplies contracts is likely to have on the free movement of goods. The system of the reserved quota of public supply contracts falls foul of Article 30 EC. It cannot be justified under the rule of reason of Article 36 EC, nor under Article 26 of Directive 77/62. It also stated that it is inconsistent with Article 30, even if it is considered as aid within the meaning of Article 92 EC. The second case[52] concerned

---

[49] See J.M. Fernadez Martin and O. Stehmann, *Product Market Integration versus Regional Cohesion in the Community* European Law Review, 1991, Vol. 16, p. 216.
[50] Case 84/86, *Commission v. Hellenic Republic*, not reported.
[51] Case 21/88, *Dupont de Nemours Italiana S.p.A v. Unita Sanitaria Locale No.2 di Carrara*, judgment of March 20, 1990, [1990] ECR 889.
[52] Case 351/88, *Lavatori Bruneau Slr. v. Unita Sanitaria Locale RM/24 di Monterotondo*, op.cit.

whether the reservation of a percentage of public supplies contracts (30%) to undertakings located in a specific area is incompatible with Article 30 EC, even if the measures fall under Article 92 EC.[53] The Commission also brought an action against Italy[54] in 1989 for declaration that the Italian Law laying down special provisions for accelerating the completion of public works was incompatible with Article 59 EC and European Directives on Public Works.[55] That law reserved a proportion of public works to sub-contractors whose registered offices were in the region where the works were to be carried out. The Court ruled that such provision had an actual or potential discriminatory effect on undertakings outside that particular region and other undertakings from Member States, thus being inconsistent with Article 59 EC. Furthermore, it represents a criterion of selection that is not mentioned in the Works Directives[56] and in particular does not reflect any of the requirements of an economic or technical nature provided for in Articles 25 and 26 of Directive 71/305. In 1990 Italy was again brought before the Court in Luxembourg for two cases; the first[57] concerned an application lodged by the Commission, and a declaration by the Court was sought that, Italy failed to fulfil its obligations under Directive 77/62 and 88/295. The *Unita Sanitaria Locale XI Genoa* (health authority) stipulated that, in order to enable tenderers to participate in a public supply contract, 50% of the minimum amount of supplies required to have been made over the preceding three years should have been supplies to public administration authorities. Although such a condition is absolutely inconsistent with the Supplies Directives, the Court did not proceed on the substance of the case and declared the action inadmissible, as the Commission did not observe the proceedings laid down in Article 169 EC.

There has been a great deal of controversy at European level whether preference schemes could ever conform with European Law and Policy. There are suggestions that the operation of preference schemes violates fundamental principles of the Treaty of Rome such as the free movement of goods, the right of establishment and the freedom to provide services; there is also the blunt violation of the principle of discrimination on grounds of nationality. On the other hand, the Treaty itself stipulates

---

[53] The same judgement as in 21/88 Dupont Case.
[54] Case 360/89, *Commission v. Italy*, [1992] ECR I 3401.
[55] Directives 71/305 and 89/440
[56] Articles 23 to 26 of Directive 71/305.
[57] Case 362/90, *Commission v. Italy*, judgment of March 31, 1992.

provisions for the development of economic and social cohesion and the operation of regional policies, mainly through market intervention mechanisms. There is also the provision relating to state aids, of course, within the limitations imposed by Community competition law and policy. The above framework reveals the interaction of the application of preference purchasing schemes with Community law and policy. A clear-cut distinction of what is and what is not compatible with Treaty provisions as far as preference schemes is concerned is not an easy exercise. As the Treaty of Rome and its amending Treaty of Maastrich comprise a set of legal and policy agendas which often appear contradictory in principle, a detailed analysis of the thrust of preferential purchasing schemes may shed some light on the picture.

One could suggest that the utilisation of preference schemes may fall under the ambit of state aids, which under the Treaty of Rome and the Maastricht Treaty are perfectly legitimate, provided they do not contravene with the principles, law and policy of competition in the common market. Hence, instead of grants and other forms of financial assistance to regions which are deemed in need of industrial restructuring and adjustment, public procurement may represent an alternative. State aids directed to less favoured regions rather constitute a *passive* form of restructuring, as the recipient of financial assistance (a particular industry or a particular public authority) would not have any direct or indirect or very limited involvement in the industrial restructuring process. Grants and direct financial assistance from Member States or from European Union Funds perpetuate the sub-optimal division of the European Union in different types of regions. It could be maintained that instead of encouraging economic growth and economic alignment of less favoured regions with developed ones, they continue to support uncompetitively peripheral areas in Europe. Public procurement as a form of state aid in pursuit of industrial policy objectives can benefit industries which are located in less favoured regions.[58] Such industries may not have access to opportunities for specialisation and to know-how, which constitute an enormous advantage and reinforce the position of the centrally located

---

[58] The *Du Pont de Nemour* case (case C 21/88, *Du Pont de Nemours Italiana SpA v. Unita Sanitaria Locale N.2 di Carrara*, [1990] ECR 889) implied the possibility of using public procurement as state aid. See the analysis of J.M. Fernadez Martin and O. Stehmann, *"Product Market Integration versus Regional Cohesion in the Community"*, European Law Review, 1991, Vol. 16, p. 216.

areas. The fact that in less favoured regions wages are low does not compensate the expectation for higher productivity, as production output either stagnates or decreases. Less favoured regions also lack the required infrastructure which will serve industrial development and as a consequence competitiveness is low. Furthermore, with the completion of the internal market, less favoured regions are also challenged to reach the average European performance level, when standards of quality and efficiency in traditional labour intensive industries are evolving rapidly. Regional policies based on traditional forms of financial assistance to less favoured regions in the European Union can only achieve a temporary balance between them and the fully developed - industrially intense regions. Such a balance will inevitably have sub-optimal effects, as neither production nor productivity is expected to increase. State aids do not contribute to industrial restructuring and adjustment, unless there is provision for spatial distribution of economic activities.

Although the utilisation of public procurement as a means of regional development policy in the form of state aids may not breach directly or indirectly primary Treaty provisions on free movement of goods, the right of establishment and the freedom to provide services, it is far from clear whether the European Commission and the Court of Justice could accept public procurement as a means of state aids. Prior notification of the measures or policies intended to be used as state aid to the European Commission, does not apparently legitimise such measures and absolves them from the draconian framework of Article 30 EC. The parallel applicability of Articles 92 EC and 30 EC, in the sense that national measures conceived as state aids must not violate the principle of free movement of goods, renders the thrust of regional policies through state aids practically ineffective. The Court of Justice seemed to have experimented with the question of the compatibility of Article 92 EC (state aids) with Article 30 (free movement of goods) in a number of cases where, initially, it was held that Article 90 EC and Article 30 EC are mutually exclusive, to the extent that the principle of free movement of goods could not apply to measures relating to state aids.[59] The acid test for such mutual exclusivity was the prior notification of such measures to the European Commission. However, the Court apparently departed from such position, when it applied Article 30 EC to a number of cases concerning

---

[59] See case 74/76, *Ianelli & Volpi Spa v. Ditta Paola Meroni*, [1977] 2 CMLR 688.

state aids, which had not been notified to the Commission.[60] Quite surprisingly, the Court brought notified state aids measures under the remit of the provision of free movement of goods in the *Du Pont de Nemours* case and reconsidered the whole framework of the mutual exclusivity of Articles 92 EC and 30 EC.

In addition to the above considerations, there is enough mileage in the argument that, if preference schemes, according to European Commission's data, appeared to have had a minimal effect on the market performance of firms in the less-favoured regions, their actual or potential effect on competition should be minimal. Thus, a *de minimis* formula could be applied. The attack of the inefficiency of preference schemes should focus rather on the method and the thrust of their application and less on their availability itself. It is important here to reiterate that the application of preference schemes, if properly planned, can achieve a desirable spatial policy at both domestic and European levels.[61]

The European Commission had declared the temporary character of such schemes and explicitly abolished them after the completion of the single market (1992). Preference schemes should be replaced by incentives for the participation of small and medium sized firms in public markets. These incentives should be backed up with clear and understandable policies and, of course, legislation. Indeed, the European Union has realised the importance of the above transition from preference schemes to incentives for regional firms' participation in public procurement. Apart from a number of Communications to the Council of Ministers referring to the problem of Small and Medium Sized Enterprises (SMEs) in the European Integration context, it has, in its legislation on public procurement, introduced provisions that could be regarded as an hybrid form of legislation on the small and medium sized firms in public procurement. All Directives on Public Procurement, influenced by the European Commission's Communications encourage the use of sub-contracting in the award of public contracts. Particularly, in public supplies contracts, the contracting entity in the invitation to tender may ask the tenderers on their intention to sub-contract to third parties part of the

---

[60] See case 18/84, *Commission v. France*, 1985, ECR 1339; case 103/84, *Commission v. Italy*, 1986, ECR 1759; also, case 244/81, *Commission v. Ireland*, 1982, ECR 4005.

[61] see J.M. Fernadez Martin and O. Stehmann, *Product Market Integration versus Regional Cohesion in the Community*, op.cit.

contract.[62] This reveals the importance of sub-contracting for regional development in public procurement.[63] In public works contracts, contracting authorities awarding the principal contract to a concessionaire may require him to subcontract to third parties at least 30% of the total work provided for by the principal contract. Additionally, the sub-division by public entities of contracts into lots could facilitate SMEs participation in their award and finally, the reduction of cost of tendering for public contracts through the introduction of simplification and standardisation procedures will give SMEs an equal access to public contracts.

A number of suggestions[64] that might take the form of legislation or policy by either national or European authorities with a view to overcoming the above obstacles and promoting regional economic development through the strategic application of public procurement have been proposed. It should be mentioned that these suggestions find their origin in the spirit and to some extent the wording of the Directives, but the relevant provisions cannot from the appropriate framework for their successful implementation. All the recommendations proposed have their advantages and disadvantages and the attempt to select one or more brings into play questions of legal compatibility, particularly with reference to European Community Law.

- *creation of certain thresholds in the European Public Procurement Directives for SMEs only*. This will guarantee a certain percentage of public contracts to SMEs, but at the same time will exclude them from large public contracts. However, such a scheme will also pose considerable administrative difficulties in its implementation.
- *provisions that impose on contracting entities a minimum target number of contracts for SMEs by means of a positive obligation for awarding authorities to divide a certain percentage of public contracts into lots and to require successful tenderers to subcontract a certain part of the contract*. Such provisions could improve SMEs' chances of participation in and award of public contracts, although they may

---

[62] Articles 17 and 20 of the Public Supplies (93/36) and Public Works (93/37) Directives respectively.

[63] D. Mardas, *Sub-contracting, Small and Medium Sized Enterprises (SMEs) and Public Procurement in the European Community*, Public Procurement Law Review, 1994, Vol. 3, CS 19.

[64] C. Bovis, *Public Procurement and Small and Medium Sized Enterprises in the United Kingdom and the Republic of Ireland*, ACCA, Research Paper 17, 1996.

contravene Public Procurement Directives by avoiding the stipulated contract value thresholds.
- *preference in favour of SMEs in certain areas by means of price advantage or government subsidies.* The advantage could be the limitation of regional disparities and provision of a minimum of financial security in certain industries in certain regions but is should be recalled that preference schemes have been abolished since 1993 as incompatible with the single market. Subsidies may be incompatible with Article 92 EU Treaty.

**The industrial policy dimension in public procurement**

The implementation of industrial policies through public purchasing focuses on either the sustainment of strategic national industries, or the development of infant industries. In both cases, preferential purchasing patterns can provide the economic and financial framework for the development of such industries, at the expense of competition and free trade. Although the utilisation of public procurement as a means of industrial policy in Member States may breach directly or indirectly primary Treaty provisions on free movement of goods and the right of establishment and the freedom to provide services, it is far from clear whether the European Commission and the Court could accept public procurement as a means of state aid. In the light of the *Du Pont du Nemour* case,[65] the possibility of qualifying public procurement as state aid in pursuit of the industrial policies of the Member States appears.[66] Although the Court adopted a very restrictive approach in determining the compatibility of state aid with Article 30 EC, it left the door open for the application of public procurement as state aid, provided it does not contravene the principle of free movement of goods or the freedom to provide services

The industrial policy dimension of public procurement is also reflected in the form of strategic purchasing by public utilities. Public utilities in the European Community, which in their majority are

---

[65] Case C 21/88, *Du Pont de Nemours Italiana SpA v. Unita Sanitaria Locale N.2 di Carrara*, [1990] ECR 889.
[66] See, J.M. Fernadez Martin and O. Stehmann, *Product Market Integration versus Regional Cohesion in the Community*, op.cit.

monopolies, are accountable for a substantial magnitude of procurement, in terms of volume and in terms of price. Responsible for this are the expensive infrastructure and high technology products that are necessary to procure in order to deliver their services to the public. Given the fact that most of the suppliers to public utilities depend almost entirely on their procurement and that, even when some degree of privatisation has been achieved, the actual control of the utilities is still vested in the state, the first constraint in liberalising public procurement in the European Union is apparent. Utilities, in the form of public monopolies or semi-private enterprises appear prone to perpetuate long standing over-dependency purchasing patterns with certain domestic suppliers. Reflecting the above observations, the reader should bear in mind that until 1991, utilities were not covered by European legislation on procurement.[67] The delay of their regulation can be attributed to the resistance from Member States in privatising their monopolies and the uncertainty of the legal regime that will follow their privatisation.

The industrial policy dimension of public procurement evolves around public monopolies in the Member States which predominately operate in the utilities sectors (energy, transport, water and telecommunications) and have been assigned with the exclusive exploitation of the relevant services in their respective Member States. The legal status of these entities varies from legal monopolies (where they are constitutionally guaranteed) to delegated monopolies (where the state confers certain rights on them) and during the last decade they have been the target of a sweeping process of transformation from monolithic and sub-optimal public corporations to competitive enterprises. Public monopolies very often possess a monopsony position. As they are state controlled enterprises, they tend to perform under different management patterns than private firms. Their decision making responds not only to market forces but mainly to political pressure. Understandably, their purchasing behaviour follows, to a large extent, parameters reflecting current trends of domestic industrial policies. Public monopolies in the utilities sector have sustained national industries in Member States through exclusive or preferential procurement. The sustainability of "national champions", or in other terms, strategically perceived enterprises, could only be achieved through discriminatory purchasing patterns. The

---

[67] Utilities were first regulated in their procurement by virtue of EC Directive 90/531, O.J. 1990, L 297.

privatisation of public monopolies, which absorb, to a large extent or even entirely, the output of such industries will most probably discontinue such patterns and will result in industrial policy imbalances as it would be difficult for the "national champions" to secure new markets to replace the traditional long dependency on public monopolies and it would take time and effort to diversify their activities or to convert to alternative industrial sectors.

The protected and preferential purchasing frameworks between monopolies and "national champions" and the output dependency patterns and secured markets of the latter have attracted considerable foreign direct investment,[68] to the extent that Community Institutions face the dilemma of threatening to discontinue the investment flow when liberalising public procurement in the common market. However, it could be argued that the industrial restructuring following the opening-up of the procurement practices of public monopolies would possibly attract similar levels of foreign direct investment, which would be directed towards supporting the new structure. The liberalisation of public procurement in the European Community has as one of its primary aims the restructuring of industries suffering from overcapacity and sub-optimal performance. However, the industries supplying public monopolies and utilities are themselves, quite often, public corporations. In such cases, procurement dependency patterns between state outfits, when disrupted can result in massive unemployment attributed to the supply side's inadequacy to secure new customers. The monopsony position when abolished could often bring about the collapse of the relevant sector.

Industrial policies through public procurement can also be implemented with reference to defence industries, particularly for procurement of military equipment. The Procurement Directives cover equipment of dual-use purchased by the armed forces, but explicitly exclude from their ambit the procurement of military equipment. It should be also mentioned here that every Member State in the European Union pursues its own military procurement policy by virtue of Article 223. In the light of the Maastricht Treaty on European Union, the creation of a framework within which a common European Defence Policy should be established, defence contracts and procurement of military equipment by member states should be harmonised, to the extent that a centralised

---

[68] European Commission, *The Effect of the Opening-up of Public Procurement to Foreign Direct investment*, 1995.

mechanism regulating them should take over independent national military procurement practices.[69]

Attempts have been made to liberalise, to a limited extent, the procurement of military equipment at European level under the auspices of European Defence Equipment Market. This initiative is a programme of gradual liberalisation of defence industries in the relevant countries and has arisen through the operation of the Independent European Programme Group, which has been a forum of industrial co-operation in defence industry matters amongst European NATO members.[70] The programme has envisaged, apart from collaborative research and development in defence technology, the introduction of a competitive regime in defence procurement and a modest degree of transparency,[71] subject to the draconian primary Treaty provisions of Article 223. Award of defence procurement contracts, under the EDEM should follow a similar rationale with civilian procurement, particularly in the introduction of award criteria based on economic and financial considerations and a minimum degree of publicity for contracts in excess of ECU 1 m.

The establishment of a Common European Defence Policy could possibly bring about the integration of defence industries in the European Union and this will inevitably require a change in governments' policies and practices.[72] Competitiveness, public savings considerations, value for money, transparency and non-discrimination should be the principles of the centralised mechanism regulating defence procurement in Europe. The establishment of a centralised defence agency with task of contractorisation, facilities management and market testing are all examples of new procurement policies which give an opportunity to the defence industry for new business but at the same time create greater risks to contend with. New directions on existing policies such as risk

---

[69] A. Cox, *The Future of European Defence Policy: the Case for a Centralised Procurement Agency*, Public Procurement Law Review, 1994, Vol. 2, p.65.

[70] The Independent European Programme Group has been renamed to Western European Armaments Group and its operation has been transferred under the auspices of the Western European Union (WEU) in 1992.

[71] Excluded from the EDEM regime are nuclear and chemical weapons, propulsion systems and warships. Exceptions from the policy commitments could also be justified on grounds of "emergency" and "national security".

[72] J.B. Wheaton, *Defence Procurement and the European Community*, Public Procurement Law Review, 1992, Vol. 1, p.432.

management, contracting for reliability and cost represent considerable challenges for the defence industries to meet.

# Concluding Remarks

In December 1996, the European Commission published the *Green Paper on Public Procurement: Exploring the Way Forward*. In this document the Commission has reflected on the law and policy of public procurement particularly since the completion of the internal market. The Green Paper does not proclaim a huge success by the regime or any unprecedented impact upon the demand and supply sides of the public purchasing equation. It rather acknowledges the modest effect of the law and policy on the principles envisaged in the opening up of the public sector markets in the European Community. Remarkably, it invited all interested parties to submit written evidence on the effect of the regime upon them and possible suggestions as to future improvements.

The Green Paper has recognised the complementarity of public procurement with other Community and national policies. Because of the economic importance of public procurement, an effective regulatory regime on the law and policy of public purchasing in the European Community is considered as fundamental to the success of the common market. The effectiveness of the public procurement regime would bring about cost-efficiency gains for the public sector, which could consequently affect the success of fiscal deficit reduction policies imposed by the Maastricht convergence criteria. Thus, the European Commission has made clear the possible links between public sector savings and convergence criteria of the European Monetary Union. However, to what extent the success of monetary integration in the European Community would be affected by the outcome of the public sector integration process of the common market deserves thorough and in-depth quantitative and qualitative research for the years to come.

Although the Commission acknowledged some improvements in the transparency of the public procurement process as a result of the obligatory publicity and advertisement requirements, substantial progress in the implementation of the Directives within domestic systems has not been recorded. The Green Paper raises the thorny question of *qualitative implementation* of the public procurement regime into national legal orders. To what extent the Member States have failed to meet the expectations of European Institutions and share their aspirations for an integrated procurement system in the common market, is a matter for the European Court of Justice to decide. The reservations of the successful implementation of the regime expressed by the author in relation to the limited amount of litigation and the relatively low number of complaints in public procurement, could perhaps trigger the need for a new approach to Member State's obligations arising from Directives. The acid test for the *qualitative implementation* of the public procurement Directives is *access to justice* at national level. Moreover, the expectations of the new regime in relation to the actual or potential savings for the public sector have not been fully materialised. The author has pointed out the relatively limited economic impact of the public procurement law and policy on the demand and supply side respectively and in particular the effects on price convergence and the public sector import penetration.

Nobody has suggested that the integration of public markets in the European Community would be an easy exercise. The vital importance of public purchasing for domestic policies, as well as the complexity of the field contribute to the modest progress so far. However, this should not be construed as a criticism directed to European Institutions or even Member States, which sometimes seemed to reject the envisaged regime. The integration of public markets in Europe through the regulation of public procurement of the Member States represent perhaps the bravest attempt of the Community to finalise the completion of the common market and achieve the objectives stipulated in the Rome and Maastricht Treaties. What has been so far achieved is unprecedented and credit should be given to all those who strive for the accomplishment of the ultimate goal in Europe.

# Index

Abnormally low tenders, 139, 165-168
Advertising, 34, 56, 60-62. 74, 77, 111, 113, 169
Advisory Committee on Public Procurement, 156, 167
Affiliated Undertakings, 78, 79, 110
Agreement on Government Procurement, 40, 55-57, 73, 81-85, 92, 156, 202
Association Agreements, 86
Attestation, 80, 153
Authorities, See Contracting authorities
Award Criteria, 12, 25, 58, 60, 62, 64, 78, 94, 107, 111, 130, 146, 180, 199, 204, 222
Award of damages, 122, 125, 130, 134, 143, 150-156

Award Procedures, 19, 24, 34, 56, 61, 74, 78, 94, 98, 101, 104, 111, 118, 126, 155, 163

Call for Competition, 76, 109, 169
Cechini Report, 4, 26, 32, 42
Common Commercial Policy, 55
Common Product Classification, 75, 178
Common Procurement Vocabulary (CPV), 178
Concession Contracts, 60-62, 71, 77, 111
Conciliation, 76-77, 82, 141, 155
Constraints, 22, 68, 160, 197, 208
Construction Projects under International Agreements, 57, 63, 65, 73, 74, 85, 157
Contract Notice, 113
Contracting Authorities, 14, 25-39, 41, 49, 55-58, 60, 70-77, 83-89, 99

Contracts, 11, 15, 23, 24, 27-30, 32-45, 46-50, 53-81, 83-104
Co-ordination, 31, 36, 37, 49, 53, 59, 60-61
Customs Union, 1, 4

Damages, see award of damages
Design Contests, 74, 111
Directive on Public Services, 34, 59, 68, 73, 74, 75, 87, 206, 207
Directive on Public Supplies, 21, 34, 53-59, 75, 82-83, 92, 102, 112, 117, 148, 151, 172, 2213, 214, 218
Directive on Public Utilities, 33, 34, 45-52, 56, 57, 65-71, 96, 134, 175, 220
Directive on Public Works, 34, 59-69, 80-85, 91-97, 102, 111, 142-148, 179, 204-205, 214, 218

Eligibility requirements, 99, 100, 101
Enforcement, 15, 17, 21, 82, 114-120, 150-153, 156, 162, 180-184
Estimation of contract value, 92-97
European Free Trade Association (EFTA), 81-86
Excluded Sectors, 65, 67, 73, 85
Exclusion of contractors, 98, 110, 152, 203, 205
Exclusive Rights, 23, 70, 87, 92, 93, 106, 171-173
Extra-territorial effects, 21, 82, 156

Financial and economic standing, 40, 100-107, 199
Framework Agreements, 104, 109, 168-171
France, 44, 46, 162, 283-194
Freedom of establishment, 91
Freedom to provide services, 14, 25, 53, 59, 60, 91, 102, 215, 216, 219

GATT, 21, 40, 41, 55, 57, 69, 73, 74, 81-89, 156-159, 202
Germany, 44, 47, 49, 141, 162, 183-194
Greece, 44, 48, 50, 143, 163, 183-194
Green Paper on Public Procurement: the way forward, 22, 205, 224, 225

Impact assessment, 12, 21, 159, 212
Industrial Policy, 4, 11-18, 29, 66, 67, 176, 186, 197, 210, 215, 219
In-house Contracts, 10, 110, 207, 208
Internal Market, 3, 4, 12, 14, 18, 19, 32, 58, 64, 67, 115, 127, 130, 216
Ireland, 44, 48, 116, 144, 183-194
Italy, 44, 49, 117, 145, 183-194

Japan, 29, 39, 41, 68, 69, 81, 89
Judicial review at European level, 17, 115-128
Judicial review at national level, 128, 132, 139, 140-149, 156

Legal requirements, 77, 101
Liberalisation, 18, 69, 74, 82, 85, 159, 177, 202, 206, 221
Local labour employment, 112
lowest offer, 165
Luxembourg, 44, 49-50, 102, 138, 162, 183-194

Market Access, 9, 28, 30, 40, 60, 62, 81, 87, 88, 198
Monopolies, 3, 6, 22, 43, 160, 175-177, 220
most economically advantageous tender, 12, 25, 64, 106, 107, 112, 156, 166, 170, 198, 204

National Treatment, 84, 86
negotiated procedure, 25-58, 62, 95, 104-111, 163, 168-175, 198
Netherlands, 44, 50, 107, 162, 180, 183-194
Nomenclature: NACE, 60, 178, 188-194
Non-discrimination, 212, 213, 222
non-priority services, 77, 78
Non-Tariff Barriers, 2, 3, 4, 14, 18, 24, 26, 32, 42, 84, 130, 160, 170-178, 186, 195, 202

Official Journal, 25, 45, 46-58, 62, 80, 94-95, 105, 153, 160-170, 184
open procedures, 104, 105, 146, 168, 170, 198

Portugal, 44, 50, 51, 139, 162, 183-194

Post-tender Negotiations, 106
Preference schemes, 12, 64, 204, 212-217
Principles of the Directives, 27
priority services, 77, 78
professional qualifications, 98
Public Authorities. See Contracting authorities
Public Housing Schemes, 113, 205
Public Service, 34, 59, 68, 73, 74, 75, 87, 206, 207
public service concessions, 77
Public Supplies, 21, 34, 53-59, 75, 82-83, 92, 102, 112, 117, 148, 151, 172, 2213, 214, 218
Public Undertakings, 23, 86, 87, 92, 93
Public Utilities, 33, 34, 45-52, 56, 57, 65-71, 96, 134, 175, 220
Public Works, 34, 59-69, 80-85, 91-97, 102, 111, 142-148, 179, 204-205, 214, 218
public works concessions, 61, 70
Publication of Public Contracts, 93-95, 109, 161-169, 171-174

Qualification Criteria, 62, 11, 113
Qualitative Selection, 62, 111, 131
Quantitative Restrictions, 3, 54

Recognised Contractors, 101-103
Regional development, 12, 14, 33, 72, 112, 196, 209, 212-218
Remedies, 34, 79, 82, 86, 122, 125, 128, 130, 135, 140, 144-157
restricted procedures, 25, 58, 62, 104-111, 168-170

Secret Public Works Contracts, 64, 109, 173, 175
Selection Criteria, 74, 98, 111, 113, 204
Services contracts, see public services
Setting aside procurement awards, 121-125, 144-150
Single European Act (SEA), 3, 4, 33
Small and Medium Size Enterprises (SME's), 39, 40, 112, 209, 217
Social Policy, 177, 198-206
Spain, 44, 51, 107, 117, 138, 162, 173, 182-194
State monopolies, see monopolies

Sub-contracting, 10, 112, 176, 214, 218
Subsidiarity, 15, 42
Subsidised Works Contracts, 64

Technical capacity, 99-103
Technical Specifications, 34, 54, 56, 60, 61, 98, 179
Telecommunications, 32-40, 45-56, 60, 65, 70-85, 134, 148, 176, 220
Tendering procedures, 33, 58, 60, 81, 102, 104, 141-145, 170, 203, 212
Tenders Electronic Daily (TED), 24, 44, 95
Third Countries, 57, 73, 81-96, 153
Threshold Values, 88, 96
Tokyo Round, 41, 55, 81-96, 156, 202

Transparency, 14, 18, 19, 25, 27, 28, 34, 60, 84, 87, 93, 161, 184, 222, 225

United Kingdom, 44, 52, 119, 143, 162, 183-194
Uruguay Round, 41, 69, 74, 85, 156, 202
USA, 69, 81, 126, 133-141, 174

Volume of public procurement, 12, 38-53, 141, 168, 175, 181, 220

White Paper on Completing the Internal Market, 3, 14, 18, 32, 58, 67, 177
WTO, 41, 86, 96, 156-158